THE STORY OF CHOGORIA

JOHN WILKINSON

THE HANDSEL PRESS
Avalon, 35 Dunbar Rd, Haddington EH41 3PJ

© John Wilkinson 1994, 2008

All rights reserved. No part of this publication may be reproduced, stored in a retrieval system, or transmitted in any form by any means, electronic, mechanical, photocopying, recording or otherwise, without the prior permission of the Handsel Press Ltd.

ISBN 1 871828 50 3
EAN 978-871828-50-4

British Library Cataloguing in Publication Data:
A catalogue record for this publication is available from the British Library

Typeset in 11pt Garamond at The Stables, Carberry

Printed in Scotland by W M Bett Ltd, Tillicoultry

Reprinted 2008 by MPG Books Ltd, Cornwall

To the memory of

CLIVE IRVINE

and

JOY IRVINE

CONTENTS

LIST OF ILLUSTRATIONS	vii
ABBREVIATIONS	viii
FOREWORD	ix
PREFACE	x
MAP OF ORIGINAL MISSION STATIONS	xii
CHAPTER ONE: FROM KRAPF TO KIKUYU	1

  The Three Pioneers
  The East African Scottish Mission
  In Kikuyu Country
  The Kikuyu Mission Develops

CHAPTER TWO: INTO CHUKA-MWIMBI COUNTRY	11

  The Chuka-Mwimbi People
  The Chuka-Mwimbi Country
  The Mission Arrives
  The First World War
  After the War

CHAPTER THREE: THE PROSPECT OF HELP	21

  The Army Doctor
  The New Missionary
  The Missionary Bride

CHAPTER FOUR: IN CHUKA-MWIMBI	27

  The Generous Benefactor
  The Station Established
  The Doctor Begins Work
  The Mission Industrialised
  What did the People Think?
  What did the People Believe?
  The New Faith
  A Roadside Encounter

CHAPTER FIVE: EARLY DAYS AT CHOGORIA   37
  Bush-Pigs
  Locusts
  The Supply of Food
  The Milk Supply
  Visitors
  Prayer
  The Family Arrives

CHAPTER SIX: THE FIRST SEVEN YEARS (1922-1928)   43
  Publicity & Support
  Industrial Developments
  Agricultural Experiments
  The Model House
  The Women's Lot

CHAPTER SEVEN: THE FIRST SEVEN YEARS (cont.)   51
  Medical Work Established
  The Church Founded
  Educational Work Begun
  The Chogoria Area Defined

CHAPTER EIGHT: OPPOSITION ARISES (1929)   63
  The Land Question
  Kikuyu Customs
  Female Circumcision
  The Issue at Stake
  Opposition at Chogoria
  The Chogoria Promise in Retrospect
  The Results of Opposition

CHAPTER NINE: RECOVERY & PROGRESS (1930-39)   75
  The General Situation
  The Daily Routine
  The Works Department Carries On
  The Church Survives the Crisis
  The New Church Built

CHAPTER TEN: RECOVERY & PROGRESS (cont.)   87
  The School Situation
  The Hospital Recovers

CHAPTER ELEVEN: WAR & REVIVAL (1939-1949)   95
   The Wartime Situation
   The Indigenous Church
   The East African Revival
   Revival Comes to Chogoria
   The Revival and the PCEA

CHAPTER TWELVE: POST-WAR DEVELOPMENTS   107
   Food, Stone and Administration   **(1944-1952)**
   The Semi-Jubilee of Chogoria
   Chogoria Becomes a Small Town
   The Church Takes Over the Schools
   The Hospital Staff Increases

CHAPTER THIRTEEN: THE CHURCH ADVANCES   119
   The Revival in the 1950s   **(1952-1960)**
   The Presbytery of Chogoria Formed
   School Matters
   Education in Kenya
   Hospital Affairs
   The Nurse Training School

CHAPTER FOURTEEN: PROGRESS OF NATIONALISM   128
   Nationalism in Kikuyuland   **(1929-1952)**
   Nationalism becomes Militant
   Chogoria and the Mau Mau
   The Emergency Ends

CHAPTER FIFTEEN: EMERGENCY TO INDEPENDENCE
   Political Developments   **(1956-1963)**   136
   Land Consolidation
   The Growth of the Church
   Changes in the Schools
   The Hospital Carries On
   Dr Irvine Retires

CHAPTER SIXTEEN: KENYA AFTER INDEPENDENCE   145
   Education after Independence   **(1964-1970)**
   The Schools at Chogoria
   Health Care in Kenya
   Chogoria Hospital Redevelopment
   The Challenges to the Church

CHAPTER SEVENTEEN: COMMUNITY HEALTH CARE AT CHOGORIA (1970-92) 156
The Chogoria Dispensary System
The Community Health Department
Chogoria Attracts International Attention
The Community Health Care Programmes
The Community Nurse Training School

CHAPTER EIGHTEEN: CHOGORIA AFTER 1980 165
Community Development
The 'Urbanisation' of Chogoria
The Hospital Services Expand
The Hospital Chaplaincy Team
Three Grades of School
The Church and its Mission Areas
The Woman's Guild

EPILOGUE 177

APPENDIXES 179
One: Significant Dates in the History of Chogoria
Two: Senior Staff at Chogoria Hospital

NOTES AND REFERENCES 184

INDEX 194

POSTSCRIPT (2008) 201

Thanks are expressed to the Pollock Memorial Missionary Trust, to the Hope Trust and to others for assistance with this publication, including the Drummond Trust of 3 Pitt Terrace, Stirling, through whose support it was possible to sell copies of the first edition in Kenya in aid of Chogoria Hospital.

ILLUSTRATIONS

1. Dr Clive Irvine (1962)
2. Mrs Joy Irvine
3. Dr Geoffrey Irvine
4. The Bungalow (1922)
5. The first Church (Built 1923)
6. The Church at Chogoria (Built 1930)
7. The Chancel
8. The Deacons's Court (1928)
9. Group after the Signing of the Chogoria Promise (September 29th 1929)
10. The Chogoria Kirk Session (1935)
11. The Chogoria Revival Team (1949)
12. The Woman's Guild (1936)
13. The Boys' Primary School at Chogoria (Built 1936)
14. Mr Grieve teaching Class of Standard VI boys (1946)
15. Chogoria Boys' High School Jubilee Block (1987)
16. Chogoria Girls' Boarding Primary School and its Headmistress, Mrs Irene Ndiga
17. Girls' Boarding School at Chogoria (Built 1937)
18. Chogoria Girls' High School Administration Block (1970)
19. The first permanent Hospital building (1926)
20. The five Hospital Orderlies (1927)
21. The first Leprosarium at Gatheru (1926)
22. The Leprosy Dispensary at Chogoria (1929)
23. The Quadrangle of the old Hospital about 1950 (now the Nurse Training School)
24. The Injection and Dressing shelter (Built 1930)
25. Sister Clark Wilson, Dr Irvine and staff (1939)
26. Dr Irvine, Sister Fergusson and Adiel with male patient
27. Sister Margaret Burt
28. Jackson Chabari
29. Francis Muruja
30. Dr Irvine taking Service at a Dispensary (1929)
31. Dr & Mrs Wilkinson at Mukuuni Dispensary (1949)

32 The Women's Ward (1941)
33 The Women's Medical Ward (1971)
34 The Men's Ward (built 1939)
35 The Surgical Wing (built 1971)
36 The old Operating Theatre (built 1926)
37 The modern Operating Theatre (built 1971)
38 The Medical Wing (built 1971)
39 The Hospital Chapel (built 1983)
40 Mrs Helen Raini, Matron
41 The Outpatient Clinic
42 Dr Alastair Sammon, Medical Officer-in-charge (1988-94)
43 Mr Festus Nkonge, Hospital Administrator

ABBREVIATIONS

AIM	Africa Inland Mission
CHD	Community Health Department
CMS	Church Missionary Society
CSM	Church of Scotland Mission
EASM	East African Scottish Mission
FMC	Foreign Mission Committee of the Ch. of Scotland
IBEA	Imperial British East Africa Company
KAU	Kenya African Union
KCA	Kikuyu Central Association
KMV	Kikuyu Missions Volunteers
LNC	Local Native Council
PCEA	Presbyterian Church of East Africa

FOREWORD

I came to Chogoria disillusioned and disappointed with the direction of health care in another part of Africa and frustrated at my inability to affect it. I found it illogical that tertiary health care should often be established at the expense of primary health care, and that cure was more respected than prevention. The result was that I voted with my feet, and found them being led firmly to Kenya and to Chogoria.

Immunisation rates are as high in the catchment area of Chogoria Hospital as in most of Europe, and an isolation ward has become unnecessary in the hospital. The health knowledge of the community is good, and is kept so by a large number of health care volunteers, people motivated by the respect of their communities and the enthusiasm of those who teach them.

I found the attitudes and achievements at Chogoria quite staggering after the medical poverty of my previous experience. When I was forced to look for reasons for this, certain recurrent themes became clear to me as I worked at Chogoria and began to understand its history - prayer, persistent hard work, innovative style, and faith in the unlimited ability of local people to develop.

The impetus for this book came from the hospital, but health is much broader than medicine alone can provide, so the story of Chogoria begins with the preaching of the good news of God's love and its practical expression in education as well as in health care.

The story of Chogoria needs to be told for the sake of health in Africa, but also for our own lives, because the things that belong to the success of Chogoria may offer the same to us as individuals. It is told by someone who is himself part of the story.

PCEA Chogoria Hospital   *Alastair Sammon MD, FRCS*
PO Box 35   Medical Officer-in-Charge
Chogoria, Kenya.   May 1994

PREFACE

This book is at once a contribution to the history of the rise and progress of the Christian Church in East Africa and a biography of the missionary who gave forty years of his life to its establishment and upbuilding at Chogoria on the eastern slopes of Mount Kenya.

The origins of the Christian Church amongst the Chuka-Mwimbi people with which this book deals can be traced to the year 1916 when Kenyan Christian missionaries first went to live and work amongst them. These missionaries came from the mission stations at Kikuyu and Tumutumu where the Church of Scotland had begun missionary work some years before. The missionary policy of the Church of Scotland was the promotion of evangelism, education and health care amongst the people to whom its agents were sent and this policy was pursued from the beginning of the work amongst the Chuka-Mwimbi.

As we shall see, the work first began at Mweria, but in 1922 it was decided to move to a new site at Chogoria which became the permanent location for the Mission. In October of that same year, the first European missionary was posted to Chogoria in the person of Dr Clive Irvine. Dr Irvine was a man of strong Christian convictions, vigorous personality and many and varied talents, including those of leadership and technical ability. How actively and effectively he and his Kenyan and European colleagues made the concerns of evangelism, education and health care their own, will appear as the story of Chogoria unfolds in the chapters which follow this preface.

I lived and worked at Chogoria at different times which totalled almost seven years in all. For three of these years I was a close colleague of Dr Irvine, sharing with him in the work of the Church, the schools and the hospital. When Dr Irvine retired in December 1961, I succeeded him as Medical Superintendent of the hospital. One source, therefore, of the material on which this book is based is the personal reminiscences and the written records which my wife and I have preserved.

Other sources are detailed at the end of the book in the section headed *Notes and References* and need not be listed in full here. Some, however, should be mentioned. Two invaluable sources are available for the period 1922 to 1958, namely the Scottish Mission journal *Kikuyu News* and the *Chogoria booklet*. Both these publications contain important and detailed information for the period they cover. Almost every issue of *Kikuyu News* during this period contained an article on Chogoria written by Dr Irvine, and the *Chogoria* booklet was, of course, all about Chogoria. The earlier pages of *Kikuyu News* also contain details of how the work at

Chogoria was planned and begun there during the decade or so before Dr Irvine arrived. Two further sources from which information was derived were the minutes of the Church of Scotland Foreign Mission Committee and the annual reports of this Committee to the General Assembly of that Church from 1898 to the present.

In 1993, my wife and I visited Chogoria when I received much information and assistance from a large number of people. Of these I would specially mention the Revd Elias Kabii, the Revd Dr Julius Nkonge and the Revd Jediel Micheu, together with Mr Francis Muruja and Dr Geoffrey Irvine - who along with his brother Anthony (now living in England) supplied details of the Irvine family history for which I was very grateful.

I am particularly indebted to Mrs Ankie Jansen whose husband, Dr Gerrard Jansen, is at present on the staff of Chogoria Hospital. Mrs Jansen has spent a great deal of time examining the records of the hospital and tracing documents and reports relating to Chogoria, now held at the Kenya National Archives in Nairobi and elsewhere. She very generously made her notes and findings available to me for my use in writing this book and also took time to read through critically, earlier drafts of its chapters.

The original suggestion which led to the preparation of this history came from Dr Alastair Sammon, the current Medical Officer-in-Charge of Chogoria Hospital, who has written the Foreword which introduces the book.

I am grateful to the officers of the Church of Scotland's Board of World Mission (especially its Africa Secretary, the Revd James Wilkie), and also to those of the Presbyterian Church of East Africa for their interest and their permission to prepare and publish this account of the Story of Chogoria. I received much encouragement from the present Moderator of the General Assembly of the Presbyterian Church of East Africa, the Right Reverend Bernard Muindi.

The production and publication of this book would not have been possible without the support of the several Trusts which kindly gave grants for this purpose. These included the following:

The Drummond Trust, 3 Pitt Terrace, Stirling;
The Hope Trust, Edinburgh;
The Pollock Memorial Missionary Trust, Glasgow.

To the trustees of these three bodies I wish to record my grateful thanks for their support.

A final word of thanks must go to the publisher, The Handsel Press, and its editor (the Revd Jock Stein) for his interest and encouragement during the writing of the book.

John Wilkinson

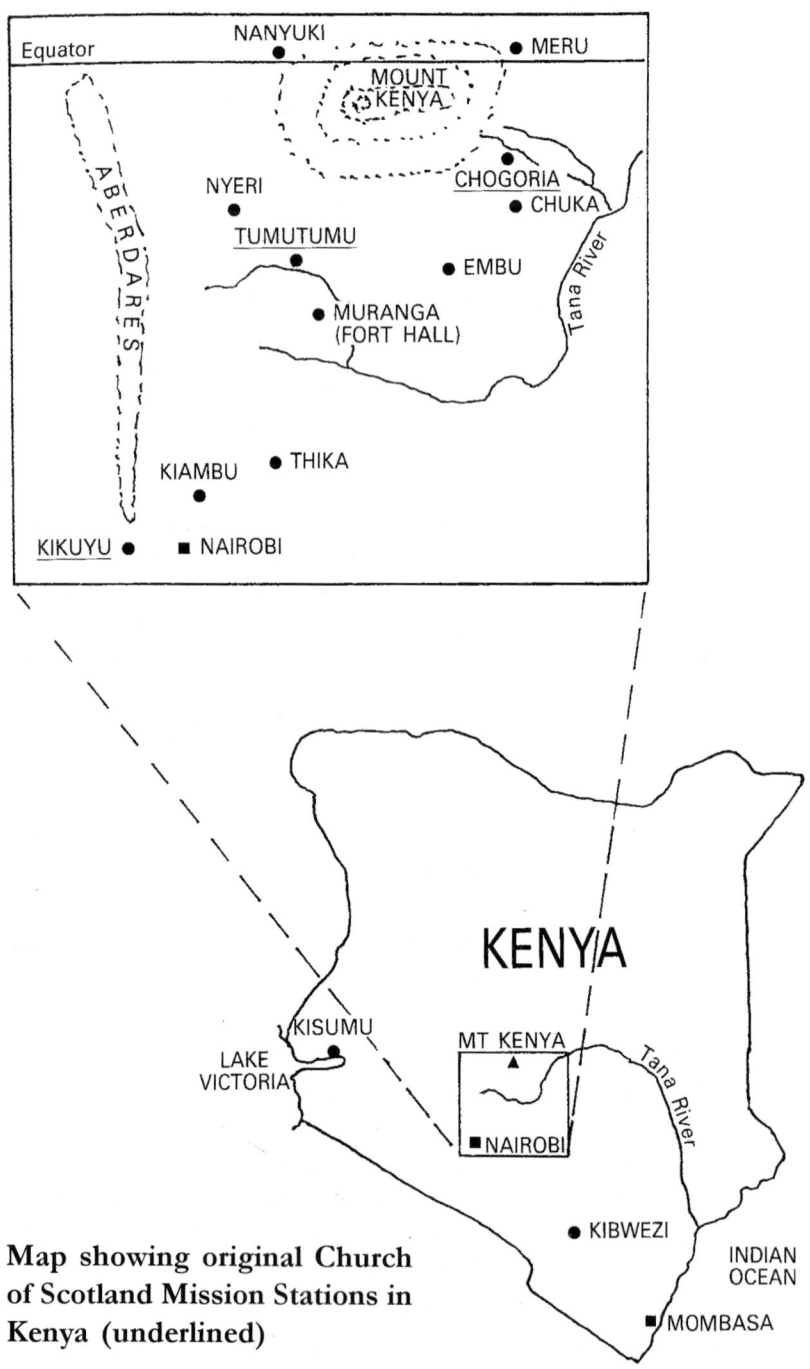

Map showing original Church of Scotland Mission Stations in Kenya (underlined)

CHAPTER ONE

FROM KRAPF TO KIKUYU

> We are not Traders, but Preachers of God's Word, who desire to spread the Gospel throughout the whole of Africa.

These were the words by which Lewis Krapf explained the purpose of his coming to East Africa to a local African chief in 1844.[1]

With the arrival of Krapf, the modern western Protestant Christian missionary movement reached the shores of East Africa. The main source of this movement in Britain was the Evangelical Revival which had resulted from the work of John and Charles Wesley and George Whitefield in the eighteenth century. As a result of their work, the Churches were faced with the challenge presented by those peoples of the world who had never heard the gospel of Jesus Christ. The mainstream Churches were reluctant to accept the challenge and so those within their membership who wished to do so, formed missionary societies.

The first of these to include the word Africa in its title was The Society for Missions to Africa and the East formed by evangelical members of the Church of England in 1799. In 1812 this title was changed to The Church Missionary Society for Africa and the East, and finally the second part of the title was dropped and the name became The Church Missionary Society (CMS).[2]

The Three Pioneers

The CMS was at first unsuccessful in finding missionaries from England who were willing to work in East Africa, and had to depend on recruiting German missionaries who had been trained at the Basel Missionary College which was established in 1815 to train Lutheran and Reformed missionaries. The first of these to be recruited was Johann Ludwig (Lewis) Krapf, a German Lutheran pastor from Württemburg in south Germany. In 1838 Krapf joined the CMS Abyssinian Mission and spent a frustrating six years, first in Abyssinia and then in the Muslim kingdom of Shoa to the south-east of that country. It was in Shoa that he became interested in the Galla people, a Hamitico-Semitic people who eventually occupied all of southern Abyssinia and also migrated south across the Tana River. As a result of religious intrigue, he was expelled from Shoa in 1842 and crossed over to Aden. From here Krapf and his wife sailed to East Africa in the hope that he might be able to reach the Galla people by working northwards from Mombasa.

He arrived in the port of Mombasa from Aden on January 3rd 1844 after being shipwrecked on the way. From here he immediately went on to Zanzibar to obtain Sultan Seyyid Said's permission in person to begin missionary work on Mombasa Island and on the East African mainland. The Sultan was very impressed by this gaunt European stranger and gave him a letter of introduction to the Arab governors on the mainland. It was written in Arabic by Ahmed, the Sultan's secretary, and read as follows:

> This comes from Seyyid Said Sultan: Greeting to all our subjects, friends and governors. This letter is written on behalf of Doctor Krapf the German, a good man, who wishes to convert the world to God. Behave well towards him and be everywhere serviceable to him.[3]

Krapf then returned to Mombasa in May of the same year and he took a house for his wife and himself on Mombasa Island. With this as his base, he began to make plans for the evangelisation of the Swahili, Nyika and Galla peoples. Within two months, his wife Rosina and their newly-born child were dead of malaria and they were buried at English Point on the mainland opposite the Old Town of Mombasa. He carried on the work they had come to do, and after two years he had translated the whole of the New Testament into Swahili and had compiled a grammar and dictionary of that language.

In June 1846 he was joined by Johann Rebmann, another Lutheran pastor from Germany, and during the next five years these two pioneers between them made eight safaris into the East African interior. On May 11th 1848, Rebmann became the first European to see the snows of Mount Kilimanjaro. His report of this was not believed in Europe where it was maintained that perpetual snow could not exist so near to the equator. On December 3rd of the following year, Krapf became the first European to see Mount Kenya when he was staying with the Kamba Chief Kivoi at Kitui. In his report he describes how he saw an enormous mountain surmounted by 'two large horns or pillars' and covered with snow.[4] It was on the eastern slopes of this mountain and within sight of those two large horns or pillars that Chogoria was to be established over seventy years later.

Two other German missionaries arrived in June 1849 but soon contracted malaria from which one named Wagner died during the following month. The other one, named Jakob Erhardt, survived and provided welcome reinforcement for the two lonely pioneers.

In February of the following year, Krapf and Erhardt sailed southwards down the coast from Mombasa to the mouth of the Rovuma River in search of possible routes to the interior. Later, Erhardt landed at Tanga and stayed there for some time. From the information he gathered on these two occasions, he was able to prepare a map of East Africa which was published in a German missionary paper in 1855. It was then reproduced in the CMS newsletter in the following year and became the main inspiration of the explorers Burton and Speke in their expedition of 1857, when Speke became the first European to see Lake Victoria Nyanza, which in 1862 he demonstrated to be the source of the River Nile.

Krapf had to return to Europe from East Africa in 1853 owing to ill health, and he was followed by Erhardt in 1855. Rebmann stayed on until March 1875 in spite of increasing weakness and blindness. Before he left for Europe, Rebmann had reduced three vernacular languages to writing and compiled a dictionary in each.

The faithful work of these three men had established bases for the CMS on Mombasa Island and at Rabai on the nearby mainland, and their linguistic work and geographical explorations had laid a solid foundation for their successors. Krapf regarded their coastal mission as the first link in an equatorial chain of missions which would stretch right across the African continent from east to west. More links would be forged as the missions moved inland. However, it was David Livingstone "and not the CMS missionaries with their twelve years' start and their powerful society behind them, who set in motion the missionary invasion of East Africa".[5]

The East African Scottish Mission

In his address to the University of Cambridge on December 4th 1857 David Livingstone ended with the following appeal:

I go back to Africa to try to make an open path for commerce and Christianity; do you carry out the work which I have begun. I leave it with you.[6]

It was partly in response to this appeal that the British East African Association was formed in 1887. In the following year this became the Imperial British East Africa (IBEA) Company incorporated under a royal charter from Queen Victoria. This Company acquired trading rights and administrative responsibility for the territory between the East African coast and the eastern border of the Congo Free State, and also for that part of the coast which included the port of Mombasa. The flag adopted by the new company consisted of a blue and white background on which were superimposed a crown above a blazing sun with the motto *Life and Liberty* set out beneath.

The chairman of this new company was Sir William Mackinnon who was a staunch member of the Free Church of Scotland, a body which had separated from the Established Church of Scotland in 1843 on the issue of State interference in Church affairs in Scotland. Mackinnon was concerned for the spiritual welfare of the peoples for whom his company had now become responsible and his fellow directors of the Company shared this concern. One of these directors was Alexander Low Bruce who had married Anna Mary, the youngest daughter of David and Mary Livingstone.

Although George Mackenzie, the Administrator of the new Company in Mombasa, had invited the CMS to plant mission stations all along the Company's trade route into the interior,[7] the directors in Scotland decided to establish their own independent undenominational Mission to be called the East African Scottish Mission (EASM). They formed a small committee of directors with Mackinnon as chairman and Bruce as honorary secretary and treasurer. The result was that in 1891 they approached the Free Church of Scotland to request the services of the Revd Dr James Stewart who was at that time on leave in Scotland. Dr Stewart had been the companion of David Livingstone in 1862 on his Zambesi expedition, and was now the Principal of the Lovedale Missionary Institution in South Africa. This request was granted and Dr Stewart accepted the invitation to go to East Africa, although it meant that he would be unable to attend the Lovedale Jubilee celebrations in July 1891. In April of that year, Dr Stewart left Scotland and sailed for Mombasa.

On September 19th 1891, he set out from Mombasa with what his instructions called "a pioneer Missionary Expedition". The expedition numbered in total 273 men, including six Europeans in addition to himself. They had printed instructions issued by the EASM committee in Edinburgh which ordered them to

> proceed inland to the locality proposed as the district in which the Mission is to be settled. This at present is Machako's, about 300 miles northwest of Mombassa. The first station may be a temporary one, to be occupied only while the surrounding country is being fully and carefully examined.[8]

The expedition reached Kibwezi in Kamba country (*Ukambani*), about two hundred miles or two weeks' march from Mombasa, on October 15th. There they stopped and set up a temporary camp whilst Dr Stewart examined the choice of localities for the establishment of the permanent mission station. He reveals in his report that before he left Scotland for Africa, the Mission Committee had specially indicated to him two possible localities, namely Dagoretti in Kikuyu country and Machakos in Kamba country. On behalf of the IBEA Company, Captain Frederick (later Lord) Lugard and George Wilson had built a fort at Dagoretti in October 1890, but from the reports he received about Dagoretti, Stewart decided that settlement in that locality was "quite impracticable at present". The local Kikuyu people were in arms against the Company's agents who manned the strongly-built stockade there, and it had had to be evacuated twice in the previous year because of local hostilities. He concludes, "We shall reach Dagoretti by and by, but not just yet".[9] He and the guide to the expedition (the same George Wilson just mentioned) visited Machakos but decided against settling there as it was much further from the coast and therefore more expensive to keep supplied. Also the area was almost treeless and had only a scanty water supply. So Dr Stewart decided to stay at Kibwezi, a place of "great beauty and rich vegetation" and above all a place of "excellent water in abundance".[10] Land was purchased from the Kamba Chief Kilundu and the mission station was established on the caravan route from Mombasa to Machakos and Uganda.

The choice of Kibwezi proved to be disastrous. The place was unhealthy and the population sparse. The periodic arrival of the Company's caravans maintained the malarial infectivity of the local mosquitoes which bred in great numbers in the nearby Kibwezi river, in the irrigation channels dug to water the Mission gardens and in a large swamp which began to form beside the mission station about a year after the Mission arrived, due to ground subsidence. The result was that the staff suffered from chronic malaria which occasionally was complicated by blackwater fever. The occurrence of blackwater fever at Kibwezi was attributed to the temporary poisoning of the wells by locusts. In addition, these caravans brought other infectious diseases of various kinds including occasionally the dreaded smallpox. For various reasons, within about twelve months, only Thomas Watson remained of Dr Stewart's original party and it had become clear that Kibwezi could not be regarded as the permanent site of the Mission.

Meantime the situation around Dagoretti had improved and in September 1894 Watson travelled up to Dagoretti to seek a possible site for the Mission. However, he was urgently recalled to Kibwezi when Dr David Charters, who was head of the Mission, mysteriously disappeared on a hunting expedition. Charters' body was never found but his Express rifle turned up later at Arusha which suggests that he had been killed by a war-party of Masai warriors.[11] Watson then succeeded him as head of the Mission. In April 1895 Watson was joined at Kibwezi by Dr Matthew Wilson and later that year the two of them visited the area of Dagoretti and chose a site for the Mission near the Company's fort there. Lugard's original fort had been rebuilt on a different site about two miles north of Dagoretti by Captain Eric Smith in 1891 and was now called Fort Smith. Watson wrote a full report on this visit to the directors of the Mission Committee and set out the reasons for a change of location for the Mission from Kibwezi to Dagoretti. He sent off this report on October 28th 1895 and it reached Glasgow on December 18th. The directors considered the report but were reluctant to agree to the change of location. There the matter rested until Watson went on leave to Scotland and was able to report personally to the Committee. He left for Scotland on July 7th 1896 and in due course sought and obtained the permission of the Committee for the change of location.

In Kikuyu Country

Armed with the necessary permission, Watson returned from Scotland in September 1897 only to experience several frustrating delays, including one due to his contracting smallpox. A year later he was at last able to report that on September 11th 1898 he had transferred the Mission from Kibwezi to a site near Dagoretti called Baraniki. However, Watson's troubles were not yet over for, when Dr Thomas Homer arrived to serve with the Mission, he at once condemned the site as too low-lying, and another site had to be sought. This new site was one and a half miles to the west of the Baraniki ridge and higher up, and came to be called Thogoto locally, but it became better known as Kikuyu after the name of the people it served.[12]

Meantime, both Sir William Mackinnon and Alexander Bruce had died in 1893 and the EASM Committee had already begun to feel that they could no longer carry responsibility for the Mission. In December 1893 an approach was made to the Edinburgh Medical Missionary Society, but this Society was unwilling to take over responsibility for the Mission. Then on December 4th 1900 Thomas Watson died of pneumonia, and on the 15th of the same month the directors approached the Church of Scotland with the request that this Church might become responsible for the staffing and administration of the Mission. In May 1901 the General Assembly of the Church of Scotland agreed to accept this request on the recommendation of its Foreign Mission Committee (FMC).

So it was that on January 1st 1903 the Church of Scotland FMC assumed responsibility for the Kikuyu Mission. However, it was not until May 9th 1907 that the final legal transfer of the Mission with its endowments in Scotland and its assets in East Africa was completed. The Church of Scotland took over the Mission from the Mackinnon trustees on the understanding that it would be maintained apart from the resources of the FMC, and in July 1907 the FMC set up a special board of management, made up of nine members from the FMC and nine from amongst the subscribers to the Mission. This body was called the Kikuyu Subcommittee. This special arrangement continued to operate until January 1st 1937 when it was changed to allow the Mission to come directly under the FMC like all the other mission fields of the Church of Scotland. This meant that the financial support of the Mission would now come from the funds of the FMC where formerly it had come from the private subscriptions of those interested in its work. However, following this change, the subscribers to the Kikuyu Mission were allowed to appoint a representative of their interests to the FMC, and for many years this was Miss Agnes B. Bruce, the daughter of

Alexander Bruce, the original secretary of the EASM, and a granddaughter of David Livingstone.

In 1901, the Revd Clement Scott DD had recently returned to Scotland from Africa where he had been the head of the Blantyre Mission of the Church of Scotland in British Central Africa (later called Nyasaland and now Malawi). He was appointed as the Superintendent of the new Kikuyu Mission of the Church of Scotland.[13] On November 15th 1901 he embarked with his wife and their two daughters on the British India *SS Matiana* and reached Mombasa in the following month. His appointment and arrival forged yet another link with David Livingstone after whose home town in Scotland, Blantyre had been named.

The Kikuyu Mission develops

Now that the future of the Mission at Kikuyu was assured, development proceeded along the lines which had been followed by Scottish missionaries at Lovedale, Livingstonia and Blantyre. This meant that its work was to be a combination of religious, educational, medical and industrial activity. Thus it was that Clement Scott, and the colleagues who soon joined him, set about developing the work with the aim of making Kikuyu a training institution for African ministers, teacher-evangelists, hospital assistants and artisans. Much of this training was practical and technical, so that in its early days the Mission was often referred to as the East African Scottish Industrial Mission, the title which Mackinnon would have preferred for the Mission. Scott was able to obtain additional land at Kikuyu, to promote an extensive agricultural development in order to make the Mission self-supporting, as well as to train the local people in efficient agricultural methods. He also set up other technical training departments including a carpentry workshop, a forge for metal-working and a printing press.

When Clement Scott died of pulmonary embolism on October 13th 1907 at the age of 54, he was succeeded by the Revd Dr Henry Scott, a namesake but not a relation. Henry Scott arrived at Kikuyu from Nyasaland on 28th December 1907. He had studied theology and medicine concurrently, as Dr Robert Laws of Livingstonia had done before him. After qualifying in both disciplines he served in Nyasaland (modern Malawi) as a missionary, first at Domasi and then at Zomba. He proved to be the kind of missionary statesman which the Kikuyu

Mission needed at this time. He promoted co-operation between the various missionary societies working in Kikuyuland. In his own Mission he introduced a programme of village preaching in which the missionaries went out to the villages within reach of Kikuyu each evening and explained the gospel round the village fire using a lamp and Bible pictures.[14]

Meanwhile, Krapf's vision of a chain of mission stations across Africa with an extension northwards into Abyssinia had not entirely faded. Shortly before his death, Clement Scott had made plans for two of his colleagues to go up to the Meru area to the north-east of Mount Kenya and open what would be the first of a series of mission stations in the direction of Abyssinia. With his death these plans were abandoned. Nevertheless his successor was soon conscious of the need to establish a mission station further into Kikuyu country once this became possible in 1908. It was only in that year that missionaries were permitted to cross the Tana River into northern Kikuyuland because the Government administration had previously believed that the state of this area was too unsettled for this to be allowed.

Soon after Dr Henry Scott arrived he obtained a site for a mission station south of Mount Kenya on the lower slopes of Tumutumu Hill in Nyeri District. On the top of this hill was a sacred fig tree at which the local Kikuyu elders offered sacrifice and prayers in times of distress such as drought and famine. The new station was called Tumutumu and was in the midst of a population of about fifty thousand African people. The first members of staff at this new station were Petro Mugo and Danieli Wacira, both of whom had been assistants in the printing department at Kikuyu and had been recently baptised. Petro went alone there in October 1908 and then was relieved by Danieli a few months later. Then in July 1909, Arthur Ruffell Barlow ('Bwana Baaru') arrived at Tumutumu. Barlow was Clement Scott's nephew by marriage who had come out from Devon to Limuru at Scott's invitation in December 1903 and soon made himself proficient in the Kikuyu language. When he arrived at the new station he found that a small day-school had already been started by Petro and Danieli which had an average daily attendance of twenty-five pupils. Dr Horace Philp arrived from Scotland in April 1910 and began to develop the medical work at Tumutumu. In 1912 Dr Philp was one of the first doctors to train African medical assistants and demonstrate to sceptical Government officials that Africans could readily learn medical skills and use them effectively to serve their own people.[15]

The next stage in the expansion of the work of the Church of Scotland Mission was its extension into Chuka-Mwimbi country.

CHAPTER TWO

INTO CHUKA-MWIMBI COUNTRY

Travelling north from Tumutumu round the eastern slopes of Mount Kenya, we pass successively through country occupied by a number of agricultural peoples who are also members of the group of the Kikuyu people. These are the Ndia, the Embu, the Chuka, the Mwimbi and the Meru, with the Mbere and the Tharaka on the plains below the mountain.

The Chuka-Mwimbi People

The Kikuyu people, of whom the Chuka-Mwimbi form a part, are themselves part of the large family of Bantu peoples who now occupy about three-quarters of Africa south of the Sahara. The name Bantu is a linguistic one and was first used by Wilhelm Bleek in a book on the languages of South Africa in 1862. It does not denote a homogeneous ethnic group but those peoples whose word for a human being is derived from the root *ntu* denoting humanness, as, for example, the word *muntu* which means a person in the Mwimbi language (*Kimwimbi*). The word Bantu thus literally means 'people'. The language of the Bantu people is characterised by two features which are not found in other languages. These are the division of its nouns into a number of classes distinguished from each other by their prefixes and by a law of alliterative concord. By this law the prefixes of all the words of a sentence are determined by the prefix of the subject noun.

There are two main theories about the origin of the Bantu peoples which we may distinguish as the West-East theory and the North-South theory. The West-East theory is the older one and derives the proto-Bantu from West Africa where they are believed to have originally occupied south-eastern Nigeria and the central Cameroons.[1] About three thousand years ago they began to move gradually into the area of the Congo-Zambesi watershed and then travelled south and east. In the south they went to Angola and Zambia where they arrived about 500 BC. In the east they came to the head-waters of the White Nile. Some of the Bantu then moved directly south again into Zimbabwe and South

Africa. Others migrated east to reach the East African coast and then they moved northwards until they reached the Juba River and settled in an area called Shungwaya in the vicinity of modern Kismayu (Port Durnford). From here they were pushed south again by the Galla and the Somalis until they came back to the Tana and the Athi Rivers about AD 1200-1300. On reaching these rivers, they moved inland up their valleys and spread out fanwise to occupy the land which the rivers drained. It is believed that the Kamba people represent those who moved up the Athi River valley, whilst the Kikuyu group of peoples consist of those who moved up the valley of the Tana River. According to this view, the Chuka and Mwimbi peoples were settled on the eastern slopes of Mount Kenya by about AD 1300. The Kikuyu group of peoples thus originally entered Kikuyu country from the east and formed the north-eastern part of the eastern Bantu migration.

The North-South theory suggests that the proto-Bantu came from the middle Nile valley, and more specifically from the Cushite kingdom of Meroe.[2] About the year AD 350, this kingdom was conquered by Axum, a state of north-east Ethiopia, and its people began to migrate south. They moved gradually through Ethiopia to reach East Africa. Eventually about the fifteenth century or earlier they migrated across country to reach Tigania and Igembe or up the Tana River valley until they arrived at the foothills of Mount Kenya. Then they moved slowly south across the eastern foothills of the mountain. As the migration progressed, groups of people separated off from the main migration and either stayed on the plain or moved up the ridges on the mountain. Those who stayed on the plain became the Tharaka and the Mbere, whilst those who moved up the ridges became the Mwimbi, the Chuka and the Embu. The rest moved on further south and became the ancestors of the
present-day Kikuyu.

A variation of this theory suggests that there were in fact two migrations. The first and main one from the north as we have just described which produced the Tharaka, Chuka and Embu people.[3] The second migration which occurred about the eighteenth century came from the coast up the Tana River. This migration passed through Tharaka country and up the ridges of Mount Kenya and became the Mwimbi and the other smaller peoples of the east side of the mountain. Support for this suggestion of two migrations is found in the distinct physical differences between the Chuka and the Mwimbi which have been noted by numerous observers. The Chuka people are stockier in build and their skin is blacker in colour than that of the Mwimbi.

According to both views, the people who form the present-day Kikuyu moved on and reached the area of Murang'a (Fort Hall) about AD 1550. Some of them then moved north to Nyeri where they arrived about 1700, and others moved south to the Kiambu area where they settled about 1800. They were still in the process of occupying the land in the Kiambu area when the Europeans first arrived.[4]

Thus eventually we find the Chuka-Mwimbi people settled in the location which they occupy today, although they continued to extend that location westwards by a steady encroachment on the forest above them. They were not, however, the first people to live there. According to Kikuyu tradition they were preceded by a hunter-gatherer people whom they called the Aathi (a word meaning 'hunters' in Kikuyu) and the Masai called the Ndorobo. These people lived in the forests of Mount Kenya and it was from them that the Kikuyu claimed to have purchased the land on which they settled and with whom they probably intermarried. Before the Aathi, the land was occupied by the Gumba people whom Leakey describes as a prehistoric people of the late Stone Age and early Iron Age. They were pygmies who lived in underground pit dwellings in the forest around Mount Kenya where they hunted wild animals and kept bees.[5] It has been suggested that the Aathi resulted from the intermarriage of the Kikuyu and the Gumba.[6]

The meaning of the name Chuka is unknown, but may be related to the name of the River Naka which flows through the Chuka country on its way to join the Ruguti and forms part of the Tana River system. The original name of the Government station established in Chuka was Fort Naka. The name Mwimbi comes from that of the traditional mother of the Mwimbi and may be compared with that of Muumbi, the mother of the Kikuyu. The father of the latter people was Gikuyu from whom the name of the Kikuyu people is derived. No satisfactory explanation has ever been offered of the reason why the ancestors of the Kikuyu were called Muumbi and Gikuyu.

The most plausible explanation available is that
> a man met a woman who was making pots (*kumba*), and that this woman discovered that the man was sheltering under a wild fig tree (*mukuyu*). On marrying they called each other

nicknames, a usual Kikuyu custom, associated with the circumstances of their initial meeting. Thus the man called the woman Muumbi ('potter'), while the woman called the man Gikuyu ('of the fig tree').[7]

The size of the Mwimbi population in 1914 was estimated by the Government administration to be about twenty-five thousand, whilst the Chuka were said to number about fifteen thousand. A more accurate estimation by the Kenya Colony Survey Department in 1929 gave the figures as somewhat lower, with the Mwimbi numbering over eighteen thousand persons occupying about one hundred and fifty square miles of land, and the Chuka totalling over thirteen thousand persons occupying one hundred and fifteen square miles.[8]

The Chuka-Mwimbi Country

The Chuka-Mwimbi country is dominated on the west by the large upthrust mass of Mount Kenya which rises above the hot yellow plains which surround its base. The people gave several names to this mountain which are all derived from the appearance of the perpetual ice and snow which can be seen covering the rocks and valleys of its summit. It is called *Kirinyaga* which means 'mountain of light or brightness' or 'mountain of the white-plumed male ostrich' because of the white glaciers which surround its black peaks.[9] The name of the country today is derived from the name *Kirinyaga*. It is said that the first European explorers employed Kamba guides who did not pronounce the 'r' and the 'g' in the name *Kirinyaga*. The result was that when they were asked the name of the big mountain, the guides answered 'Kenya' and that is what the Europeans called it.[10]

Mount Kenya is a long-extinct volcano which lies astride the equator. The walls of its crater have long since been worn away by wind and rain, so that its highest point now is not the crater rim as in the case of Mount Kilimanjaro, but the mass of hard rock which plugs the former vent of the volcano. This massive plug of rock now forms the three main peaks of the mountain - Batian (17,058 feet), Nelion (17,022 feet) and Lenana (16,355 feet) - which lie immediately south of the equator. Ridges radiate out from the area of the peaks, and the perennial streams and rivers from the glaciers and the wet moorlands have carved out numerous valleys and ridges as they ran down through the forest to drain into the Tana River to reach the sea, or into the Ewaso Nyiro River to end in the Lorian Swamp and disappear into the sands of northern Kenya.

When the Kikuyu peoples arrived at Mount Kenya from the east they found it covered by a great belt of indigenous forest at the altitudes between four and eight thousand feet. It was in this forest zone that they settled and began to fell the trees to uncover the rich fertile volcanic soil. The Kikuyu in common with the other Bantu peoples had brought with them a technology and a skill. That technology was the smelting and working of iron which may originally have come to them from the Nile valley. The soil of Mount Kenya was not only fertile, it also contained iron oxide which gave it a characteristic reddish-brown colour and was the source of the iron metal which the people obtained by smelting. The trees they felled provided the firewood they needed for warmth and cooking, and the charcoal they needed for iron-smelting. The skill they possessed was that of tropical agriculture by which they were able to cultivate crops such as millet, cassava, beans and maize. The felling of the trees gave them space in which to plant these crops for they were essentially agriculturalists, amongst whom the iron-working was a specialised activity confined to only one clan. It is also believed that they brought with them oxen and the domestic fowl. As they reached the East African coast during their migration they also became familiar with the banana and the Asian yam which had been introduced from Indonesia into Madagascar and then to East Africa in the early Christian centuries.

The Mission Arrives

The CMS regarded the area on the eastern slopes of Mount Kenya as part of their 'sphere of influence' and in 1910 had already set up mission stations at Kabare and Kigari amongst the Embu people. They had not, however, been able to expand to the north across the Thuchi River into the area occupied by the Chuka and Mwimbi people. This was partly because the people there occasionally showed hostility to Government officers on safari. By 1913 the situation had improved and a new Sub-district of Chuka-Mwimbi was formed as part of Embu Administrative District, and a Government station or *boma* was established at Chuka (Fort Naka). In September of that year, Dr John

W. Arthur, who had succeeded Henry Scott as head of the Kikuyu Mission when he died from malaria and dysentery in March 1911, approached the CMS and requested that the CSM be allowed to take over missionary responsibility for the Chuka-Mwimbi area. The CMS agreed on condition that the area should be occupied immediately. Dr Arthur then visited the area concerned in October of that year along with William Tait, an industrial missionary from Kikuyu, and they were assigned two possible sites for a mission station. One was at Chief Kabangango's location about two miles from the Government station at Chuka and the other in Chief Mbogoli's location in Upper Mwimbi.[11] The result was that in March 1914, the Kikuyu Mission Council requested approval from the Foreign Mission Committee of the Church of Scotland for the opening of a Mission amongst the Chuka-Mwimbi people. The Committee regretted that it was unable to approve this request. A year later, Dr Arthur was on leave and went with his father, who was the convener of the Kikuyu Subcommittee, to present the case for opening a mission station in the Chuka-Mwimbi area to the parent Committee at the Church's headquarters at 88 Queen Street in Edinburgh. This time the Committee agreed to the request, provided the work was "of an experimental kind and on a modest scale".

Following this decision by the Foreign Mission Committee, the Kikuyu Mission Council in September 1915 agreed that Dr Stanley Jones, who had recently arrived at Kikuyu, should be transferred to Chuka-Mwimbi, and that he should be joined later by another missionary. In preparation for this, Dr Jones, William Tait and Nurse McMurtrie with Daudi Makumi visited Chuka-Mwimbi in October 1915 and chose a third possible site for the Mission at Mweria in Chief Gaitungi's location in Lower Mwimbi, several miles lower down the mountain than Mbogoli's. They felt that the site at Mbogoli's was not sufficiently in the centre of the Mwimbi population. In the event, Dr Arthur decided that Dr Jones could not be spared from Kikuyu Hospital, and so the first members of staff to be posted to Mweria in March 1916 were Daudi Makumi, Wilson Waweru and Samsoni Maingi. Daudi and Wilson were teacher-evangelists from Kikuyu and had been members of Clement Scott's catechumen's class there. Samsoni was from Tumutumu and the brother of Danieli Wacira. He had been trained as a hospital assistant at Tumutumu by Dr Philp. He was one of the fourteen young men admitted to the catechumen's class there by Dr Henry Scott in March 1911. All three of these men were accompanied by their wives. A school was built at Mweria, the first in Mwimbi, and in 1919 it had a roll of sixty boys and fifteen girls. In later years, Dr Irvine spoke of how much the Chogoria Mission owed to these men and their wives who started the work in Chuka-Mwimbi and held on there until more support was forthcoming, in a situation of loneliness and sometimes of danger.

The First World War

However, by this time the First World War was in progress and the Foreign Mission Committee ruled that any further involvement in Chuka-Mwimbi should be delayed because of the present strain on the Mission staff and resources.

As the war in German East Africa progressed, the strain on the Mission staff and their resources increased. In March 1915 a Carrier Corps Hospital was built of temporary materials at Kikuyu with four wards of twenty-five beds each of which were looked after by Dr Jones. Early in 1916 Dr Philp was appointed Provincial Medical Officer for the Kenia Province until the end of the war in East Africa. Finally, in March 1917 the Government issued a Compulsory Service Order to conscript forty thousand young African men for service in the Carrier Corps in the military campaign in German East Africa. After this order came into effect, Dr Arthur successfully proposed to the military authorities that the Missions in Kikuyuland should form a Kikuyu Missions Volunteer (KMV) Carrier Corps. This unit was duly formed with a strength of about nineteen hundred young African men from the various Missions.[12] About five hundred were from the CSM, nine hundred from the CMS and the rest from the AIM and other Missions. Dr Arthur, Barlow and Tait were given leave of absence from the Mission to serve as its officers. They were duly commissioned as Captain and Second Lieutenants respectively. Handley Hooper of the CMS Kahuhia station also became a Second Lieutenant and five other missionaries were given non-commissioned rank. The unit was mustered at Kikuyu on Saturday April 14th and each recruit was given a copy of *Tuthomo*, an elementary reading book in Kikuyu to help them learn to read. After about a month's training the Corps left for Mombasa from where it sailed to Dar-es-Salaam and then moved upcountry to Dodoma and then to Iringa where they supplied Belgian troops of the Iringa Force with food and ammunition. After only about six months' service in the field, the Corps was disbanded in February 1918, but the missionaries were not able to return to their stations until April.

The historian of the Carrier Corps comments that "the KMV played a part out of all proportion to their small numbers or the short time that they served".[13] He also comments that the KMV casualty rate of 5.5% was much lower than the 14.6% rate recorded for the Carrier Corps as a whole, and suggests that even this figure was an underestimate and that the overall casualty rate was about 22%.[14] The low casualty rate of the KMV is a reflection of the care which their missionary officers took of the men under their command.

It might be thought that this absence of missionaries on service with the KMV Battalion of the Carrier Corps would have been a great hindrance to their work. So it was, locally and temporarily, but ultimately it proved of great benefit. There was great keenness on the part of young African men to join the mission unit voluntarily rather than be conscripted by their chiefs into units where they might have to serve under uncongenial officers. The number of young African men who volunteered to serve in the battalion was far greater than the total of those who had so far been baptised as a result of the work of the missions.[15] Service in a common cause and in face of common dangers, brought the missionaries closer together with more African young men than had so far been possible at this early stage of missionary work. In later years, these young men often said how grateful they had been to the missionary officers for their care of them, and for all that they had learned from them. The result was that when they returned home after the war, they were far more open to the message of the missionaries than they had been before. This common service and expatriate experience also gave rise to a new political awareness amongst them with consequences to which we shall refer later.

In the meantime, in November 1916 the Kikuyu Mission Council had requested permission to proceed with the occupation of Chuka-Mwimbi as soon as possible after the close of the war in German East Africa, but this permission was still not forthcoming from the Foreign Mission Committee. Even so, Chuka-Mwimbi was not forgotten and the Mission Council prepared estimates for the further development of the work there and submitted them to the Committee in 1917. During this period Dr Arthur visited Chuka-Mwimbi once each term to keep in touch with the work there.

In the middle of 1918, the Provincial Commissioner of the Kenia Province (now called Central Province) wrote to the Mission Council to say that the Government was proposing to close their *boma* or substation at Chuka because of the shortage of administrative staff. The Provincial Commissioner suggested that the Mission might take over this site and buildings in place of the site at Gaitungi's previously assigned to them, but on which no permanent buildings had so far been erected. The Foreign Mission Committee agreed to this arrangement and gave the Mission Council authority to negotiate terms on its behalf. However, by 1921 the Government had changed its mind and the *boma* site was no longer available.

After The War

Once the war was over, the question of the further development of Chuka-Mwimbi was considered and in 1919, estimates were drawn up by the Mission Council for the the continuation of the work which had been begun there in 1916.

The matter became urgent in 1920 for the Government insisted that the time had come for a European missionary to be stationed in Chuka-Mwimbi. If this were not done, the previous permission for the establishment of a Mission there might have to be withdrawn. Finally, following this threat, in November 1921 the Foreign Mission Committee gave permission for the Mission to be developed further, but only on the lines of medical work and under the Government's Native Reserves' Medical Scheme which had been introduced at the end of the war. Under this scheme the Government provided an annual grant of £1,572 for both Kikuyu and Tumutumu CSM Hospitals, and it was hoped by the Mission that any medical work begun in Chuka-Mwimbi would eventually qualify for a similar grant. This grant would then supplement the financial support from the Church of Scotland which had indicated that it could provide only a minimum of the support necessary.

Once there was the prospect of the appointment of European missionary staff and the development of a permanent mission station, the Mission Council drew up revised estimates for the Chuka-Mwimbi station for the year 1922 totalling £320. The Foreign Mission Committee voted £100 towards this amount in the expectation that funds would also be available from the Government's medical scheme already mentioned. In addition, a Scottish lady, Mrs Stewart of Culgruff at

Crossmichael in Scotland, had given a donation of £600 for the erection of buildings at Chuka-Mwimbi.

However, the situation was soon about to change dramatically with the appearance of a doctor and the offer of financial support for the new Mission.

CHAPTER THREE

THE PROSPECT OF HELP

East Africa was one of the lesser-known theatres of action in the First World War. In the European 'Scramble for Africa' of the nineteenth century, East Africa had been divided up between the British, the Germans and the Portuguese. At the outbreak of war in August 1914, German East Africa (later called Tanganyika and now included in Tanzania) found itself surrounded by territories held by hostile forces. At first, it was hoped that the war would not involve the overseas territories of Britain and Germany, but this was not to be. German forces deliberately attacked British East Africa to make Britain divert resources from the European theatre of war in order to defend her East African interests.

The German forces were led by General Paul von Lettow-Vorbeck, an able and resourceful military commander, who was able on numerous occasions to outwit the British forces. However, Britain gained command of the East African coastal waters and so was able to blockade the ports of German East Africa and cut off his supplies and reinforcements. She was also able to call in the help of South African troops under General Smuts who took over as supreme commander in 1916 and began a new offensive against the German forces. By November of the following year, all German troops had been driven out of German East Africa or taken prisoner, and military operations had moved south into Portuguese East Africa (now Mozambique) and eventually into Nyasaland and Northern Rhodesia. During this time British troops were still being sent out as reinforcements to Dar-es-Salaam as the main port of German East Africa which was now under British control.

The Army Doctor

Amongst the troops which disembarked at Dar-es-Salaam early in July 1917, was a young doctor who had been commissioned in the Royal Army Medical Corps. He had left Britain in May 1917 on the *SS Durham Castle* calling at Sierra Leone and then rounding the Cape of Good Hope to reach East Africa. On arrival in German East Africa he was posted first to a medical unit at Itigi and then to the Carrier Corps hospital at Dodoma. From here he went in November to take charge of a medical post at Matikiro in the Iringa sector of the battlefield. And here he first met Captain John W.Arthur of the KMV Carrier Corps when the latter was out looking for water for his men at Matikiro. Dr Arthur records this meeting in his diary for Thursday 13th December 1917.[1] The doctor's name was Archibald Clive Irvine, recently graduated in medicine at Aberdeen University. Soon after his graduation he was called up for military service and after a short period of training he was sent out for service to the East African theatre of war.

Dr Irvine was the son of the Revd John Archibald Irvine and Lilian White who were married in Limerick in southern Ireland in 1892. He was born in 1893 in Liverpool, where his father was minister of Princes Road Presbyterian Church of England. He was the eldest in a family of three sons and three daughters. He was educated at Birkenhead School until his father moved to the charge of the South Street United Free Church of Scotland in Aberdeen in April 1908. This Church had a membership of eleven hundred and supported a missionary in China. After the family moved to Aberdeen, Archie (as he was known then) entered Aberdeen Grammar School for two years to complete his secondary education.

His sister Lyn has left us an account of the home life of the Irvine family in her book entitled *So Much Love: So Little Money*.[2] They were a large family, closely-knit and full of life. As the title of the book implies, they had little to spare of material wealth but they were able to enjoy a happy and secure family life with kindly and devout parents who were always concerned for their welfare. In the family, Archie was notorious for his sociability and unquenchable spirits which made a great contribution to family life. This is reflected in a comment that he made in a letter written much later in life when he admitted that "I have so often let my sense of humour get me into hot water". As an undergraduate he always played a full part in the annual University rag day when he would dress up in some outrageous costume to go collecting in the student procession down Union Street in Aberdeen.[3]

In October 1910 he entered Aberdeen University which he was able to attend from home. In October 1913 he graduated MA after completing a course which included Latin, logic, and pre-medical science subjects. Four years later, on March 23rd 1917 he graduated MB ChB passing the fourth professional examination "with much distinction".[4] When we first meet him in East Africa he is twenty-four years old. However, it was whilst he was an undergraduate that he became a committed Christian after an interview with a young American visitor to the Irvine home, named Fosdick, and it was after this that his thoughts began to turn to eventual missionary service.[5]

The New Missionary

At the end of hostilities in East Africa, Dr Irvine assisted with the repatriation of African members of the Carrier Corps and during this time he visited several mission stations in Kenya including the Church of Scotland Mission at Kikuyu. When his time came for demobilisation, he chose to be demobilised in East Africa.

He then offered to the Kikuyu Mission for missionary service. On July 19th 1919 he was posted to Tumutumu to assist Dr Philp in the medical work there, and took up residence in the large stone-built manse there. At this time he bought a Douglas motor-cycle and sidecar for use as transport. Because of the presence of two doctors, that year saw a great expansion of the medical work at Tumutumu and the opening of the first three outstation dispensaries in that area.

In November 1919 the Church of Scotland Foreign Mission Committee agreed to the request of the Mission Council that Dr Irvine should be engaged locally in East Africa on temporary appointment for two years. At the end of this period he would return to Scotland on leave with a view to his permanent appointment as a missionary of the Church of Scotland.[6]

The Missionary Bride

One of the best-known brands of biscuits in Britain for many years has been Carr's biscuits. The Carr firm was a family firm of Quaker origin and the youngest son of the Carr family was Ernest Carr. Since his other brothers were well-established in the management of the firm, Ernest was advised to branch out into some line of business other than the manufacture of biscuits. He chose jam, and in 1912 formed Carr,

White & Company Ltd, Jam and Preserve Manufacturers, who built a factory in Wigton near Carlisle. His business prospered, particularly during the First World War.

His firm sold the Wigton factory in 1920 and Carr decided to move with his family to a pleasanter climate than that of England. At first he considered emigrating to California, but finally decided on Kenya which he had heard about on his business trips to Madagascar to buy fruit for the jam factory. Kenya had just been declared a Crown Colony and its name changed from that of British East Africa to Kenya Colony and Protectorate. The Protectorate was the coastal strip which still belonged to the Sultan of Zanzibar.

In December 1920, therefore, Ernest Carr and his wife arrived in Nairobi with their son and four daughters. They stayed first in the Muthaiga Club until they found a small stylish stone-built house set in a garden amid a small area of indigenous forest in Lenana Road. It was called *Woodlands*. The family was very hospitable and soon built a wooden *banda* in the garden to accommodate the many missionary and other guests who visited them. Before long, Carr became involved in business affairs in Nairobi and was a partner in Carr, Lawson Ltd which eventually became Hughes, the well-known agents for Ford motor cars in East Africa. He also developed interests in tea and sisal production and in the company supplying electricity to Nairobi and Mombasa.[7]

On the first Sunday after their arrival, the family attended the African service in the CMS Church in Nairobi and soon became familiar with Church activities in Nairobi and in the country generally. One day in 1921 Mrs Carr read in *The Life of Faith*, a Christian periodical, about a spiritual revival which was occurring at the Church of Scotland Mission at Tumutumu. This had begun at a watch-night service on New Year's Eve 1919 and had led to a remarkable quickening of the spiritual life of the Church there.[8] Mrs Carr wrote to Tumutumu to learn more about this work, with the result that the second-in-command of the hospital came to visit Woodlands, namely, Dr Clive Irvine. Following this visit, Carr drove his family up to Tumutumu where they met the staff and stayed overnight.

On Friday, May 6th 1921, Dr Irvine was married to the eldest of the Carr daughters, Margaret Joyce (Joy), in All Saints' Church, Nairobi (which became All Saints' Cathedral in 1927). The service was conducted by the Revd Canon George Burns of the CMS in Nairobi and the best man was Dr Stanley Jones of Kikuyu Hospital.[9] After a short honeymoon at the Brackenhurst Hotel in Limuru they returned to live at Tumutumu in a *banda* with walls of banana bark lined with papyrus reeds, a thatched roof of grass and a floor of undressed stone. Their colleagues called it 'Banana Castle'. Dr Irvine then became Medical Officer-in-charge of the hospital whilst Dr Philp and his family went on leave to Scotland. Mrs Irvine later recalled one significant change that his marriage had made to her husband's situation. Up till then, his salary as a Church of Scotland missionary had been £225 per annum, and when he got married he was given an extra £25 to cover the cost of his wife!

In August 1921, Dr and Mrs Irvine offered to go to Chuka-Mwimbi when they returned from leave in Scotland in the following year. In that same month, Ernest Carr went out to Tumutumu and offered to take his son-in-law to see the area. They set off early one morning in Carr's open four-seater Ford motor car with the back full of camping equipment. Seven miles down the road Dr Irvine happened to glance round and notice that his father-in-law's sun helmet was no longer in the car. In those days this was an essential item of clothing for Europeans in the tropics and so they turned round and soon came across an African young man dressed in a blanket and carrying a sun helmet, which they gratefully took over from him, giving him a huge tip because neither of them had any small change. They eventually reached the Government station at Chuka and camped there and were able to gain some impression of the countryside and the Chuka people. They did not, however, get as far as Mwimbi.

In October Dr and Mrs Irvine went on leave to Scotland for a year. On February 28th 1922 Dr Irvine appeared before the Church of Scotland Foreign Mission Committee and was appointed a missionary to Chuka-Mwimbi "to commence work on medical lines as already approved by the Foreign Mission Committee".[10] In April of that year they became proud parents of their firstborn son Anthony and spent a great deal of time and energy on deputation work around the Churches in Scotland in order to stimulate interest in the new Chuka-Mwimbi mission to which they were to go on their return to Kenya. On September 1st they embarked on the *SS*

Modasa for their return to Kenya. The *Modasa* was a sister ship of the *Matiana* which we have seen brought Clement Scott and his family to Mombasa in 1901. Both these ships belonged to the British India Steam Navigation Company which was founded in 1856 by Sir William Mackinnon whom we have already met as the chairman of the Imperial British East Africa Company and of the East African Scottish Mission.

CHAPTER FOUR

IN CHUKA-MWIMBI

Now that the missionary doctor had been found for Chuka-Mwimbi, the question of financial support for the work became urgent. The Foreign Mission Committee in Edinburgh had made clear to Dr and Mrs Irvine when they were appointed that they could provide only a bare minimum of support to the new Mission and that to begin with, the work must be on medical lines only and on a modest scale. The situation was made even more serious by the refusal of the Government to provide a grant for any medical work at the new Mission under the recently-introduced Native Reserves' Medical Scheme.

The Generous Benefactor

At this point Ernest Carr intervened. He offered to guarantee the sum of one thousand pounds annually for the five years 1922 to 1926 inclusive to enable the work to go forward on both medical and educational lines.

Whilst this generous offer was gratefully accepted by the Foreign Mission Committee, they laid down the following conditions before the work should go forward:

1   The work should be wholly financed locally including the cost of the overseas missionary staff.
2   There should be no transfer of overseas missionary staff to the new station from either Kikuyu or Tumutumu.
3   More permanent local support should be sought than then existed.[1]

These conditions were accepted by the Mission Council and the way was now open for the further development of the work in Chuka-Mwimbi which had been so patiently pioneered by Daudi Makumi and his wife Priscilla, Wilson Waweru and his wife Rebeka, and Samsoni Maingi and his wife Naomi.

Carr took a keen interest in the work at Chogoria and his name will occur again and again in our story. He also kept a close watch on its finances. So we find his son-in-law writing to the Secretary of the Foreign Mission Committee to ask him to delay sending invoices for drug purchases until the following quarter so that he would not overspend in the current quarter, for "as you know, my father-in-law will be very annoyed and will distrust me in future if I go beyond my estimate". It may be that Dr Irvine wrote this with his tongue in his cheek, but he not only wrote, he also sent a cablegram to the same effect.

The Station Established

Now that it had been agreed to expand the work in Chuka-Mwimbi, the first question to be settled was the definitive location of the mission station. In February 1922 whilst the Irvines were in Scotland on leave, Carr with Dr and Mrs Arthur and Barlow went with the local Government officers from Embu to decide where the Mission should be located. Three sites had previously been considered and we have already seen how evangelistic, educational and medical work had been begun on the site at Mweria in Chief Gaitungi's location selected by Dr Jones. However, Gaitungi had not proved to be very co-operative with the work of the Mission. The three sites were now examined afresh and the one preferred was one of the two originally chosen by Dr Arthur in 1913 and described then as "a beautiful green sward".[2] This site was in Chief Mbogoli's location in upper Mwimbi near his village at Mutindwa and was called Chogoria, a name of unknown derivation.[3] It stood about two miles below the forest line on Mount Kenya at an altitude of five thousand feet. The party then negotiated with the land owners in the presence of the Provincial Commissioner for the lease of a plot of forty acres for the new Mission. Carr and Barlow returned in March and the latter prepared a survey of the new plot which had to be in two parts to avoid the African homesteads and gardens (*shambas*) which were present on it.

The next question was that of accommodation for the doctor and his wife and family. To meet this need, Carr had a wood and corrugated iron bungalow prefabricated in Nairobi and taken out to Chogoria in sections by a convoy of seventy ox-carts. The 146 mile journey of this convoy was undertaken in March 1922 in the middle of the long rains, along narrow cart-tracks and over many rickety wooden bridges, some of which were damaged by the heavy ox-carts. This convoy was followed by six motor cars containing Carr and Barlow and other Europeans for the purpose of the survey just referred to, but which also conveyed Indian carpenters whose task was to erect the new bungalow on the smaller of the two plots. Carr and Barlow then camped on the new site for two weeks in order to ensure that a good start was made with the building of the bungalow. Carr returned later to supervise the completion of the building.

Dr and Mrs Irvine and Anthony arrived by ship at Mombasa on September 27th 1922 and came up to Nairobi the same day by train and then stayed for ten days with the Carrs at Woodlands. Then on Monday, October 9th they set off for Chogoria at 5.30am in an open Dodge motor car laden with their belongings. After a long day of driving they turned off the main Meru road and drove for another two miles along a narrow track with the bush meeting overhead. As they crossed a small clearing they saw the red-painted corrugated iron roof of the bungalow and knew they had at last reached Chogoria. Their long dusty journey of 146 miles had taken them just over twelve hours.[4]

Two or three days later their household goods arrived on two ox-carts from Banana Castle at Tumutumu and they began to settle into their new home. It was a new experience for Mrs Irvine who although she had had music training, had no training at all in setting up house out in the blue amongst a people who, though friendly towards their new neighbours, had no knowledge of their ways and needs. Fortunately, they began to have a number of European visitors who were able to help them in their settling-in process and in the early development of their work.

The Doctor Begins Work

Whilst his wife was busy organising the home and looking after the young Anthony, Dr Irvine was beginning to plan the development of the mission station. He had a number of advantages which aided him in this work. First, he was beginning on a virgin site. The only building which existed when he arrived was the bungalow which became the home of himself and his family. This meant that he was stepping into no-one else's shoes and was free to develop the work and the site as he wished. Second, he was already familiar with the Swahili and Kikuyu languages from his experience in the Army and at Tumutumu and this made communication with the local people possible from the start. As the Mwimbi people were members of the Kikuyu group of peoples they readily understood Kikuyu, even though their own language was a distinctive dialect of that language. Thus, for instance, their words of greeting were different from those of the Kikuyu. Third, he was able to call on the assistance of men who had already been trained at Kikuyu or Tumutumu in the various skills which were required to establish a mission station. Daudi, Wilson and Samsoni, for instance, had already gained the respect and confidence of the people.

The new doctor lost no time in getting things organised. The Chogoria ridge was treeless, but it was covered by dense bush which reached higher than a man's head and so on the day after his arrival when six men were sent by the local chief, Dr Irvine got them to clear the bush from the mission plot to form a garden and an area on which buildings could be erected. Soon he had about twenty men and they became the nucleus of the workforce which gradually transformed the Chogoria ridge and its bush into an organised mission station. He held a daily service for the workmen from the beginning. One of those original workmen told afterwards how they did not close their eyes during prayer because they were not sure what the good doctor would do whilst they had their eyes closed!

Soon after he arrived in October 1922 he was joined by more African staff who had been trained at Kikuyu or Tumutumu. These included two teachers, two hospital assistants (Suleiman Nanju and Paulo Wohoro), one evangelist (Daudi) and one carpenter (Ayubu Nguiai).[5] In the following year they were joined by another two teachers, one hospital assistant, and a stonemason named Maina who was an elder from Tumutumu who became a very valuable member of the staff.[6]

The Mission Industrialised

As we have already seen, there was a tradition within the Scottish Mission of industrial activity and training, and so it is not surprising that this side of the work at Chogoria was developed early. Indeed such activity was essential for the development of a mission station situated so far away from supplies and so distant from a railway which might bring these supplies.

Here once again, Ernest Carr stepped in to help. On his original visit in February 1922 to decide the site of the new Mission in Chuka-Mwimbi, he had noted that one feature in favour of Chogoria was the presence of a small waterfall on the nearby Kamara River. The result was that when Chogoria had been secured as the site for the Mission, he ordered a small hydroelectric 20 kilowatt DC generator from the Anglo-Swedish Electric Company in Sweden which was brought out to Chogoria from Nairobi on twenty ox-carts and installed at the waterfall in February 1924. The flow of water over this waterfall proved to be barely sufficient in the dry seasons to operate the 22½ horsepower Pelton wheel which ran the generator. The result was that later in 1924 a furrow was dug from the South Mara River to bring water across to increase the amount of water in the Kamara.

The availability of electricity allowed the building and equipping of an industrial workshop. Once again, Carr provided the means to purchase most of the heavy equipment needed, so that by August 1924 Dr Irvine could write: "We now have a first class workshop; it looks like a factory!" The earliest items of equipment to be installed were a large circular saw for cutting up logs, a smaller saw for finer work and a twelve-inch electric planer. Other items were added as they became available and by 1927 there were no less than nine power-driven machines in the workshop. These included a grindstone, a sand-crusher and sifter, and a clay-mixer to which was added a small hand-pumped forge for metal work. To begin with, the workshop was set up not very far from the bungalow and Mrs Irvine comments on the noise the machines made, and how sometimes it was impossible for her to work in the house as a result. She compared the noise made by the electric planer to that of a mighty organ. However, by 1927 the workshop building had become too small and was rebuilt on a site further away from the house. The workshop became known locally as the *tinga*, an obvious onomatopoeic indication of the noise made by the machines.

Apart from the wood-and-iron bungalow, the first buildings at Chogoria were of mud and wattle with thatched roofs, but the facilities provided by the workshop soon allowed the planning and erection of more permanent buildings than had been possible in the early development of the mission stations at Kikuyu and Tumutumu. In the indigenous forest above Chogoria were trees such as the Kenya cedar and camphor which were resistant to termites, and the Mission now had the means needed to prepare wood from them suitable for building. So trees were felled in the forest and their trunks brought down by ox-cart to be sawn into planks in the workshop and then planed for use in the erection of buildings. Some of these early buildings at Chogoria were made of wood with roofs of wooden shingles and were partly paid for out of the donation given by Mrs Stewart of Culgruff already mentioned.

What Did The People Think?

It may well be asked at this stage, what did the local people think about what had begun to happen in their midst? When the Methodist missionaries began to work amongst the Meru people to the north of Chogoria, the attitude of the local people was said to have been one of indifference.[7] When Chogoria was established, however, the attitude of the people there was "friendly and co-operative".[8] On one occasion Dr Irvine described it as "amused tolerance".[9] He also recorded that there was little opposition from the local medicine men and they were even outwardly friendly.[10] Much of this friendly reception can be put down to Dr Irvine's own natural friendliness and warm interest in people. He was never given a nickname by the local African people as several other missionaries were, but was simply called *rigitari witu* ('our doctor') when he went out on preaching tours or on medical safaris. The use of this name gave him special pleasure. He was also referred to as 'Aveni' which was an obvious local attempt to pronounce his surname.

Few of the local people had seen Europeans before. When the African people first came into contact with Europeans they called them *athungu* which means 'those who move around' and comes from the Swahili verb *zunguka*, to go around.[11] What had impressed the African people when they first came into contact with Europeans was their ability to move readily from place to place.

What Did The People Believe?

But what did they believe about God, and how did this relate to the message of the gospel which these newcomers had come to bring?[12]

The Chuka-Mwimbi people believed in *Ngai* or *Murungu*, the great, all-powerful, supernatural, impersonal, invisible being who was the creator and giver of all that exists.[13] He had no father or mother, or any companions. He lived in the sky but had temporary resting-places on the four boundary mountains of Kikuyuland. His main one was on the top of Mount Kenya and so he was called *Mwene-nyaga*, the lord of the ostriches, a name derived from that of the mountain. He manifested himself in such natural phenomena as rain and thunder and lightning, and in the sun, moon and stars. Thunder was *Ngai* cracking his joints as he prepared for action against his enemies, and lightning was the sword by which he cleared his way.

Ngai was remote from ordinary existence and took but little interest in individuals and their daily lives. Only major catastrophes or important crises of life warranted an appeal to him for his assistance. Even on these occasions he could not be approached by individuals but only by the family, clan or age group as appropriate. Thus at the four major events in the life of the individual, namely, birth, initiation, marriage and death, it was the family group which approached *Ngai* for the spiritual assistance which the individual required. Before he was approached, every other means of dealing with the situation had to be exhausted for "*Ngai* is not to be pestered". This was a saying much used in Kikuyu life.[14]

There was no idea that humans might have a continuing personal relationship with *Ngai*. There was no demand for a personal act of trust in the love and goodness of *Ngai*, only a requirement of trust in the power and work of the medicine man who was the means by which humans could contact the spirit world.

The people also believed in a world of ancestral spirits which mirrored the earthly world and was in communication with it. There were three types of spirits: the spirits of the family, the clan and the age-group, all of which could affect the life of the individual. These spirits could be pleased or displeased by the behaviour of an individual or family or age group. Also, these spirits could bring misfortune or sickness on an individual or family. When this occurred the services of a professional medicine man (*mundu mugo*) were called upon to determine which spirit was responsible, why it had been offended and how it could be appeased.

The people had no sense of personal responsibility towards *Ngai*. Sin was a mistake which threatened the welfare of the community, not an act against *Ngai* and so he did not need their repentance nor they his forgiveness. Guilt consisted of ceremonial uncleanness (*thahu*) incurred by the breaking of law and custom, of taboos and religious injunctions, whether deliberately or unintentionally. This was regarded as an individual matter and *Ngai* was not approached to deal with it. The removal of the ceremonial uncleanness was undertaken by the individual concerned who would call in the services of a medicine man; he would find out what had happened and then conduct an act of ceremonial cleansing or purification which always involved the sacrifice of a sheep or goat.

"Throughout the whole scheme of relationship with the spirit world, whether with the ancestral groups or with *Ngai*, ran the scarlet thread of sacrifice."[15] Without the sacrifice of a sheep or a goat there could be no reconciliation between human beings and the spiritual powers. Sacrifice was thus necessary to obtain the intervention of *Ngai* in situations of drought, famine and plague, and for the appeasement of the spirits which were producing family misfortune.

The New Faith

The new faith was based on the written tradition in the Bible and not on oral tradition as in the religion of the Chuka-Mwimbi. Once the people had the contents of the Bible explained to them they recognised some elements in it which resembled those of their own ancestral faith, especially the idea of a all-powerful creator and of the need for sacrifice. But there were very significant differences too.

In contrast to *Ngai*, the God of the Bible was personal and anxious to have fellowship with human beings. He was interested in all human affairs and had actually come to live amongst men and women in the person of his Son Jesus Christ. He loved all people individually and could be approached by individuals through prayer at any time. But originally, humankind had rebelled against him and fallen into sin, and it was this sin that kept us from enjoying fellowship with him, and sin could only be removed by sacrifice. At first, as the Old Testament showed, he had accepted animal sacrifices, but then he had given his own Son Jesus Christ as a final and sufficient sacrifice so that people could be forgiven if they accepted that sacrifice for themselves.

There was no place for the ancestral spirits in the new faith and no work for the medicine man. There were spirits indeed, but these were the Holy Spirit, the third person within the Godhead, and the Devil and his evil spirits or demons, who were subject to the Holy Spirit.

The gospel taught too that each person was responsible before God for his or her own daily life and conduct and that each needed to come before God in repentance and faith in order to be accepted by God and enjoy fellowship with him. The basis of that acceptance was the sacrifice of Jesus Christ on the Cross.

This was the new faith which the missionaries had come to bring and to invite the Chuka-Mwimbi people to accept.

A Roadside Encounter

A good illustration of how the old religion prepared the way for the new faith is provided in an incident which Dr Irvine described in 1929.[16]

One day he was driving the Mission lorry down to lower Mwimbi to collect a load of maize. As he drove along, he came on a group of young Mwimbi men, some of whom were dressed in war paint of grease and red ochre with their hair in pigtails fore and aft. They were performing a slow dance led by one of them who was singing in a high falsetto voice. He stopped the lorry and got down to ask about what they were doing. They explained the dance and then performed it again for him. Dr Irvine invited them to sit down and chat and they did so. He then took out his Kikuyu New Testament and showed it to them saying, "This is God's book which tells us how good and pure God is". They agreed that God was good. He went on to speak about how evil humans were, and of this they were not so sure until he gave them some examples which showed that humans were evil. He pointed out that since God was good and humankind was evil this only led to war and fighting. He asked them what could be done about our evil and they said they did not know. He then went on to say, "If a man is sick, don't you sacrifice a goat and trust that he will get better?" They agreed and then he went on to read the verse John 3.16 which showed how God himself had provided a sacrifice for our sin, and if we accepted that sacrifice for ourselves, we could be put right with God. They were very interested in this and Dr Irvine encouraged them to pray to God every morning and evening for forgiveness and for strength to know and to do the right. They were all friendliness and said that it was a good matter that they had heard. At this he invited them to come to the Mission to hear more, and climbed back into the lorry and went on his way to collect the maize.

CHAPTER FIVE

EARLY DAYS AT CHOGORIA

Life at Chogoria in their early days was very different for Dr and Mrs Irvine from the life they had left behind them. It is of interest to record the various aspects of their life there, on which they commented in the letters and reports sent to friends and supporters.

The Bush-Pigs

When they first arrived, the countryside was overrun by wild bush-pigs which lived in the forest. The people hunted them with spears, but could not control their numbers. The bush-pigs dug up and ate the food being grown by the people in their gardens. They loved yams especially. One man came to Dr Irvine to beg his help. He grew yams for sale; the bush-pigs were eating them all; he could not now raise the money required to pay the hut tax which the Government now demanded from the people. Others said they had not enough food to feed themselves and their families.

Dr Irvine sent an urgent message to the Secretary of the Foreign Mission Committee in Edinburgh to ask him to send out two pounds weight of strychnine nitrate. When this arrived he began to issue it to the local people to use in bait which they laid out for the bush-pigs to eat. The people paid for the strychnine in kind for they were not yet used to a money economy. Foodstuffs that were obtained in this way were used to feed the patients in hospital.

This method of eliminating the bush-pigs was very effective although even in 1935 they were still damaging local crops. Today these animals are rarely seen in the Chogoria area. The people, of course, were very grateful to the doctor for this kind of help.

Locusts

Another threat to the food supply in Chuka-Mwimbi, and to that of Kikuyuland as a whole, was the invasion of locusts. These were the desert locust variety which bred in the desert areas of Saudi Arabia and then flew across the Red Sea in great swarms into the Horn of Africa. From here they came south into Kenya and caused great damage to crops. Although locust invasions were always serious because of their effect on the food supply of the people, there were two occasions when they were more serious than usual because they were combined with other disasters. The first occasion was in 1898-1900 when a locust invasion occurred at the same time as other disasters to produce economic and political consequences to which we shall refer in Chapter Eight. The second was in 1918-19 when the locusts appeared during a period of drought which coincided with the great pandemic of influenza of those years. The result of this combination was a greatly increased mortality rate amongst the people living in the area of Mount Kenya. Every year locust invasions are mentioned in the Mission reports until the late 1940s when the efforts of the Desert Locust Control Service were successful in preventing locust invasions. This they did by controlling the breeding and swarming of the locusts in their breeding grounds in the Arabian peninsula.

The Supply of Food

Once there were fewer bush-pigs around locally, the Irvines began to plant a vegetable garden and to employ local men to look after it. Since Chogoria was just south of the equator it had two rainy seasons and therefore two harvest seasons, for crops grew very quickly. The two rainy seasons were distinguished locally as the rains of the beans in March to May (the long rains), and the rains of the millet (the short rains) in October to December. The short rains were usually the heavier rains around Chogoria. The crops which the Irvines planted in their garden included potatoes, French beans, bananas, oranges, strawberries, figs and passion fruit.

Mrs Irvine describes how they commonly obtained meat in their early years. The nearest butcher's shop was at Meru, forty miles to the north. It was kept by a Somali butcher and its meat was inspected by the local Government Health Department staff before being put on sale. After Meru became their post office, a member of the Chogoria African staff went there on foot twice a week to post and collect mail. He would also buy meat at the butcher's shop and bring it to Chogoria wrapped in banana leaves, but by the time it arrived in Chogoria it was often too far gone to be used. However, it was immediately put into a solution of potassium permanganate to sterilise it, and then usable portions were cut off from it and the residue disposed of. An alternative source of meat was from the local people who on occasions would kill a sheep or a goat and bring the hindquarters or other parts of the carcase for sale to the missionaries at Chogoria. The local people also kept hens and would also bring chickens for sale. Also, once they realised that the missionaries ate eggs, these also became a ready source of food.

Food from the garden and other sources was supplemented by tinned food which was brought up from Nairobi. It was several years before refrigerators became available at Chogoria to allow the storage of perishable foodstuffs.

No bread was available locally and so Mrs Irvine began to bake her own. She had not been taught how to bake until one day they had a European visitor who offered to teach her. She became a very talented baker and trained her house servants in the art too, as well as teaching it to the wives of many missionary colleagues. It is interesting to find her recipe for bread-making still being used at Chogoria today.

The Milk Supply

The supply of milk from the local cows posed a particular problem in the early years. The cows were in the control of the male heads of the local families, usually elderly men who adhered closely to their traditional ways. When approached they said that they could supply milk but it must be according to local Mwimbi custom. Thus the cow must be milked into a calabash. If the milk were received into any other kind of vessel, then the person who drank it would be overtaken by misfortune for which the owner of the cow would be held responsible. Also the calabash must be cleaned by using a mixture of cow's urine and ash from the village fire. If this were not done, the cow would die. Finally, the milk must not be boiled or cooked or mixed with any other substance or the supplier's family will incur *thahu* and this would be expensive since it would have to be removed by the *mundu mugo*.

Obviously the acceptance of a local supply of milk proved to be difficult and so to begin with, the staff had to use tinned milk. However, the prospect of receiving payment for the milk was so attractive that the old men came up with a solution. Although the above customs meant that Mwimbi cows could not be used to supply milk, they would buy cows from Chuka so that any bad effects would be passed on to the

Chuka families and the Mwimbi families would not be affected! This was done and milk was supplied. However, with the economic depression in the 1930s, Chuka cows became too expensive and so Mwimbi cows came to be used without any of the expected bad effects. Of course, the milk had still to be boiled before drinking, just as all drinking water had to be.[1]

Visitors

Once Chogoria was established it began to have a great number of visitors. One reason was that Chogoria provided a convenient base from which to climb Mount Kenya from the eastern side. Mrs Irvine tells of one young man who turned up alone one day and said he had come to climb the mountain and would they please supply the necessary equipment for him to do so. They supplied what they could and he set off. When he came down the mountain he then asked them to buy from him the tins of food which they had originally supplied him with, some of which he had already opened. They did not feel they could disappoint him!

There were also visitors who came with their cameras to photograph wild game and the mountain peaks. They often published books which described their safaris and displayed their photographs with never a mention of their Chogoria hosts whose hospitality they had enjoyed and sometimes just taken for granted.

There were still other visitors who had expertise of great value to Dr Irvine in his plans for the development of Chogoria. Some visitors were Government officers of various kinds who paid formal or informal visits to the new Chogoria Mission. Other visitors were missionary colleagues from the other stations or from other missions, such as the Methodist Mission which had been established at Kaaga near Meru in 1913.[2] There was no ordained missionary at Chogoria for several years and so when the services of an ordained missionary were needed for the celebration of the sacraments, either Dr Arthur from Kikuyu or Dr Philp or Mr Calderwood from Tumutumu would come as welcome visitors.

Travel to Chogoria was not always easy in these early days. There was only one road of access to the Chuka-Mwimbi area and that ran north from Sagana on the Nairobi-Nyeri road through Embu and Chuka to Meru. Chogoria was situated on a side-road which branched off this main road some twenty miles or so north of Chuka. The roads were earth roads and often not much wider than cart-tracks. They became impassable in the rainy seasons which left them deeply-rutted; and they could be blocked by landslides. The bridges across the innumerable rivers and streams which came down from Mount Kenya were made of wooden logs and planks. These wooden logs and planks would be attacked by white ants (termites) and then the bridges would collapse under a heavy load. They would not be repaired for some time, and so Chogoria would be cut off by road for up to three months until they were repaired.

Prayer

One of the most significant activities of the daily life of Chogoria was prayer. Within a few months of his arrival at Chogoria we find Dr Irvine writing in his second circular letter:

> A fine work may be built up of energetic labour in the field and hospital and classroom, but the far harder work of winning souls is done by the far harder work of praying. If I would name a gift, as Solomon did, I would ask, I think, that I might have a mighty "joy in prayer, and liberty and power to continue in intercession for others".[3]

Eighteen months later we find him saying that his circular letters are not intended to raise money but "to raise prayer".[4] The work at Chogoria was begun and continued in prayer. As we have already mentioned, Dr Irvine began each working day in prayer with the workmen. As the work developed and the staff increased, definite times of day were set aside for prayer in the life of the station. These varied from time to time. At one period it was at 8am; at another time it was midday; and at other times in the evening when a prayer meeting would be held in the Church twice a week.

This practice of prayer in the daily routine of the Mission arose from the Irvines' firm belief in the efficacy of prayer and from their own practice of personal prayer and Bible study.

They could give many examples of answered prayer in the history of Chogoria. Thus in 1946 Dr Irvine recorded that "we prayed together in our morning prayer-meeting about the asked-for increase [in the Government grant] for hospital, and the grant was put up from £324 to £600. We prayed for stone-cutters (now that stone had been found at

Chogoria) and two appeared the day we began to pray.... In 1936 we prayed definitely for £400 to build girls' boarding quarters and three months later we got word that two legacies of £300 and £100 had been left for Chogoria, so we believe that He will provide now for the same thing for our boys."[5]

Dr Irvine became well-known for his practice and belief in prayer as the natural expression of the Christian life. In the obituary written by his sister Elizabeth, she quotes the comment of a Nigerian working in student circles in Nairobi: "Few Christians in Nairobi do not know of praying Irvine".[6] This comment refers particularly to Dr Irvine's ministry of prayer in Nairobi after he left Chogoria, but it is a true description of his whole life.

He often spoke on the importance of prayer in the Christian life, especially to students. On one occasion he addressed the Christian Union at Makerere University College in Uganda on this subject, and then published an expanded version of this address under the title *Telephone to Heaven*. This booklet was first published in 1967 and has been reprinted several times since then.[7] The booklet is written out of the practice and experience of prayer in the daily life of the Irvines and their staff at Chogoria. In it Dr Irvine speaks of prayer as a "telephone to Heaven" which is never engaged, never cut off and never out of order. He goes on to speak of the basis of prayer in God's love for his people expressed in the promises about prayer we find in the Bible, and the need to persevere in prayer. Prayer should be specific so that we can know when God answers.

The Family Arrives

We have already seen how Dr and Mrs Irvine came to Chogoria in October 1922 with their first-born son Anthony, born in Aberdeen. In November 1923 a second son Geoffrey was born at Chogoria. As there was still no registered nursing staff at Chogoria, Sister Milligan came over from Tumutumu for the birth. In June 1925, a third son arrived, Kenneth; the family was complete.

In due course, the three boys went to kindergarten at Limuru and then to primary school at Pembroke House in Gilgil. They then attended the Prince of Wales' School in Nairobi for their secondary education. Anthony went on to Cambridge University to study physics, whilst both his brothers qualified in medicine and will appear again in our narrative.

CHAPTER SIX

THE FIRST SEVEN YEARS

From the beginning, the name of the Mission had been the Chuka-Mwimbi Mission, but in 1926 it was agreed that it would henceforth be known as the Chogoria Mission, or simply Chogoria. This change of name gave the Mission a more individual identity as well as a shorter name. Also from the beginning the Mission was associated with the name of Dr Clive Irvine as the pioneer European missionary at Chogoria. This is why the history of Chogoria is also part of the story of his life.

Publicity and Support

Chogoria had been launched originally on a very slender budget and then on a guarantee of funding for only five years. What lay beyond those five years was still uncertain, but it was clear that the work at Chogoria would have to be much more self-supporting than that at Kikuyu or Tumutumu had ever been.

Dr Irvine realised this from the start and used his talents of authorship and of photography to promote and sustain the interest of the members of the Church of Scotland and other Christian people in the work at Chogoria. When he was on leave in Scotland in 1927 he produced a few copies of a handmade booklet of annotated photographs covering the years 1922 to 1927. In 1930 he published the first number of what became an annual booklet entitled simply *Chogoria*. In the year 1934, 1350 copies of this booklet were printed and sent out at a total cost of about thirty-five pounds sterling. He continued to produce this booklet in September of each year until 1957 in which year seven hundred copies were printed. However, in that year the Church of Scotland Foreign Mission Committee decided that it was no longer able to give grants towards the cost of publications issued by its individual mission fields. No issue, therefore, appeared in 1958, but a final number appeared in 1959. This final number, which was the thirty-second issue, was produced free of charge by the printing firm G.& W. Fraser Ltd of Belmont Street Printing Works in Aberdeen which had printed all the previous numbers from 1930, "as a thank-offering to God for his goodness".[1] Every issue of the booklet contained photographs of the work of the Mission in Chogoria and its area, except when the shortage of photographic film made this difficult during the Second World War. Thus there were no photographs in the 1942 booklet, and a reduced number in the following three years when films were still in short supply.

Already, of course, during their first missionary leave and before they had begun work at Chogoria, both Dr and Mrs Irvine had spoken at many meetings and with many people in Scotland about the new work among the Chuka-Mwimbi people. On their return to Kenya Dr Irvine continued to maintain contact with those who had expressed an interest in supporting the work. During his second leave from February 1927 to March 1928 he was authorised by the Foreign Mission Committee of the Church of Scotland to appeal direct to Church congregations in Scotland for the work at Chogoria. This kind of permission was not usually given to missionaries on leave, but was given in the case of Chogoria because the Committee was finding difficulty in providing support, now that the Carr benefaction was about to cease. The result was that by the time they had returned from leave, Dr and Mrs Irvine had raised funds which would cover the cost of the work at Chogoria for the next two years. After their return from leave in 1928, Dr Irvine records that he personally wrote about seven hundred letters to supporters in Scotland to keep them informed of the progress and needs of Chogoria.[2]

Industrial Development

In the last week of the year 1922, Ayubu the carpenter came to Dr Irvine with a lump of blue clay in his hand which he had found in the valley below Chogoria. For the next few months they experimented with the making of sun-dried bricks, and they used these to form the floor of the new Church which as we shall see was opened in June 1923. In the next year a visitor came to Chogoria named Perry who was an expert in brickmaking. Following his advice, Dr Irvine continued with the experiments in brickmaking with the bricks now fired in a kiln. Different mixtures of clay and earth were tried and wooden box-moulds were made. The clay and earth were mixed in the clay-mixer and came out as smooth soft material which was then pressed into the box-moulds.

When the bricks were formed they were laid out in long drying-sheds to dry off before being fired in the kiln. By December 1923, Dr Irvine was able to report that they were producing a good quality of large-sized bricks with two holes down the centre of the length of each brick to facilitate drying. A later visitor to Chogoria said that these bricks were the best he had seen in the country except for those made by the railway workshops in Mombasa. Another visitor said that the type of clay they had at Chogoria was that in which diamonds were often found, but none were ever found at Chogoria.

As the work developed, it became clear that Dr Irvine needed the help of a qualified artisan to run the workshop and to supervise the erection of the new buildings required to house the different departments which were being set up and to provide accommodation for the staff of these departments. However, it will be recalled that when Chogoria was established on the basis of Ernest Carr's guarantee, the Foreign Mission Committee had laid down certain conditions for the acceptance of that guarantee. One of these was that there should be no transfer of overseas missionary staff to Chogoria from either Kikuyu or Tumutumu.

It so happened that at this time there was a free-lance European artisan temporarily employed in the industrial department at Tumutumu named G.C.Cobb, who was not an overseas appointment. Dr Irvine successfully requested permission to employ a local artisan and so was able to employ Cobb when he left Tumutumu.[3] He came to Chogoria in February 1924 and stayed for the best part of four years. His help was invaluable and with the help of the African craftsmen who had come from the other two stations, including Maina the stonemason from Tumutumu, he was able to begin the technical training of local Mwimbi young men. By the time he left in 1928 to join the CMS, Cobb was able to hand over supervision of the workshop and building work to Gaitungu who was one of the earliest workers at Chogoria and very competent and reliable. At this time, the usual establishment of the works department was about ten people. However, when the time came in 1928 to build the new Church, the department was employing no fewer than forty men including three Indian carpenters. By 1929 Dr Irvine was able to report that there were now twenty-five permanent buildings at Chogoria, all of which had been designed by himself and erected by the works department under his supervision.[4]

Both Kikuyu and Tumutumu had well-established industrial training departments and as early as 1909 Kikuyu had introduced a three-year apprentice scheme for the technical training of local young men. In 1926 it was decided to introduce a similar scheme at Chogoria and sign on apprentices for training. Twelve apprentices were taken on for training in carpentry and brickmaking. However, this scheme did not prove attractive to the Mwimbi young men who were unwilling to serve an apprenticeship for three years at what they saw as too low a wage. The result was that the scheme was abandoned. However, although there was now no official training scheme, suitable local young men were taken on and trained in such skills as carpentry, brickmaking and metal-working.

Agricultural Experiments

With so plentiful a rainfall in Chuka-Mwimbi country, Dr Irvine was anxious to introduce cash crops for he soon realised that the Chuka-Mwimbi were basically an agricultural people and that prosperity would only come to the area if appropriate cash crops could be introduced. Thus we find him writing in 1923:

> In the belief that the future of the African lies in agriculture, a weekly lecture is given on this subject, and an acre or an acre and a half is being planted with mulberry, groundnuts, etc. in an endeavour to find and teach the cultivation of a new crop.[5]

In that same year there is a reference to an outschool which had a garden where the growing of cotton was being tried. In the event this crop proved unsuitable for the altitude of Chogoria, although it is grown lower down the mountain in Tharaka country today. The mulberry trees did however flourish and became the source of the mulberry wine which was made by Mrs Irvine for use in communion services.

Dr Irvine was able to encourage the planting of maize in an indirect way. We have already seen how Ernest Carr had provided the heavy equipment for the workshop at Chogoria. Soon after this new equipment was installed, Dr Irvine was presented with a stone mill for grinding maize by a European farmer in Limuru who became interested in Chogoria. The arrival and availability of this mill had the effect of encouraging the local people to grow more maize since they could now have it ground into flour more easily than before. Up till then the main staple cereal had been millet.

His great contribution to the agriculture of the Chogoria area was, however, the introduction of coffee-growing. In 1927, Dr Irvine reported that he had experimented with the planting of coffee.[6] He had brought coffee seeds from Kikuyu and planted them experimentally in Chogoria. The first coffee to be grown in Kenya was planted at Kibwezi by John Paterson, the agricultural missionary of the East African Scottish Mission. He had obtained the coffee seeds from the Sheikh Othman Mission of the Church of Scotland in Aden.[7] It is not recorded exactly when this planting was first done, but it must have been early in the development of Kibwezi for in March 1893 Dr Charters reported that some coffee seedlings were ready for transplanting. When the Mission moved upcountry from Kibwezi to Kikuyu the growing of coffee continued to be one of its agricultural activities.

Coffee-growing proved to be very suitable for the Chuka-Mwimbi area and coffee eventually became one of the main cash crops which was to bring much prosperity to the area. However, African people were not at first allowed to plant coffee, and it was only in 1935 that Dr Irvine obtained permission for coffee to be planted within a three-mile radius of Chogoria. The reason for this restriction was the lack of Government agricultural staff to ensure that the coffee trees were properly cared for and did not become diseased. By May 1938, the first crop of coffee berries was ready for picking.[8]

The Model House

Another contribution which Dr Irvine made to the local community is illustrated by an article he wrote on 'Huts and Houses' in the edition of *Kikuyu News* for December 1928.[9] In the introduction he commented as follows:

> One of the first signs of advancement in the African is building a better house. It is a very practical form of Christianity, because it definitely helps to improve his wife's condition - a valuable object because the wives commonly hang back from any innovation more than the husbands.

The traditional Chuka-Mwimbi hut was built of mud-and-wattle walls with a thatched roof of grass. It was circular with a conical roof and built on the ground with a low wall and with low thatched eaves which protected the mud wall from the rain. It had no windows and the door-opening was closed by logs placed across it horizontally and held in place by upright poles. These logs were very difficult to remove quickly if the hut went on fire, and several cases of severe burns had been admitted to hospital as a result. Also, there was no provision for ventilation and the smoke from the fire in the middle of the earth floor of the hut found its own way out through the door or seeped through the thatched roof.

To avoid these disadvantages, Dr Irvine designed and built an experimental house on the Mission. It was rectangular in shape and stood up off the ground on wooden piles to reduce the destructive activity of white ants (termites). It had mud-and-wattle walls, with bracken stitched over the outer surface of the walls to protect the mud from the action of the rain. The thatched roof was ridged and the eaves were cut short. Window-openings with wooden shutters were set in the walls and a proper opening door provided. The fire was removed from inside the house to a small mud-and-wattle kitchen outside where the cooking was done. The house was made entirely of local materials and no nails were used in the construction, for the materials were bound together by local twine made from vegetable fibre. No special tools were necessary apart from the panga or large cultivating knife which every family possessed. The floor of the hut was made of wickerwork which was then plastered over with mud to produce a smooth surface. This new design of house had several advantages over the old traditional round hut. The obvious one was the improved hygiene possible in the house. There was now provision for good ventilation and the entry of daylight and sunlight, both of which were important measures for the prevention of the transmission of infection. There was no accommodation for sheep and goats and cattle which all could be sources of human disease, notably tetanus. The new design also made it possible for husband and wife to live together rather than in separate huts as they did traditionally.

This new design of house attracted a lot of local interest and several of the local young men built houses of this type for themselves and their families. Eventually as the prosperity of the district increased, houses came to be built of stone with corrugated iron roofs but they were often built on the basic pattern of the Chogoria model house except for the piles.

This design was also used for buildings erected at outstations for the accommodation of staff and for the provision of dispensaries and other small buildings, when small verandahs were often added.

The Women's Lot

This design of a model house is a good illustration of Dr Irvine's concern for the family life of the African people and especially for the domestic burden traditionally borne by the wife.

Water for household use was obtained by the African people from the local rivers and carried in earthenware pots (and later in *ndebes* or four-gallon paraffin tins) by the women and older children from the river to their huts, often quite a long walk and a steep climb away. Realising what a burden this daily chore of fetching water was for the women, Dr Irvine began to encourage the men to buy donkeys for their wives which could carry the heavy containers full of water up from the river. However, this idea was not taken up and few donkeys are to be seen in Mwimbi country today.

Later on, when corrugated iron became available for roofing, he also began to encourage the husbands to install corrugated iron rainwater tanks beside their houses to collect the rainwater which ran off the roof. This was to provide a convenient and immediate source of water for the family, and so reduce the heavy work of fetching the water expected of the wife and older children.

Another chore of the wife was the collection of firewood which often meant a journey into the forest from which she returned bearing a heavy load. This was another responsibility of the African women with which a donkey could help. As we have just mentioned, donkeys did not prove popular and so today the women are still to be seen carrying bundles of firewood on their backs. Such bundles may weigh anything up to a hundred pounds and may have to be carried for several miles.

When the growing of coffee was introduced in the Chogoria area, Dr Irvine was not slow to realise that this too added to the burden carried by the women. It was they who were expected to harvest the coffee berries and had to transport them to the local coffee factories when these were established. Again the donkey could help with the transport and so there were many reasons why Dr Irvine never ceased to encourage people to buy donkeys, but without success.

On one occasion he commented on how the coming of civilisation had only increased the work of the women. Before civilisation came, the people dressed in skins and these did not need washing and did not need frequent changing. With the coming of clothes made of various fabrics, garments had to be washed and repaired and from time to time replaced. All this meant more work for the wife especially if she were to keep her children well-clothed. Dr Irvine said that he was always glad when a husband bought a sewing machine for his wife, even though he might expect the Doctor to buy it for him in Nairobi (as he often did) and bring it out to Chogoria for him. And, of course, when it needed repair the Doctor was always available! [10]

CHAPTER SEVEN

THE FIRST SEVEN YEARS (cont.)

Medical Work Established

The medical work began in 1923 in four little mud-and-wattle huts.[1] One of these served as an operating theatre and another as an injection room.[2] By August of the following year a dispensary-cum-operating theatre of brick had been built. To begin with, the medical work was mainly outpatient in character for hospital admission was a new experience for the Mwimbi people and they were unwilling to commit themselves to an overnight stay in the new building in the care of a strange European doctor. The new doctor had also to gain their confidence. Nevertheless during the year 1923 almost seven thousand outpatients were seen by Dr Irvine and the medical assistants who had come to Chogoria from Tumutumu.[3]

The Government had established medical facilities at their substation at Chuka in 1921. They had erected a mud-and-wattle building and sent a European medical officer with supporting African staff to man it. However, Government retrenchment forced the closure of these facilities and in 1925 Dr Irvine was appointed Acting District Medical Officer for Chuka. This withdrawal of Government medical services resulted in an increase in the number of patients coming to Chogoria. Some of these patients were Akamba who came across the Tana River from Kamba country to reach the hospital. They were wealthy and willing to pay a small fee for hospital treatment which made a welcome addition to the income of the hospital. Also, early in 1926 Dr Irvine was asked to supervise four Government dispensaries in the Embu District as the Government medical officer at Kerugoya was not able to provide the supervision they required. This took him away from Chogoria for two days each month and also further increased the numbers of patients who came to Chogoria for treatment. Later, the Government medical officer found he was able to supervise two of these dispensaries, leaving the remaining two to be looked after by Chogoria. This arrangement continued for some years for we find that in 1932 Chogoria was still providing drugs and supervision for two dispensaries in Embu District.

In April 1925 Dr Irvine began to build the first permanent hospital building. This was built of brick now that brick-making was well under way at Chogoria. The main building was completed in March 1926 and consisted of two large wards set at an angle to each other and connected together at the angle by a consulting room, a large dispensary, an operating room, a bathroom and a blanket store. The two wards between them had accommodation for a total of thirty patients. [4]

At the same time Dr Irvine planned and built a small home for leprosy patients on the spur of land which projected out into the Kamara valley below the hospital and was called Gatheru. This leprosy home was built of brick with a roof of wooden shingles and had four rooms with two beds each, with its own kitchen and store. The cost of this new home was borne by the Mission to Lepers (now The Leprosy Mission), who began to give an annual grant of £240 to the leprosy work at Chogoria. Dr Irvine had treated his first cases of leprosy at Tumutumu before he came to Chogoria. He was interested to find that the Mwimbi people did not know what this disease was and had no fear of it in spite of its disabling features.[5] In 1951 he wrote an article for the *East African Medical Journal* on his experience of running a small leprosarium at Chogoria. In this article he said that he had observed that a third of his leprosy patients had tapeworm and wondered if this condition predisposed a person to leprosy infection. However, he later realised that there was no significant connection between the two conditions.[6]

Dr Irvine reported in 1928 that the local people now had less fear of admission to hospital. Also in this year more buildings were added to the hospital compound. These included a small isolation ward, a kitchen and a ward for the accommodation of Indian patients for which the Indian community at Meru subscribed one hundred pounds. There were now seven hospital assistants at Chogoria who had come from either Kikuyu or Tumutumu.

The following figures show the number of patients seen and treated at the hospital during this period:

	Inpatients	Outpatients	Operations
1923	50	6,965	
1924	96	11,090	28
1925	311	16,446	16
1926	221	13,234	13
1927	332	14,128	17
1928	275	14,356	21
1929	315	15,570	64

The principal communicable diseases reported at this time were leprosy, yaws, tuberculosis, tick-borne relapsing fever and malaria. Whilst Dr Irvine was on home leave in 1927, Dr Janet Welch who had been working temporarily at Tumutumu was transferred to Chogoria to be responsible for the medical work. She reported treating 774 cases of yaws in 1927 as compared with 413 cases in 1926. Also she had treated 491 cases of malaria during medical safaris. Of these diseases, one of the most satisfactory to treat was yaws, for this disease readily responded to the intramuscular injection of Galyl, a preparation of bismuth sodium tartrate. With the introduction of this treatment and the collection of patients in yaws camps to apply it, the disease was eventually brought under control. The medical staff at Chogoria were largely responsible for the disappearance of the disease from Chuka-Mwimbi country. Dr Irvine developed a special interest in yaws which he first met at Tumutumu where three-quarters of the population were said to suffer from the disease. In 1925 he submitted a thesis on 'Yaws in East Africa' to the University of Aberdeen for the degree of MD. This was accepted and he graduated MD *in absentia* on July 9th of that year.

In this early period there was but little operative surgical work, but Dr Irvine describes one patient with an enormous tumour of the face arising from the lower jaw which he attempted to remove. He called on Mrs Irvine to assist him with the operation in the course of which he had to tie the carotid artery to control the bleeding. The patient died later. There were also many wounds and injuries to deal with due to men falling out of trees, and falling out with each other. In one case a child was brought in who had been trodden on by an elephant. Previously there were no hospital facilities on the eastern side of Mount Kenya for injuries like these. The Government hospital at Kerugoya was only opened in 1929 and that at Meru in 1930.

Another patient in this early period was an old woman who one night had carefully shut herself in her hut with the goats and a calf as was the custom, and then gone off to sleep. In the middle of the night she was wakened by a commotion in the hut and in the dim light of the fire she saw the calf standing up. She grabbed what appeared to be its tail to get it to lie down again when the owner of the tail, which happened to be a fully-grown leopard, turned on her and mauled her. She grabbed a glowing log from the fire and fought off the leopard which then fled. She was brought into the hospital and Dr Irvine was called to see her and he proceeded to stitch up her wounds under a local anaesthetic. She lay quite still as he worked and so he asked her did she feel the needle. She said that she did, but added, "What's the good of complaining when you are being helped?"[7]

The Church Founded

Nine months after the arrival of the Irvines at Chogoria, a Church building was erected and was dedicated in June 1923. It was a large cruciform mud-and-wattle building with rounded short sides and a porch in the middle of one of its long sides. It had a thatched roof which was ridged. At the centre point of the ridge there was a hole for ventilation which was covered over by a small roof of thatch to keep out the rain. The local people were very intrigued by this extra little roof, the like of which they had never seen before. Some of them copied the idea when they built themselves new huts for they found that the ventilation it provided reduced the smoke-laden atmosphere inside the huts. This was only one of the innovations which Dr Irvine was to introduce into local architecture and practice.

From the beginning, Dr Irvine began regular services and Church instruction classes. Each morning as the day's work began he would gather the workmen for prayer before allocating the work to be done that day. The Church had been built to seat over a hundred people and soon each Sunday morning service was being attended by sixty to a hundred people. At the end of 1923 he reported that thirty people were attending classes for instruction in the Christian Faith which were held on Wednesday and Sunday afternoons.

The result of this patient and intensive Christian teaching was seen in September 1924 when the first candidates to present themselves for baptism came forward. Dr Irvine was not yet ordained and so he invited Dr Arthur who was ordained to come from Kikuyu to carry out the baptisms. He came and on September 28th he was able to baptise twelve men, one woman and five children.[8] The name of the woman was Marion wa Musa. Also a further significant number of people were enrolled in the classes for Christian instruction. Mrs Irvine noted that there was great enthusiasm amongst the Mwimbi women, especially those who were married.

A year later Dr Arthur returned and was able to baptise a further eleven people and to admit twelve to the Lord's Table to partake of Holy Communion.[9] It was then arranged that in future when the services of an ordained missionary were required, they would be provided by the Revd George Calderwood or Dr Philp from Tumutumu. However in March 1926 the first African minister was posted to Chogoria. The Revd Jeremiah Waita was one of the first eight Africans to be ordained by the Presbytery of Kenya which had been set up in 1920 under the authority of the General Assembly of the Church of Scotland. Their ordination came at the end of a three-year course of training by Mr Calderwood at Tumutumu. After the Revd Jeremiah had been ordained at Tumutumu, he immediately offered to go to Chogoria where he was warmly welcomed by Dr Irvine. His coming allowed the formation of a Church committee to oversee the administration of Church affairs. Mrs Irvine recorded in her diary for 4th April 1926 that on that day for the first time a service of Holy Communion had been conducted by an African minister at Chogoria. This was another milestone in the progress of the Church there.

In 1925 Dr Irvine reported that up to one hundred and seventy people were now attending the Sunday morning services. However, he was disappointed with the collection which usually had amounted to one shilling until one Sunday he preached on giving and tithing, after which it increased to four shillings. Most of the collection was given in kind and so whilst there might be few coins or eggs in the plate, there would be piles of maize cobs, bananas and sugar-cane on the floor. These items were sold after the service and the money added to the total collected as coins.

Beginning in 1923, regular visits were paid to the nearby villages to talk with the people and to hold services on Wednesday and Sunday evenings. Sometimes it was not possible to hold a service as on the occasion when Dr Irvine and a medical assistant found the villagers making beer from sugar cane and all the men already drunk. By 1925, regular Sunday evening evangelistic safaris were being organised. Seven teams of three to seven Christian lads would go out on foot to preach in the villages within a five-mile radius of Chogoria. In 1929, Dr Irvine reported that these safaris were still being held and by this time the team of about twenty young Christians were taken out by lorry. They would be dropped off in pairs at strategic points and would hold services in two or three villages before being picked up and brought back to Chogoria. This allowed them to cover a much wider area.

A convention was held at Chogoria in September 1926. This was led by the Revd William Rampley and his family from the CMS station at Kabare near Embu. Mrs Rampley held special services for the women and the two young Miss Rampleys for the children. People came from all the outstations and the Church was crowded for most of the meetings.

The year 1926 was notable for another event in the history of the Church in Kikuyuland for it was in that year that the Kikuyu translation of New Testament was published by the National Bible Society of Scotland and the British and Foreign Bible Society.[10] Before this, the only parts of the New Testament available in Kikuyu and bound together were the Gospels and the Acts of the Apostles which were published in 1920. The New Testament translation was mainly the work of Ruffell Barlow and the Revd Harry Leakey of the CMS. Barlow had also published a book of Old Testament stories which he called *Mohoro ma Tene Tene* ('Stories of Long Ago'). The language of this translation of the New Testament was that spoken in the south and west of Kikuyuland and so it differed from the language of the Chuka-Mwimbi people which showed differences in dialect from the language spoken by the Kikuyu in these other areas. However, it was decided by the Bible Societies that these differences were not great enough to warrant a separate translation of the Bible for the Chuka-Mwimbi people. The Church at Chogoria therefore adopted the new Kikuyu translation as its official version.

The Church already had a hymnbook for in 1915 a Kikuyu hymnbook had been published with the title *Nyimbo cia Kuinira Ngai* ('Hymns to Sing to God'). These hymns were mainly translations from English, but original Kikuyu hymns were added in successive editions of the book. The latest revision of the hymnbook was published in 1974.

The first Church Service Book was published in 1926 to coincide with the ordination of the first eight African ministers to which we have already referred. The latest revision of this book was published in 1975.

The first Christian marriage at Chogoria was celebrated in 1927 after the banns had been proclaimed on Christmas Day. Because there were as yet so few Christian girls, Christian men had to take non-Christian girls as wives and be married according to African custom. Following this first Christian marriage, no fewer than twenty-four married couples came forward to have their marriage blessed in Church.

In June 1928 the Revd Jeremiah Waita left Chogoria and was replaced by the Revd Solomon Ndambi.[11] Also in this year seven deacons were appointed to form a Deacons' Court for the Church at Chogoria to supersede the Church committee which had been formed when the Revd Jeremiah had originally come to Chogoria. The names and work of these deacons were Ayubu (teacher), Filipo (evangelist), Gerishom (evangelist), Jonathan (evangelist), Maina (stonemason), Willie (evangelist) and Musa who was the first Christian to be baptised at Chogoria.[12]

On August 4th 1928 Mrs Ernest Carr laid the foundation stone of the new Church which was to be built in brick to replace the original mud-and-wattle structure of 1923 which was now falling into disrepair due to white ants, age and weather.[13]

The Church statistics which are available for this period are as follows:

	Baptisms	In Church classes
1923		30
1924	18	---
1925	11	110
1926	39	92
1927	48	363
1928	11	193

Educational Work Begun

The school at Chogoria was opened in 1923 with a roll of thirty-five young men. At first it met in the open-air, and then moved to the mud-and-wattle Church building which had just been built, but in July 1925 a separate building was erected for the school. The pupils were taught by the African teachers sent from Kikuyu. One of these teachers was Willie Kanini who originally came from the Embu area but had gone to Kikuyu to train as a teacher. He came to Chogoria only two months after Dr Irvine and became the teacher at Tungu outschool when this was opened. Eventually he was asked to take charge of the workshop stores, a position of great trust and responsibility which he held for over thirty years.

To begin with, the pupils were almost all in their late teens or young adulthood and married. Sometimes they brought their wives with them too, who in turn brought their babies. The classes were sometimes interrupted by the local chief seeking young men for labour and other purposes, and regarded the school as a convenient place to find a few suitable young men readily available. The school subjects included reading and writing in English and Kikuyu, with hygiene and Bible teaching.

The educational work soon spread from Chogoria into the surrounding district and by June 1923 Dr Irvine can list the following centres at which educational work had begun:[14]

Place	Teacher	Medical worker
Gaitungi's	Esau (a.m.)	Kanegene
Nyaga's	Esau (p.m.)	Nahashon Mwangi
Mutwanjema's	Ruhito	
Muthambi	Jonathan Mara (a.m.)	
Mutwathara's	Jonathan Mara (p.m.)	
Chuka *boma*	Harrison Kariuki (a.m.)	
Mutwarugamba's	Harrison Kariuki (p.m.)	
Kiambati's	Jonathan Kiambati	

At first the teachers for these schools also came from Kikuyu and Tumutumu but soon local Mwimbi teachers were being trained. The report for 1924 mentions that five had been recruited for training at Chogoria in that year. Once they were trained, the new teachers were given a smart khaki uniform with the initials CS (for Church of Scotland) in red on the left breast-pocket.

By the beginning of 1929 it had become increasingly difficult to recruit teachers from the other stations to run the larger schools in Chuka-Mwimbi. During the first half of that year there was only one at Chogoria itself, Wilson Waweru, who had been one of the original teachers who had come to Chuka-Mwimbi in March 1916. However, Wilson suddenly died in October 1929, and Dr Irvine himself had to take over his teaching duties in the school until a new teacher could be found.[15]

The numbers on the roll of the schools increased year by year as the following figures show:

1923	35
1924	200
1926	260
1927	428
1928	450

There was, of course, no national school curriculum or qualifying examination at this stage, but the pupils did not escape end-of-term examinations. These were often conducted by Dr Irvine as part of his duties as unofficial supervisor of schools. He describes how in October 1928 he went with a lady colleague to conduct the end-of-term examination at the school at Chuka. There were thirty-five pupils on the roll, but only eight or nine turned up for the examination. The subjects of the examination were reading out of a Kikuyu book, writing from dictation, reciting arithmetical tables to the twelve-times table, and answering questions on the Bible, the catechism and on general knowledge.

So far we have spoken of the education of the young men. The education of the Mwimbi women and girls also began in 1923 when sewing and Bible classes were begun by Hannah the wife of Paulo the evangelist who came from Kikuyu soon after Dr Irvine arrived in 1922. At first, only three women came but the numbers increased, and when Mrs Irvine was able to take over the class for one day each week, it had to be held in the open air under a shady tree and then finally met in the Church building. Many of the women brought their children and babies with them.

In 1925 Ernest Carr offered to support a lady worker at Chogoria for five years and Miss Harrell from the Africa Inland Mission joined the staff in March of the following year. She took over the sewing class from Mrs Irvine and taught English in the school, as well as helping in the hospital. After Miss Harrell left, two successive short-term lady missionaries were appointed until the more permanent appointment of Miss Rita Butter-Malcolm was made in 1929. In addition to her work in women and girls' education, Miss Butter-Malcolm also undertook nursing duties in the hospital having had some nursing training.

When Dr and Mrs Irvine went on leave early in 1927, Miss Marion Stevenson who had just returned from home leave was asked to undertake the oversight of all the work at Chogoria. Miss Stevenson had already had twenty years' missionary experience in women and girls' work at Kikuyu and Tumutumu. As the African staff at Chogoria were all from these two places, she got a great welcome from them when she arrived in March.[16] It was at Kikuyu that she had been given her nickname of *Nyamacheki* ('The lady of the cheques').[17] She was able to continue to encourage the women's side of the educational work. When she took over she found that there was only one girl in the class, the rest were all married women. The syllabus consisted of reading, sewing, hygiene and Bible teaching. Later the class was divided into two. Those who brought babies with them were now given their own class three times a week and their syllabus was expanded to include cooking, mothercraft and child welfare. In 1928 over sixty women came to this class. The other class was thus able to continue without the distraction which the babies provided.

The older women were not forgotten and a Grannies' class was begun in 1927. This met on a Thursday morning and began with five grannies and soon there were seventeen. Several of them walked long distances in order to attend, even up to sixteen miles. They drank pailfuls of weak sugary tea and listened to the Bible stories they were told by the lady missionaries and tried to understand the pictures of Bible life which they were shown. They appreciated having their own classes with the result that they encouraged the young people of their families to seek education at the mission.

Miss Stevenson was very energetic and during her stay at Chogoria she set herself to visit every village within reach and get acquainted with all the scholars and Christians in the outschools. On Wednesday afternoons the nearer villages were visited and those far away on weekend or longer safaris. For the longer safaris she would take a tent and camp. She would hold services in the villages and attract an audience by playing a portable organ and in the evening by showing pictures by using a magic lantern and a large screen. She would often be accompanied by Dr Janet Welch who would take her medical box with her and see sick people in the villages and extract teeth where necessary.[18]

The Chogoria Area Defined

To the north of the Chuka-Mwimbi territory lay that of the Meru people who also belonged to the Kikuyu group of peoples. By agreement between the Missionary Societies and the Government, this area was allocated to the United Methodist Missionary Society. This Society had originally begun missionary work at the coast in 1862 with the assistance of Ludwig Krapf, but in 1912 they also moved up to the Meru area and in September of that year built a mission station at Kaaga about a mile from the Meru *boma*.[19]

At first there was no clear boundary between the work of the Church of Scotland Mission and the Methodist Mission. As the work of the Methodist Mission expanded southwards and the work of Chogoria extended northwards it was obviously desirable that there should be a mutually-recognised boundary between their areas. So in 1928 it was agreed that this boundary should be the line of the Kithinu River.[20] The boundaries of the work of the Chogoria Mission thus became the Kithinu River to the north and the Thuchi River to the south. The area beyond the Kithinu northwards was now the responsibility of the Methodist Mission with its headquarters at Kaaga, and that beyond the Thuchi southwards was recognised as the responsibility of the Church Missionary Society with its main station at Kigari near Embu.

The area east of Chuka-Mwimbi was where the Tharaka people lived and the 3,000 feet contour of altitude is usually regarded as the western boundary of Tharaka country separating them from the Chuka-Mwimbi people. However, no eastern boundary was defined for the work of Chogoria and it was only in later years that Chogoria assumed some responsibility for the health and pastoral care of this area under the auspices of the Presbytery of Chogoria and the Community Health Department of the Hospital. The eastern boundary thus became the line of the Tana River.

CHAPTER EIGHT

OPPOSITION ARISES

Once the Chuka-Mwimbi people had occupied the land which became their country, their migration was at an end except for a deeper penetration into the forest belt above them. They never left their land unoccupied and so it was never considered by Government for allocation to European settlers. The situation was very different in southern Kikuyuland where acute problems of land allocation and tenure arose. It was out of these problems that Kikuyu opposition to the Government (and later to the Missions) arose, and eventually affected the work at Chogoria.

The Land Question

Since the sixteenth century the Kikuyu people had been slowly and steadily advancing southwards, and by the nineteenth century they had crossed the Chania River to reach the Kiambu area of southern Kikuyuland. As they advanced they had transformed the indigenous forest into agricultural settlement, except for a belt of forest which they retained to protect them against the Masai. They claimed that the land they now came to occupy had been purchased from the Aathi, its previous occupants.[1]

At the end of the year 1898 and during the years 1899 and 1900, no less than four natural disasters affected this part of the country. These were an epidemic of smallpox amongst the population, an outbreak of rinderpest amongst their cattle, a failure of the rains for three successive years which led to a long period of drought and famine, and finally a devastating invasion of locusts which consumed all the crops growing in their *shambas* (gardens or small holdings).[2] By April 1900, Thomas Watson at Kikuyu estimated that fifty per cent of the population of that area had died from disease or starvation.[3] The result was that the people fled north to the districts of Murang'a (Fort Hall) and Nyeri, and left the Kiambu area almost deserted. Thus when the British administrators came, southern Kikuyuland appeared to be unoccupied and "to have enough land for its population for generations to come, and a good deal which could reasonably be spared for others".[4]

In June 1895 the British Government took over the administration of the country from the IBEA Company and established the East African Protectorate. At first, no dealings in land between Africans and Europeans were permitted, but in 1902 a comprehensive Crown Lands Ordinance was introduced. The basic principle of this Ordinance was "that land not in beneficial occupation at the time was at the disposal of the Crown".[5] This was not, however, the understanding of the Kikuyu people; the land may have been unoccupied by them at the time, but it was not disowned by them and still belonged to them by right. Following the promulgation of the Crown Lands Ordinance, European immigration and settlement began in earnest. Land which was apparently unoccupied and without obvious ownership was in good faith allocated to these new immigrants by the Government in many areas of the country including Kiambu.

There was little reaction to this process on the part of the Kikuyu before the First World War. However, by the end of that war a number of young Kikuyu men had had their horizons widened by service in the Carrier Corps as we have already mentioned. On demobilisation they returned home and began to give more thought to the problems of their people. This led to the awakening of the Kikuyu political consciousness and to the formation of several political associations.

The first of these associations was the Kikuyu Central Association first formed in 1920 under the name of the Kikuyu Association. In the following year it was renamed the Young Kikuyu Association with Harry Thuku as its secretary. On March 14th 1922 Thuku was arrested and later deported to Kismayu (then part of Kenya), and the Association went underground until 1925 when it emerged under the name of the Kikuyu Central Association (KCA). In 1928 Johnstone (Jomo) Kenyatta became its general secretary and the editor of its new publication written in the Kikuyu language and called *Muiguithania* ('The Reconciler'). This was the first newspaper to be published by Kenya Africans. The main battle-cry of the KCA was, "Give us back our land". This meant that by its very nature the Association was anti-Government and anti-European, and later it was to become anti-Mission even though it often held its political meetings under the guise of religious meetings.

So far as the CSM was concerned, the first overt expression of an anti-Mission attitude on the part of the KCA was seen at Tumutumu in the years 1924 to 1926 when the Mission there began to enlarge its school gardens in order to make the teaching of agriculture more practical. This was seen by the the KCA as an attempt on the part of the European missionaries to establish title to land and so lead to its alienation to European settlers. The result was that all the crops in these gardens were uprooted and attempts made to have the land reclaimed.

The land question was not the only issue which was taken up by the KCA, for the Kikuyu had other grievances. These were the practice of forced labour, the obligation of registration and the possession of a *kipande* (African registration card), the high hut or poll taxes demanded by the Government and the low wages paid by the European settlers.

The propaganda of the KCA against the Government, the Europeans and the Missions was spread throughout Kikuyuland and beyond. It infected Chuka-Mwimbi even though the people there could hardly argue that the government or Europeans had stolen their land for there was no European settlement within their borders. In a report written in 1929 Dr Irvine mentions that he has been aware of this propaganda for some three to four years, but it has not affected the work at Chogoria.[6] However, the situation was about to change for another major issue was about to be added to that of the land.

Kikuyu Customs

As the Church in Kikuyuland came into being and increased in numbers, the problem arose of how far its members could continue to observe traditional Kikuyu customs. Those customs which were regarded as incompatible with Christian principles were divided into three groups.[7]

The first group contained those beliefs and customs which whilst at variance with Christian principles, were not necessarily actively opposed to them. These could be allowed to die out of their own accord as the implications of Christian teaching were understood and accepted. They included deference to ancestral spirits, the traditional sacrificial system and the practice of magic and sorcery.

The second group consisted of customs which were completely incompatible with Christian principles and therefore unacceptable in a practising Christian community. These included polygyny and sexually-motivated dances.

The third group included those customs which were medically or hygienically undesirable and therefore must be opposed on this ground rather than on any religious ground. Amongst these were the exposure of the dead rather than their burial, and the practice of female circumcision.

Most of these customs were to fade out in time or to cause no special problems, but the custom which the KCA seized on and made the issue which justified their anti-Mission attitude was that of female circumcision. This was a shrewd move by the KCA for it concerned an issue readily understood by all Kikuyu, whether they were able to understand the other issues the KCA raised or not.

Circumcision at the stage of puberty was part of the initiation of both boys and girls into adulthood in Kikuyu tribal life. So far as the circumcision of boys was concerned, the Missions had no difficulty in accepting this practice although they may not always have been happy at the ritual and instruction which accompanied it. It certainly did not usually have any adverse physical or medical complications. However, the problem was soon solved by recommending that the circumcision of boys might be carried out in hospitals or other medical units under medical supervision and in surgically clean conditions. This has increasingly become the practice today.

Female Circumcision

The circumcision of girls was different. When a girl got married, the result of circumcision was often to interfere with normal sexual intercourse and if the girl became pregnant, it not infrequently produced difficulties in childbirth with prolonged labour which could result in the death of the child and even the death of the mother.

The fact that the CSM had doctors and hospital facilities on all its three stations made its staff very conscious of these undesirable effects.[8] The result was that at Kikuyu, even before 1910, girls at school there and their parents were being taught about the risks of female circumcision which Miss Marion Stevenson, then a missionary at Kikuyu, preferred to call "sexual mutilation".[9] Over the next twenty years or so there were many discussions between missionaries and African Christians of different Missions, and among African Christians themselves of both sexes, which always ended in a majority decisions against the practice. In 1916 the CSM made a rule that any parent in the Church who allowed their daughter to be circumcised would be suspended from Church membership. This rule was reaffirmed in 1920 and in 1928. In this latter year anyone coming forward for baptism or membership of the Church was required to take a vow saying that they had stopped all customs which did not agree with the Word of God, including the practice of female circumcision. In 1925 the Government condemned the practice and offered the protection of the law to those who refused the operation. The Government, however, always refused to introduce a law under which the practice would be specifically forbidden and criminalised, holding that the current law regarding assault on the person was adequate to cover the matter.

The problem did not arise for first-generation Christians for the women of this generation were adults who had already been circumcised. It was the second-generation Christian girls for whom the problem became acute and for whom the missionaries were concerned. As we have just seen, opposition by the CSM to the practice of female circumcision did not first arise in 1929 but dated to the years before 1910. Nor was this opposition confined to the CSM but was a view shared by all the Protestant Missions although the CMS was divided on what action should be taken. It is not true, therefore, to say that the issue arose because in 1929 the CSM suddenly attacked the practice.[10] The truth is that the issue arose in 1929 because the KCA suddenly seized on it in that year as another reason for which they could attack the Missions.

In March 1929 an Inter-Church conference of some forty African Church elders representing all the Protestant Missions was held at Tumutumu which resolved that the custom of female circumcision was evil and should be abandoned and that all Christians submitting to it should be suspended by the Churches. This conference called upon all the Churches to make a uniform law against the custom. A report of this conference was published in the KCA newspaper *Muiguithania* and the issue of female circumcision was immediately added to the platform of the Association for in its view, opposition to this practice was an attack on the Kikuyu people. This issue therefore was one which the KCA could and did use to increase its support amongst the Kikuyu people and to mobilise and unite its members in its campaign against the Government and the Missions. But female circumcision was "no more than a symbol of a greater issue". It was "no more than an emotional peg onto which a far wider area of social discontent could readily be hung".[11]

The Issue at Stake

At this point, the scene moved to Chogoria, but before we consider the situation there it is worthwhile to put the question of female circumcision in its larger context in order to understand why it arose at all.

We begin with a quotation from a standard biography of Jomo Kenyatta:

> In some respects the most revolutionary aspect of European contact with Africa lay in the Christian attitude towards women. The missionaries taught that wives and daughters were equal with men in the eyes of God and deserved love and respect as individuals. Only in this light could sense be made of the Bible's teaching about family life and the consequent insistence in Christian communities on monogamy, chastity, and the emancipation of women from their servile role in the tribal economy..... The question of female circumcision was one consequence of this struggle over the status of women.[12]

In other words, the issue of female circumcision was one concerned with the rights of individuals and in particular with the rights and status of women. It was concerned with the rights of Christian parents not to have their daughters circumcised, and the right of Christian girls not to be circumcised if they were opposed to the practice. This was lost sight of in the emotional and political situation of the time and the practice was overlaid with irrelevant and inaccurate propaganda. Thus it was alleged that a girl could not become a mother if she had not been circumcised; that circumcision would reduce her sexual pleasure and therefore would discourage infidelity and prostitution; that a girl was not a true Kikuyu unless she was circumcised; that it was necessary for a girl to be circumcised just as a boy was circumcised; and that the Europeans were opposed to female circumcision because they wanted to marry Kikuyu girls and so take over their family land. However, these arguments and allegations should not be allowed to obscure the real issue of human rights which was what the missionaries were concerned to uphold on a Christian basis, even in the face of much misunderstanding, misrepresentation and hostility.

So far as Kikuyu Christian girls were concerned, then, the issue at stake was whether they had the right to refuse to undergo what could be a very brutal operation carried out without an anaesthetic and with potentially serious physical effects later in life, and also the right to refuse to be involved in initiation and marriage rituals which included elements which were not morally acceptable to committed Christian believers.

The issue for the KCA and the politically-minded Kikuyu leaders was somewhat different. For them the issue at stake was the unity of the Kikuyu people. If the right of girls to refuse circumcision were conceded, they argued that this would divide the tribe at a time when the politicians amongst them wanted to unite the people in order to make their demand for the redress of their land, labour and political grievances arising from European settlement in the Kenya Highlands as effective as possible.

Opposition at Chogoria

As we have seen, European settlement did not occur in Chuka-Mwimbi country. A countryside of long ridges and deep valleys did not lend itself to the large-scale farming which the new European settlers practised in other areas. The result was that the KCA propaganda about the alienation of land did not at first produce any response in that area. It was only when KCA agents came to Chuka-Mwimbi and alleged that the setting aside of land for mission stations and outschools was only the first step to the same alienation of land which had occurred in other areas, that anti-Mission allegations began to circulate and gain some acceptance.

In 1929 the Chuka-Mwimbi people were being warned by KCA agents to watch the Mission, for they said that it had been sent by the Government to steal the land. They said also that its teaching was opposed to local African custom, especially the custom of female circumcision. The people were exhorted not to give money to the Mission, but to send their money to support the KCA.

At this time the number of baptised Church members at Chogoria was about one hundred and twenty and they were very troubled about this KCA propaganda. As we have already mentioned above, in the middle of 1928 the CSM had included a specific vow against female circumcision in the vows required of those about to be baptised. The result was that in July 1929 some candidates for baptism at Chogoria had refused to take this vow, and some Church members had objected to it. In September 1929, therefore, Dr Irvine invited Dr Arthur as the head of the CSM in Kenya to come and share with the Church at Chogoria the experience which they had had at Kikuyu in countering the KCA propaganda, and to advise the Christian community at Chogoria about what they should do. Dr Arthur set off for Chogoria on Tuesday September 24th accompanied by three elders from Kikuyu, Samsoni Njoroge, Samweli Gitau and Ernest Kamau along with Priscilla Njeri. The last-named was the widow of Daudi Makumi one of the teachers first appointed to Chuka-Mwimbi in 1916. On the way, the party visited the CMS stations at Weithaga and Kahuhia in Murang'a (Fort Hall) District and Kigari in Embu where they found conflicting attitudes to the issue of female circumcision.

The Kikuyu party arrived at Chogoria in the afternoon of Thursday September 26th and in the evening they met with about two hundred and fifty people who had come in for a season of meetings and prayer. They met with them again on the Friday morning, and in the afternoon they discussed procedure with Dr Irvine and the Revd Solomon Ndambi, the Chogoria parish minister. It was agreed that on the Saturday morning (September 28th), the deacons and the Church members should be asked to take the vow against female circumcision and to promise to have nothing to do with the KCA. In the morning they first met separately with the deacons, who said that they could not agree with the suggested procedure. Then followed a service of worship after which the whole position was put to the gathering and Dr Irvine announced that they had prepared a paper on which they had set out a promise for people to sign if they agreed with it. This promise read as follows:

> I promise to have done with everything connected with the circumcision of women, because it is not in agreement with the things of God, and to have done with the Kikuyu Central Association because it aims at destroying the Church of God.[13]

The gathering then broke up for a midday meal. During this time the local people met together on the football field where the majority decided to oppose the signing of the promise, with many saying they could not be disloyal to their people and their country. After some more discussion, a teacher-evangelist named Jonathan Muriithi, although he was the secretary of the local branch of the KCA, stood up and said he was not going to forsake the things of God and he would sign the promise. The actual words he used were reported as "I am with the Church and you can stone me if you like".[14] He was followed by his wife and six other teachers and then some others until altogether fourteen had said they would sign the promise. These then went back into the Church to await the return of Dr Irvine and the Kikuyu Church leaders. The rest of the people left the mission station. Later that evening and on the Sunday morning, several more came to sign the promise. Within a month, twenty-five others had joined the original fourteen in signing the promise, making a total of thirty-nine in all. Dr Irvine was encouraged to note that the majority of those who remained loyal to the Church were from the vicinity of Chogoria.[15]

On the Sunday morning a communion service was held, during which two women were baptised including the wife of Jonathan Muriithi. Later in the day one of these women was beaten by her father and two other men, and the other spent the day with her husband in great fear of attack. Both women were taken to Chogoria for their protection.

The party from Kikuyu returned home on Wednesday October 2nd, and on October 10th the missionary staff at Kikuyu asked all the employees of the Mission to sign a declaration similar to that which had been agreed at Chogoria. Out of fifty-three, thirty-six signed and five made a verbal declaration, but twelve teachers refused to sign and were dismissed. A week later Dr Arthur and his African colleagues reported on their Chogoria visit to the Kirk Session at Kikuyu and then to the Presbytery of Kenya. Meanwhile the news of the Chogoria 'oath' (as it was called) spread like wildfire through Kikuyuland. It soon became clear that the consequences of drawing up the Chogoria promise and asking Church members to sign it had not been foreseen. The Presbytery of Kenya somewhat reluctantly accepted the situation and allowed the use of the Chogoria promise to continue. However, when it was realised that the KCA were misrepresenting the requirement for signatures, the Mission Council agreed that signatures would not be required and that the promise could be made verbally in the form of an oath. This continued until early in 1931 when the requirement of the oath was withdrawn.[16]

The Chogoria Promise in Retrospect

In seeking to understand the background of the Chogoria promise, we need to know the situation out of which it arose. The Christian community at Chogoria in 1929 has been described as a small group of people "taking their first rather faltering steps towards applying Christian principles in their personal and community living".[17] They lived in a relatively isolated area of Kikuyuland on the eastern slopes of Mount Kenya. They were not affected by the alienation of land to European settlers. They knew little at first hand of the political agitation which was occurring in other areas of the Kikuyu country, and what little they did know was mediated to them by KCA members and agents. It was not surprising to find them uncertain of their Christian duty in the circumstances in which they found themselves in September 1929. It was natural for them to turn for advice to Dr Arthur the head of the CSM and the senior Christians at Kikuyu, which is what they did.

In the event and in the light of the consequences, it appears that the advice which they were given was unwise in two respects. The first was that they should ask people to sign a document. The second was that one of the items of that document should be a specific denunciation of the KCA.

The normal method of signing a document at this time was by thumb-printing. A thumb-print was called *kirore* in Kikuyu. It was used as a means of identification on the African registration and identity card known as the *kipande*. It was also used when European settlers and other employers engaged African employees to work on their farms. The result of its use for these purposes was that the method became unpopular and was regarded as a means of binding the signatory in ways which were not always known or agreed to by him at the time of signing.

Shortly before the visit of the Kikuyu party to Chogoria a document had been prepared by the Protestant Churches in Kiambu District for public signature. This was the result of the circulation of the report of the Inter-Church conference held at Tumutumu in March 1929, to which we have already referred, after which Kikuyuland began to seethe with unrest over the issue of female circumcision. Early in September, in an endeavour to clarify the situation and to protect Kikuyu Christian girls who did not wish to be circumcised, the Churches in the Kiambu area had prepared a petition to the Colonial Government of Kenya. This petition sought the introduction of an ordinance which recognised the right of Kikuyu Christian girls to refuse circumcision. On September 15th this petition was read in all the Kiambu Churches and people were asked to sign it with their *kirore* before it was sent to the Government. The KCA leaders attacked this *kirore* document and tried to dissuade the people from signing it by saying that anyone who signed it was in fact signing away his land, which would then be seized and taken from him. It is of interest to notice that no fewer than sixty-nine uncircumcised women signed this petition in Kiambu alone.[18]

Ten days later came the Chogoria promise with its two requirements of the repudiation of the custom of female circumcision as not in agreement with the things of God, and the rejection of the KCA because it aimed at destroying the Church of God. Those who accepted this promise were asked to sign it with their thumbprint. Thus it became a second *kirore* which the KCA lost no time in denouncing and misrepresenting.

In view of the consequences of the first *kirore* and the resentment it had provoked, it would now seem to have been unwise to have asked Church members to accept a second *kirore* whose effect could not be less than the first one had been and was equally open to misrepresentation by the KCA.

In fact, the effect of this second *kirore* was even greater than that of the first because of its content. As we have seen, the second item of the promise was a repudiation of the KCA which was specifically named. This was the first time that this body had been named and its repudiation been called for in any public Church document prepared for acceptance or signature by members of the Church.

The KCA was the only African political party in existence at this time and to demand its repudiation could be interpreted as wishing to deny the Kikuyu the means of political expression. The effect of this demand was to increase the support of the Kikuyu people for the Association in the interests of the unity of the Kikuyu people.

In this respect, too, the advice given to the Church members at Chogoria seems to have been unwise.[19]

The Results of Opposition

The immediate result at Chogoria was to undermine the effective and patient work of the previous seven years. Church attendance on Sundays was greatly reduced so that instead of the usual congregation of about a hundred in September 1929 only seventeen turned up in October. At the beginning of the school year Chogoria school had over a hundred pupils, but in October only twenty-one persons turned up for school and thirteen of these were teachers, with the result that the school was closed meantime. The outschools had previously had a total roll of about two hundred and fifty pupils but they had all to be closed for lack of pupils who were kept away by their parents. All the hospital African medical staff left without warning led by Johnstone Kiambati, the senior hospital assistant, who turned out to be a local leader in the opposition to the signing of the promise. The household staff of the missionaries also left and joined in the opposition at this time.

CHAPTER NINE

RECOVERY AND PROGRESS

Although the initial effect of the involvement of Chogoria in the female circumcision controversy in September 1929 was a setback to the activities of most departments of its work, this effect was only temporary. The Chuka-Mwimbi people were not as politically-minded as their fellow Kikuyu in southern Kikuyuland and did not generally believe the KCA propaganda. The only Europeans they knew were the missionaries and the Government officers, and the allegations of the KCA did not seem to be true of them and their activities. Within a year, Dr Irvine could speak of a new spirit and zeal within the Christian community and the return to normal of the various activities of the Mission. By 1931 he wrote that the past year had been "quite the happiest we have known".[1] Even any political bitterness there had been was subsiding and by 1933 he reported that it had disappeared. Thus the decade 1930 to 1939 was one of recovery and progress.

The General Situation

Locust invasions were troublesome during this decade. Major ones are mentioned in the years 1931, 1932 and 1939. The locusts stripped the gardens of crops and led to great shortages of food. In the early years of the decade these invasions coincided with the worldwide economic depression which adversely affected the economy of Kenya as a whole. The depression resulted in a fall in wages and in decreased opportunities for employment for those who wished to work.

Dr Irvine continued to keep the Scottish supporters of the work in Chogoria informed about developments there by his annual publication of the booklet *Chogoria*. At this time about twelve hundred copies of the booklet were printed and circulated each year at a total cost of thirty-five pounds. In preparation for going on leave in 1932 he took black-and-white cine films of the mission station and its activities, and used them very successfully during his leave. In many cases they were the first films of missionary work that people in Scotland had seen. He later commented on how this had involved both his wife and himself taking with them a very heavy cine projector on speaking engagements around the Church in Scotland, which they found very exhausting. They were, however, very successful in raising money for Chogoria which was not yet fully supported by the Church of Scotland.

The annual cost of running Chogoria had originally been one thousand pounds which was the amount guaranteed by Ernest Carr when it began. By 1932 the local cost was over two thousand pounds and Dr Irvine set out the details of this cost in an article in *Kikuyu News*:[2]

General Mission expenses	£ 100
Church	£ 25
Hospital	£ 1,100
School	£ 850
Girls' dormitory	£ 50
Travel & leaves	£ 100
Repairs and maintenance	£ 50
Total	£ 2,275

This was the sum which Dr and Mrs Irvine had to raise during their leave in Scotland to finance each year of their work at Chogoria. It was a great relief to them when in 1936 the Church of Scotland Foreign Mission Committee agreed to assume financial responsibility for the Kenya Church of Scotland Mission (including Chogoria) as from the beginning of 1937.

In 1933 the Government created a new province, the Central Province, by amalgamating the former Kikuyu and Ukamba Provinces. This involved changes in Embu District to which Chogoria had belonged up to this time. As a result of these changes Embu District was enlarged to the south by taking over part of the former South Nyeri District, whilst to the north it lost the Chuka-Mwimbi area which now became part of Meru District. Thus Chogoria became the administrative responsibility of the Meru District Commissioner who was stationed at Meru some forty miles to the north of Chogoria. As a result of this change, the Chuka-Mwimbi area was now named the Chuka Division of Meru District, with Chuka as its administrative centre.

The Daily Routine

Dr Irvine was a regular contributor to the CSM quarterly journal *Kikuyu News*. Indeed, he was the most regular of all the missionaries because he was so conscious of the need for publicity to maintain the interest and support of the Scottish Christian public. He frequently described ordinary routine things as well as those which were unusual or dramatic. On one occasion in 1931 he set out a typical weekday in his life at Chogoria at that time.[3]

- 6.00am Rising bell
- 6.30am School prayers
- 7.00am Prayers with works staff & allocation of duties for the day
- 8.00am Breakfast
- 9.00am Hospital ward round
- 10.30am Hospital service taken by African minister
- 11.00am Outpatient consultations
- 1.00pm Lunch followed by short siesta
- 2.00pm Surgical operations
          Routine and odd jobs around the station
- 5.00pm Football with schoolboys
          Tennis with family or colleagues
          Walks with visits to local villages
- 6.30pm Prayer meeting in Church
          (Mondays & Thursdays)
- 7.30pm Supper
          After supper: correspondence and reading

With regard to time, Chogoria observed a form of daylight-saving time for even though Chogoria was only just south of the equator there was a difference of about thirty minutes in the coming of daylight throughout the year. A large clock on the verandah of the Irvines' bungalow set the time for the station and this clock was adjusted as necessary to give more light in the mornings for those coming to work or more light in the evenings to allow a game or two of tennis to be played. This form of daylight-saving time continued until the late 1940s. The various divisions of the working day were indicated by the ringing of a large bell hung at the side of the workshop.

It hardly needs saying that this routine was often upset. There were frequent administrative and other emergencies. Machines stopped, accidents happened, misunderstandings arose and other difficulties occurred, all of which had to be dealt with by Dr Irvine.

Chogoria was a popular base for climbers wishing to climb Mount Kenya and Ernest Carr had financed the cutting of a track which could take motor cars through the forest and up on to the moorland above. Unfortunately a forest fire made this track impassable to vehicles, but although it was never re-opened to vehicles it remained a viable route for climbing the mountain. Carr also had provided two huts for climbers, one at Urumandi at the end of the road and the other beside the Lewis glacier. One result of this which we have already mentioned was that Europeans frequently turned up at Chogoria with plans to climb the mountain and expected the staff there to provide them with the guides, food and equipment they needed. This led to frequent interruptions and misunderstandings.

On one occasion an irate European in camp near Chogoria complained to Dr Irvine that he had been swindled by a local African lad at a shop where he had bought flour. The lad had charged him eighty cents for a pound of flour which he regarded as exorbitant. Dr Irvine called the lad in to explain. His explanation was that when the European had asked him the price of the flour he had tried to give it in English, of which he did not have very much. The doctor realised that the lad had wanted to say that the price was eight cents a pound, but since in Kimwimbi all words end in a vowel, he had naturally added a vowel so that the price had sounded like eighty cents and that was what the European had paid. Dr Irvine explained this to the man and the lad refunded the difference and so the incident ended happily.

The Works Department Carries On

The department at Chogoria which was least affected by the controversy of September 28th 1929 was the works department. There is no note in the records of anyone being absent from work on the Monday following the incident.

Their major task in 1929 was the completion of the new Church building to which we shall refer in more detail at the end of this chapter. A small wooden bungalow was built for an Indian carpenter who was engaged to make the window frames and furniture of the new Church which we describe below. In the following year some other smaller buildings were put up for the hospital and the school. In 1937 Ernest Carr asked permission to build a cottage for his use on the station; this was built of wood with corrugated iron walls and roof. It is still in use today and is known as Carr Cottage.

In his report for 1932 Dr Irvine mentions that the workshop does a large amount of saw-milling for local African carpenters and contractors. This was a much appreciated service which the Mission provided through the years, for the alternative was the laborious procedure of pit-sawing in which a tree trunk was supported on trestles over a pit and then sawn into planks by two men using a large two-handed saw. It also provided a welcome source of income for the workshop.

In 1933 a carpenter from Tumutumu named Dedan Kariuki Wangai joined the works staff at Chogoria and eventually became clerk of works. He married Rachel, the daughter of the Revd Solomon Ndambi who came to Chogoria as parish minister in 1928. Dedan was an elder of the Church and was to become a leading figure in the Revival Movement in the Chogoria area.

The Church Survives the Crisis

In spite of the events of September 1929, Dr Irvine wrote at the end of that year that he felt happier about the work at Chogoria than he had ever done. In the space of a few months, he felt that as a result of the crisis, the Church at Chogoria had been "purified from the miasma of politics" and had been given "a new liberality, a new fervour and a new zeal for evangelism".[4]

The closure of the schools due to lack of pupils meant that the teachers could now join in evangelistic outreach throughout the district. So a series of eleven monthly evangelistic safaris were arranged. One week in each month was devoted to such a safari to an outlying area of the district. On each safari would go one or two dressers from the hospital to treat the cases of malaria, yaws, relapsing fever and dysentery which they encountered.

The first of these safaris was organised in December 1929. The area chosen was that of the Tharaka people which lies about forty miles down the mountain-side from Chogoria. The people there lived under semi-famine conditions in a hot and dry countryside covered with yellow grass and thorny scrub with the occasional baobab tree. The ground was hard and stony and so one of the first tasks was to provide the evangelists with sandals to protect their feet. These sandals were made from old discarded rubber lorry tyres and were similar to those provided to protect the anaesthetic feet of leprosy patients in the leprosarium. On December 17th a party of seventeen evangelists and porters led by the Revd Solomon Ndambi set out from Chogoria on the first of these safaris. They carried three tents and walked for two days down the mountain-side to Tharaka country. Dr Irvine followed with his car carrying food and other camping equipment. Once he had met up with the others, they pitched the tents and for several days they went out in twos armed with rolls of Bible pictures to speak and preach to the people they met on the paths, in the villages and market-places. They found such keenness on the part of the people to hear the gospel that they went back to Tharaka six months later in June 1930, which was a cooler month than December. Unfortunately a number of those who went on this second tour returned with malaria because, contrary to Dr Irvine's instructions, the porters had pitched the tents too near to water on the first night.[5]

The first Easter after the female circumcision controversy was described by Dr Irvine as of special significance. During the Sunday morning service the Church leaders brought up the following items in succession: a basin and towel to commemorate Christ's last act of humility and service before his arrest; a picture of Gethsemane to remind the congregation of his agony in the garden; a rope to signify his being bound as a common criminal; a lash to represent his scourging; a crown of thorns; a cross of wood with the superscription; and finally a headcloth to speak of his burial and then of his resurrection. It was a very impressive and meaningful service especially in view of what had happened in the previous six months.

The people gradually returned to the Mission so that by the end of 1930, Church attendances at Chogoria were back to normal with about one hundred and fifty people at Sunday services, and about a third of these were women. By 1933 the attendance had increased to over two hundred. In September 1930, Sunday School classes were begun again, attracting an average attendance of thirty children. Also in 1930 a crèche for babies and young children was introduced during the morning service, so that the rest of the congregation was not disturbed by their noise. No woman was allowed to bring a baby into the service but had to leave it in the crèche which was a fenced-off area beside the Church. The mothers voted this a great success and so did the rest of the congregation.

We have already seen how the first step towards organising the Christian community on Presbyterian lines had been taken in 1928 when seven deacons had been elected. They met as a Deacons' Court on Saturday mornings once a month at Chogoria. The next step was taken in 1932. The Presbytery of Kenya of the Church of Scotland had been set up in 1920 by the authority of the General Assembly in Edinburgh.[6] In 1931 this Presbytery approved the formation of a Kirk Session at Chogoria with the result that on Sunday February 14th 1932, Dr Arthur ordained four elders from amongst the senior men of the congregation and then proceeded to set up the Kirk Session. The names of the new elders were as follows: Gerishom Mukangu, Jonathan Muriithi, Musa M'Muga and Willie Kanini.[7]

The Presbytery of Kenya also agreed to petition the General Assembly of the Church of Scotland to authorise the ordination of Dr Irvine during his leave in Scotland in 1932.[8] This was on the basis of Dr Irvine's "special qualifications and of his superintendency of Chogoria". The Commission of the General Assembly accepted this request in November 1932 and instructed the Presbytery of Aberdeen to proceed with the ordination of Dr Irvine. He was first licensed as a Preacher of the Gospel at a meeting of this Presbytery on December 6th and then ordained to the Office of the Holy Ministry "for service in the Foreign Mission Field" on January 1st 1933. The service at which he was ordained was held in his father's Church of Aberdeen South and his father conducted the public worship which preceded the ordination. He was then ordained by the Presbytery with prayer and the laying on of hands. The Moderator of the Presbytery then "addressed suitable exhortations" to Dr Irvine. This service was another link with Blantyre for the Moderator at that time was the Revd Dr Alexander Hetherwick who had succeeded Dr Clement Scott as head of the Mission there in 1898. This was the occasion when Dr Scott returned to Edinburgh and then was invited to go out to be head of the new Mission at Kikuyu as we mentioned in our first chapter. Dr Hetherwick had subsequently retired to Aberdeen.[9]

The Revd Dr & Mrs Irvine set sail for Kenya on April 14th 1933. They had had an energetic leave for part of which they had hired a caravan in Falkirk. With this they had visited places as far apart as Aviemore in Scotland, Corwen in North Wales and Sevenoaks in Kent. In the course of their leave, they had been able to raise the sum of £2,765 towards the cost of running Chogoria, which in 1931 they had estimated at £3,500.

As we have already mentioned, the first edition of the Kikuyu hymnbook had been published in 1915. It had been revised in 1929 and its contents included many hymns which were translations of well-known hymns which were set to the tunes familiar to English congregations. These tunes were written according to the seven-note or heptatonic scale common in Europe. However, Kikuyu tunes use a five-note or pentatonic scale. In 1933, the Irvines were visited by a gifted musician, Miss Gwen Martin Harvey, who re-wrote all the tunes in the Kikuyu hymnbook in terms of the pentatonic scale.[10]

In February 1936 a further five elders were ordained by Dr Irvine and took their seats in the Kirk Session. Their names were Daudi M'Raria, Jason, Joseph Gathoga, Paulo, and Phares Mutonga. Dr Irvine noted that three of the elders were now studying for the ministry.[11]

At this time few Africans wore shoes, and amongst the intimations during a Sunday morning service towards the end of 1936 was one that said that the elders had noticed that some people were coming to Church with jiggers in their feet. The intimation went on to say that in future no one would be admitted to the Church service of whom this was true. The jigger flea (*Tunga penetrans*, or *ndutu* in Kikuyu) was first noted in Kikuyuland in 1898 and is believed to have come from America by way of the slave trade of West Africa. The female flea burrows into the skin usually of the feet and produces a large number of eggs which first distend and then burst its abdomen so that the eggs are scattered on the floor. The eggs then develop into fleas and await their next victim. When the eggs are released and the flea extruded from the skin they leave a round hole or ulcer which is liable to become infected, and even to act as an entry point for the germs of tetanus. This intimation was thus an example of preventive medicine in action.

Beginning in 1936 there was a new enthusiasm for evangelism. Large open-air meetings were held at Kabeche, the large market near Chogoria. In order to attract a crowd, Dr Irvine would often take his car into the middle of the market and sit on the roof playing hymn tunes on his accordion. When a crowd had gathered one of the staff or a senior school pupil would give an evangelistic address. The evangelistic safaris were resumed at this time and on each occasion forty to fifty Church members would go on them and camp out over weekends within a radius of five miles of Chogoria to reach as many people as possible. Often they would speak in the villages without any audience visible, but they knew that many were listening in their huts and out of sight. Out of this enthusiasm for evangelism came a desire for the spiritual revival of the Church, and when a revival convention was held at Kikuyu at the end of 1938 about a dozen people from Chogoria attended. Also in an endeavour to raise the standard of preaching during Sunday services Dr Irvine began to issue typewritten sermons for use by those leading the services. This was a practice which he continued for a number of years.[12]

The New Church Built

In June 1929, Dr Irvine wrote in *Kikuyu News* that, "I am in the middle of one of the most delightful jobs I have ever had - the building of a Church".[13] The old mud-and-wattle Church building which was erected in 1923 had been damaged beyond repair by white ants and the ravages of time and weather. So the time had come for it to be replaced by a more permanent structure.

The new Church was sited on a levelled area at the southern edge of the Chogoria ridge overlooking the Kamara River which ran some two hundred feet below. It lay to the south of the road running from the Irvines' bungalow down to the hospital. The Church was designed by Dr Irvine himself who studied the architecture of All Saints' Cathedral in Nairobi and other Churches, and also such photographs of Church buildings as he could find. In general, however, he admitted that the design developed as the building progressed. The result conformed to no classic architectural style, although its windows and arches were Gothic in shape. It was constructed entirely in brick as stone had not yet been discovered at Chogoria. It was fifty feet long and forty-five feet wide and was designed to seat four hundred people, but could contain many more than this number when its wooden benches were packed to their capacity.

At the east end of the Church, the floor was raised to form the chancel which held a communion table of *muringa* wood surrounded by chairs. Immediately in front of the chancel were several short pews running along the long axis of the Church, and in the north-west corner of this area was the pulpit constructed of brick in the form of a hexagon. The chancel had seven narrow Gothic windows with blue and grey leaded lights which served to keep out the prevailing east wind. To the north side of the chancel was a separate prayer-room or chapel which opened into the Church through a door and unglazed windows so that it could be used to give extra space for the congregation if required. At the south side of the chancel was a vestry which opened into the Church and also formed the ground floor of the large square tower which rose some twenty-five feet above the height of the roof of the Church. This tower also contained a room above the vestry in which evangelists and visitors could stay overnight. The summit of the tower took the form of a shallow dome which rose to a peak in the centre.

The side walls of the Church each had fifteen Gothic windows which were protected by wire-mesh and removable wooden shutters, except for the outside windows of the prayer room which were filled in with leaded lights. Inside the Church, the rafters were supported by slender pillars made of special ornamental bricks which gave them a clustered column effect by which the pillar appeared to be formed by several columns put together. No fewer than eight different patterns of ornamental bricks were made for use in the Church and Dr Irvine comments that he found the making of these bricks "most delightful work".

The roof of the Church was made of several thousands of wooden shingles turned out by the workshop, which were painted a deep tile-red. This roof had eventually to be replaced by sheet aluminium. No ceiling was installed in the Church. The floor was made of bricks laid side by side and set in cement.

At the west end of the Church were two Gothic arches closed by wooden doors with large meshed-in windows which opened into a large rounded porch which was entered through archways on the north and south sides.

As the Church was nearing completion, the idea occurred to Dr Irvine that some cement bas-reliefs might be prepared and placed in prominent places in the interior of the Church. Seven of these were prepared. Two were placed on the panels at the front of the hexagonal brick pulpit. These were of a dove descending, to represent the Holy Spirit, and of a book and praying hands to represent Bible reading and prayer. One was placed on the wall behind the pulpit representing the apple of Eden and the cup of Gethsemane to symbolise the gospel. On this one there was a reference to John 3.16. The remaining ones were put up on four of the pillars. They were of an ox to represent service, a city on a hill to represent witness, a vine to represent abiding in Christ, and a burning sacrifice to represent yielding to God.

Electricity was installed to allow the Church to be used at night and the lights were all concealed. A harmonium was installed in the Church and was usually played by Mrs Irvine. However, the organ was frequently drowned by the volume of the singing and so eventually the singing was more often led by the beating of a big drum at the front of the Church.

On the inside of the Church the bricks were left unpainted. In contrast, the outside of the Church and the tower was painted with a white distemper which made a pleasing combination with the tile-red roof. Finally, a broad brick pavement was laid down all round the Church building, and two brick stairways were set into the bank leading down to the area of the Church from the road down to hospital. This area was then sown with grass to form a natural amphitheatre which could be used when the congregation was too large to be accommodated in the Church itself.

The Church took some eighteen months to build because of a shortage of labour, and also because the workmen were taken off for the three months March to May 1929 in order to build the new dispensary for the treatment of leprosy patients. A grant of two hundred pounds for this purpose had been given to Chogoria by the Mission to Lepers on condition that it was spent in 1929.

The cost of the new Church was about one thousand pounds and this amount had been donated by African and Scottish contributors in response to Dr Irvine's appeal for donations. These donations came in the form of contributions to the general fund for the Church building or in the form of contributions to cover the cost of specific items such as windows and doors, the communion table and prayer desk, lectern and pews. Many African Church members gave one month's wages or more towards the cost of the new Church which was opened free of all debt.

The local community had watched the building of the Church with great interest and turned out in full force for the opening and dedication of the Church on Friday January 17th 1930. The local African chiefs were present in all their finery and attended by their retainers. The District Commissioner, Mr H.E.Lambert and his wife came from Meru along with the Revd R.T.Worthington, the Superintendent of the Methodist Mission at Kaaga near Meru. Ernest Carr was in the Belgian Congo, but Mrs Carr was present. Dr Arthur was unable to come from Kikuyu because of the political situation there, but was represented by the Revd Musa Gitau.

The official procession formed up on the road leading down from the Irvine's house and moved slowly down to the new Church. It paused at the doors of the Church whilst the Revd George Calderwood from Tumutumu read the closing four verses of Psalm 24 and pushed open the doors. The congregation then sang the hymn "Let us with a gladsome mind, praise the Lord for he is kind", and the service of dedication followed during which Mr Calderwood preached the sermon. After the service, the chiefs and other special guests gathered on the lawn of the Irvine's house for tea, whilst the members of the congregation were shown round the new Church in which they showed great interest and pride.[14]

CHAPTER TEN

RECOVERY AND PROGRESS (cont.)

The School Situation

As we have already seen, one dramatic consequence of the controversy in September 1929 was a boycott of the schools at Chogoria and its outstations. Although, as a group the teachers had mostly remained loyal, the parents had in many cases withdrawn their children from attendance at school. All the outschools had, therefore, to be closed in October 1929, although two of them were reopened early in 1930. At Chogoria itself the attendance at school gradually rose to reach about thirty or forty by the end of 1929, where previously it had been about a hundred.

In August 1930 the educational staff was strengthened by the arrival of Robert Macpherson to be headmaster of the school at Chogoria and supervisor of the outschools. He had originally been appointed as an educational missionary to Kikuyu in 1924 after three years' training at Aberdeen Teacher Training College. He was a tall, gentle, wise and scholarly man who was to serve as Moderator of the General Assembly of the Presbyterian Church of East Africa from 1958 to 1961 and in 1970 was to write the history of that Church. He had served at Kikuyu and then at Kambui and just prior to his transfer to Chogoria he married Miss Alta Knapp on August 14th at Kambui. Miss Knapp was the daughter of the Revd and Mrs William P. Knapp who were the pioneer missionaries of the Gospel Missionary Society of America at Kambui in Kiambu District.[1]

The coming of the Macphersons was very welcome at this time when the educational side of the work at Chogoria needed rebuilding and expanding. Their coming also meant that Dr Irvine now had the support of a male missionary colleague such as he had not had before. A new house of wood and corrugated iron was designed and built by Macpherson in 1932 and became known as the Schoolhouse.

Eventually all the former outschools were reopened, and requests began to come from local chiefs for the establishment of outschools in their locations. It is of interest to note that most of these requests for new schools came from the places which had been visited by the teacher-evangelists during the period when the schools had to be closed because of the boycott. In some cases the school building was put up by the local people and paid for by the chief. In his report for 1934, Dr Irvine noted that they now had twenty-two boys living in a school dormitory and expected to have thirty in the following year. These were boys of age ten to fifteen where previously those who came to school had been mostly aged sixteen and over.

At Chogoria in 1932, in addition to a number of day girls, eleven girls were resident in the dormitory which had been built in order to provide protection for them against forcible circumcision. Also in the dormitory with them were three orphans for whom the girls cared. In two cases, the mothers of the orphans had died in hospital and the families had been reluctant to accept responsibility for them, and the third had been one of twins and been cast out as unlucky in accordance with Mwimbi custom. In addition to the usual range of subjects taken in school, the girls were taught sewing, cooking and hygiene. Also the opportunity provided by the presence of the orphans was taken to teach the girls how to care for children.

Under Macpherson's guidance, the educational work began to take more definite shape and conform more closely to Government standards. Thus in 1933 teachers were entered for the Education Department's Elementary Teacher's Examination for the first time. Three teachers were entered and all were successful. Also in that year, sixteen pupils sat the Elementary School Examination and fifteen of them passed.

About this time it became clear that African pupils were losing interest in vocational education and were demanding a more general and literary education. One result of this was that in 1934 the Government took over all technical training and left the mission schools to concentrate on general education. Another result was that more Government grants became available for mission schools to provide this more general education. The school at Chogoria had received no grants of this kind for education from the time of its establishment, but in 1933 it was allocated a grant of £325.

From this time forward the educational work at Chogoria was officially recognised by the Government Education Department and in 1936 the school at Chogoria was approved as a Primary School which would take pupils up to Standard VI according to the new classification of schools introduced in 1934. One result of this recognition was that a new brick school building was planned and built on the part of the Mission plot called Iteri which lay to the east of the hospital. The foundation stone of the new school building was laid by Chief Ng'entu. This building contained an assembly hall, five classrooms, an office and a store. It was in this building that the new Chogoria Primary School opened in 1937. The total cost of the building was £40.[2]

A milestone in the history of educational work at Chogoria came in 1935 when the first boy from the Chogoria School was accepted for Form I at the Alliance High School at Kikuyu. He was Erasto Mwiricia who was given a scholarship by the Meru Local Native Council to help him with his fees and expenses.[3]

The foundation of the Alliance High School at Kikuyu had been itself a milestone in the development of African education in Kenya as a whole. It was opened on March 1st 1926 and derived its name from the Alliance of Protestant Missions which had been set up in 1918 to promote co-operation between the Missions. One of the earliest proposals before this body was the establishment of a united educational institution on land belonging to the Church of Scotland Mission at Kikuyu. This institution was originally envisaged as an Alliance Medical College, and plans were prepared for such a College. These were submitted to Dr Gilks, the Principal Medical Officer for the Colony, in July 1921 only to be rejected on the grounds that the mortuary and water-closets should be separated from the main building. On their re-submission, they were again rejected because "there were now no mortuary or closets whatsoever"![4] Nevertheless the building was erected and was opened as a Medical College in March 1924 with eight students. However, the Government decided that it, and not the Missions, should be responsible for the medical training of African students and after a few months the College closed. The Government then agreed that the College should be re-opened as a High School which meant that for the first time, educational facilities at secondary school level were to be available for African pupils. Ernest Carr provided much of the finance required by the Missions to proceed with this scheme on condition that the Government also accepted responsibility for a significant share of the capital and recurrent expenditure required for the opening and development of the High School.

It was this involvement of his father-in-law in the origin of the School and his own intense concern with the higher education of the African pupils that explained Dr Irvine's great interest in the Alliance High School and its development. It was, therefore, a source of great satisfaction to him when the first Chogoria boy was accepted for admission to the School.

The political influences which had produced the controversy of 1929 still continued in education. In 1931 the Mission still felt that it had to say that its teachers may not belong to the KCA. In that same year Dr Irvine mentioned that there was a new political association which was seeking to set up its own schools in the Chogoria area.[5] By the following year this association had established seven schools in the area. These schools did provide religious instruction which was recognisably Christian in origin, but it included acceptance of the practice of female circumcision. However, from an educational point of view, the standards in these schools were very low as they had to depend on teachers who had been rejected by Government or Mission schools and on those who had no qualifications to teach at all.

A Parents' Union was formed in 1937 at Chogoria. Each parent who joined had to be a Christian and to promise to pray daily with the children and fine themselves one cent for every day they missed doing this. Members were given a brass badge. Ruffell Barlow wrote a special hymn in Kimwimbi for the Union to use. Union membership had to be renewed annually. In the first year one hundred and forty parents joined.[6]

For the first time, in 1937 special classes were arranged for adults who wished to learn to read. Previously they had joined in the normal school classes, an arrangement which had not been ideal.

In 1938 a District Education Board was set up for Meru District. This was composed of representatives of the Government, the Missions and the Local Native Council. It was responsible for approving the establishment of new schools, the allocation of education grants from central and local Government and the general promotion and improvement of African education. The creation of this Board was a great step forward, for it allowed close co-ordination of the activities of all the bodies providing Elementary and Primary Schools.

The Hospital Recovers

In September 1929 all the staff of the hospital left as a result of the stand taken by the Mission against the KCA and female circumcision. However, Dr Irvine was able to recruit six young men from amongst those who remained loyal to the Mission and to train them in hospital work such as the giving of injections and the use of the microscope, as well as basic nursing care. He was very impressed at how quickly they become proficient in their work. Whilst they were being trained in hospital work, Miss Butter-Malcolm took charge of the nursing side of the work of the hospital.[7]

The Church of Scotland FMC gave a grant of £322 for the medical work at Chogoria in 1932 and this was increased to £400 in 1938. The Government also began to give the hospital an annual grant of £250 in 1932. These grants were welcome additions to the income of the hospital.

In 1930 a small open-sided brick building was erected with a wooden shingle roof in front of the hospital building which had been built in 1926.[8] In form this building resembled the lych gate which is still to be seen at the entrance to some English parish churchyards. It was used as an outpatient injection and dressing station for patients with yaws and other conditions. Once an adequate outpatient department was built, it fell out of use and when the hospital was rebuilt in the 1970s it was moved to a site just inside the entrance to the new hospital and regarded as a historic monument.

Also in 1930 a small isolation hut was built for patients with pulmonary tuberculosis. In accordance with the then prevalent practice in the treatment of tuberculosis, the upper half of each wall was composed of open trellis-work to allow the maximum ventilation. The dietary component of the current treatment of tuberculosis proved to be difficult to provide when Dr Irvine discovered that it was contrary to Mwimbi custom for any but children to eat eggs or chicken or to drink milk, and even meat was rarely eaten.[9]

The needs of the leprosy patients were not forgotten in this period. As we have seen, in 1929 the building of the new Church was temporarily suspended in order to build a small dispensary for their use up on the hospital compound. By 1932 the accommodation in the leprosarium had been increased from eight to sixteen beds. Both of these projects were funded by the Mission to Lepers.

The hospital staff in 1936 consisted of the following in addition to Dr Irvine and Miss Butter-Malcolm:

> Jason, the senior dresser
> Henry, Justo, Jusufu and Mariko, dressers
> Jemima and Damaris, midwives
> Jackson Chabari, dispenser
> Jakubu, cook

Jason had earlier contracted leprosy, but it was diagnosed early and he was completely cured by 1934. Jackson Chabari, who had joined the staff in 1930, succeeded him as senior assistant in 1941.

The *Chogoria* booklet for 1938 records how one day at lunchtime the wind blew a red-hot cinder from the fire under the water boiler in the main hospital building on to the wooden shingle roof and set it on fire. A male nurse on duty saw it and scrambled up on to the roof and tore off the shingles which were on fire and threw them to the ground. Someone ran up to the house for Dr Irvine but by the time he arrived the situation was under control.

A major building programme was undertaken in 1938 when a large block consisting of two wards (male and female), an operating theatre and a dispensary was erected. The building which had been put up in 1926 to accommodate male and female patients was now used to house a children's ward, a maternity ward, an isolation ward, a consulting room, a laundry and the hospital kitchen. When the new block was taken into use in 1938 the patient accommodation of the hospital was as follows:

Male beds:	17	Leprosy beds:	20
Female beds:	20	Tuberculosis beds:	3
Cots:	16	Isolation:	4
Maternity:	2	Indian:	2

Total beds: 84

The hospital dealt with its first traffic accident in 1935. Daudi, an agricultural teacher at Chogoria, was returning home after dark one night on a bicycle without lights and knocked down an old man called Magiri about a mile from the hospital. Magiri sustained a compound fracture of the leg. He was given first aid by one of the hospital staff who was passing and the doctor was sent for. Dr Irvine arrived and after splinting the leg, took the man back to hospital and put the leg in plaster. The man was back on his feet walking normally in six weeks. All this was without the use of X-rays.[10]

At the end of the decade in April 1939 Chogoria Hospital welcomed its first nursing sister, Miss Jean Clark Wilson. Up till then the hospital had been run by an almost all-male staff with Miss Butter-Malcolm as matron, housekeeper and maternity supervisor. The new sister was the granddaughter of the Revd Dr Youngson, a missionary in the Punjab in India, and the niece of the Revd James Youngson who had been a missionary at Kikuyu. She was very impressed with the hospital buildings with their whitewashed walls and signal-red painted doors and window frames. She soon settled into the work of the hospital and introduced elementary nursing training for local Mwimbi girls. When she arrived, there was only one girl on the nursing staff of the hospital and she was employed in the maternity ward. When she left three years later there were fifteen girls doing nursing in all the wards of the hospital. Soon after her arrival she took on several nursing trainees and after only six weeks she was able to start teaching them in Kimwimbi. She even made contact with the local medicine man. Also at this time, white uniforms were introduced for the staff who had previously been dressed in khaki, and the men began to wear red fezzes instead of former khaki pork-pie caps.

The hospital statistics for this period are as follows:

Year	Inpatients	Outpatients	Operations
1930	413	15,366	48
1931	436	14,294	61
1932	285	13,037	50
1933	398	12,383	59
1934	618	13,054	75
1935	659	10,322	128
1936	760	11,606	129
1937	840	7,688	91
1938	1435	5,577	175
1939	1426	6,195	154

It is clear from these statistics that the female circumcision controversy of 1929 had had little effect on the work of the hospital.

Patient numbers did decrease, however, when fees for treatment were introduced. The temporary decrease in inpatients seen in 1932 was due to the fact that from the beginning of that year fees were charged for inpatient treatment. A fee of one shilling was charged for admission to hospital followed by a fee of fifty cents to one shilling for each week the patient stayed in hospital. In 1933 these fees provided an income of twenty-five pounds.

From 1st January 1937 a small fee of five cents for each outpatient was charged and this led to a similar decrease in the numbers attending the outpatient department.

Maternity cases are first recorded in 1933 when fourteen women were delivered in hospital. By 1939 that number had risen to forty-eight.

By the year 1939, we can see that the work at Chogoria had fully recovered from the effects of the female circumcision controversy and was able to report steady progress in all its departments. However by the end of that year, in spite of its isolation from the rest of the world along what was for much of the way a single-track earth road, Chogoria was about to feel the effects of the events which were occurring in the rest of the world.

CHAPTER ELEVEN

WAR AND REVIVAL

The outbreak of the Second World War on Sunday September 3rd 1939 passes almost unnoticed in the records of the Chogoria Mission at that time. However, although the immediate theatre of war was in Europe, the situation changed when Italy under Mussolini entered the war on June 10th 1940 on the side of Germany. In May 1936, Italy had annexed Somalia and formed an empire consisting of Ethiopia, Eritrea and Italian Somaliland. The result was that when Mussolini declared war against Great Britain, Kenya had a hostile neighbour along her northern border. However, even if the Italian forces in Ethiopia had decided to invade Kenya, Chogoria was not on the obvious invasion route into Kenya. This route was down the western side of Mount Kenya where a forward military base was now established at the railhead at Nanyuki. Fortunately, Italy did not invade Kenya and by May 1941 British troops had occupied Ethiopia and Italian Somaliland and the threat of invasion was over.

The Wartime Situation

Although Chogoria was not in the war zone at any time, it did not escape the effects of wartime controls and shortages.

The cost of petrol and food increased and this led to a general increase in prices throughout the country. The need for supplies for the armed forces led to shortages for the civilian population. Rationing was introduced for basic foodstuffs and for petrol. Conscription was introduced for Europeans and both Tony and Geoffrey Irvine were called up for service in the Army. Tony joined the Kenya Regiment in 1940 and was stationed at Nanyuki and then saw service in Ethiopia. Geoffrey joined the East African Artillery and went overseas to Burma. Kenneth was exempted from call-up on the grounds of his being accepted as a medical student by the University of Capetown in South Africa and was allowed to go to South Africa to study medicine.

So far as the missionaries were concerned, they were exempt from call-up although they could volunteer individually, and several did. For those who remained, the war made it impossible for them to proceed on home leave. Periods of leave were spent in other parts of Africa, thus Dr & Mrs Irvine spent their leave in South Africa in 1943. No new missionary appointments were possible during the war. European missionary colleagues from other African countries were able to visit the missions in Kenya either when they were on holiday there or when they were serving with African servicemen from their own mission area, such as Nyasaland or Nigeria. With the closure of the Mediterranean to shipping, communication with Scotland became difficult, with mail being delayed in transit and even failing to arrive.

Tens of thousands of young African men were recruited into the armed and ancillary services and were posted to theatres of war in Ethiopia, the Middle East and the Far East. The CSM sent some of its best African ministers and evangelists as chaplains and chaplain's assistants to the armed forces. In the armed forces many young men came under Christian instruction who might never otherwise have heard the gospel and many were able to profit from the educational services which the army provided.

For Church life in general, the late 1930s and the early 1940s were a period of recession. Evangelistic enthusiasm gave way to a routine conformity to habit, and individual commitment often became nominal and formal. Church attendance was not so regular as before and normal Church activities evoked little interest in many cases. Church services began with a mere handful of people present with numbers increasing as the service proceeded. Givings decreased. Theological training had to be temporarily discontinued and the decreased number of ministers available had to cover increased duties.[1]

The work in hospital in particular was affected by the war. Shortages of drugs and hospital equipment made the care and treatment of patients difficult. The hospital could not supply enough sheets or blankets for the beds in the wards and so tents were erected in the hospital compound where patients who needed hospital treatment could use their own clothes and blankets whilst they were inpatients. As one sister put it, the hospital linen cupboard was far more cupboard than linen.

The Indigenous Church

By 1939 there were fifteen bush Churches or congregations throughout the Chogoria area. The Sunday services at these Churches were conducted by elders or local Christian leaders, with regular visits from the ministers at Chogoria for the celebration of the sacraments. In 1943 Dr Irvine was still preparing typed sermons for the use of those responsible for the services at these Churches, a practice he had begun in 1936.[2]

The first minister to be ordained at Chogoria was the Revd Joseph Gathoga. Although he was a Kikuyu, he had lived near Chogoria for some years. He had been trained at Tumutumu and as a theological student he had assisted in the work of the parish at Chogoria. He was ordained by the Presbytery of Tumutumu on January 3rd 1943 and was inducted as parish minister at Chogoria.

The year 1943 also saw the setting up of the Presbyterian Church of East Africa (PCEA) and the formation of a Synod as the highest court of that Church. This was a great step forward in the history of the Presbyterian Church in Kenya. It meant that within a space of fifty years the Church of Scotland Mission had been able to establish an autonomous and indigenous African Church. In October 1945 the new Synod met in the Church at Chogoria and was attended by about fifty African ministers and elders.

In 1946 fifteen new elders were ordained at Chogoria. These included Jotham Murianki who was now the chief of Lower Mwimbi. He had been baptised in 1937 and at that time had been elected by the community as the Mwimbi area representative on the Meru Local Native Council. Four of these elders came from the Chuka area.[3]

The Chogoria area was divided into three parts in 1947 with an evangelist responsible for each part. Silas Muchina was responsible for Chuka. Silas was a Mukamba who had been trained as an evangelist at Tumutumu. Willie Kanini was in charge of the South Meru area. We have already met Willie, who came from Embu and was one of the teachers who joined Dr Irvine at the end of 1922. The third evangelist was Phares Mutunga who was responsible for the Mwimbi area.

The Church became aware in 1947 of increased pressure on its young people to accept the customs which had produced the controversy and temporary boycott of the Mission in 1929. New and undesirable types of dances were being encouraged by the non-Christian elders of the community. This was believed to be the result of the recent resuscitation in Meru District of the *njuri ya kiama* or *njuri ncheke* which was the original ruling body of elders of the Meru people. This body supported all the old customs and controlled the appointment of chiefs and LNC members. Although the resuscitation of this body was encouraged by the incumbent District Commissioner, the Church members at Chogoria were opposed to it on the grounds that it encouraged all the practices which the Church had rejected in 1929 and also it discriminated against Christians, who could not subscribe to the oath required of those who joined it, nor take part in any ceremonies which involved communication with the spirits of ancestors.[4] The same problem faced the Methodist Mission at Kaaga and produced a division of opinion there too. The Methodist missionaries, however, took a different view from those at Chogoria and were willing to accept the return of the *njuri ncheke* subject to certain conditions. These included the use of an oath which was taken on the Bible and was not associated with pagan sacrificial customs. However, the Christian members of the *njuri* were not popular with their non-Christian neighbours.[5]

Evangelistic safaris continued throughout the district. In 1947 Dr Irvine obtained gramophone records of Kikuyu hymns and talks prepared by missionaries of the Africa Inland Mission and these were played through amplifiers in the market-places on market days. These were often followed up by the showing of lantern slides of the life of Jesus on a large screen after darkness fell. Large crowds attended these open-air meetings.

The most marked feature of Church life of Kenya in the 1940s was the Revival Movement which began in Ruanda (Rwanda), then a Belgian-mandated territory. It then spread to Uganda and thence to Kenya and Tanzania. In view of its importance it is appropriate to devote the rest of this chapter to it.

The East African Revival

We first met revival on the first page of this book when we attributed the rise of the modern Protestant missionary movement in Britain to the Evangelical Revival of the eighteenth century. It was mentioned again in connection with the events at Tumutumu in 1921 for it was by reading about these that Mrs Carr became interested in the work of the CSM, an interest which led to Dr Irvine becoming her son-in-law. Revival, therefore, was no new phenomenon in the history of the CSM but it had occurred only locally and spasmodically. The phenomenon which is called the East African Revival was far more extensive and enduring than any which had occurred on the African continent before.

What is revival? This word is used in two senses. The narrower sense which is the commoner usage in America confines it to the holding of intensive evangelistic campaigns aimed at securing individual Christian conversion or commitment to Jesus Christ as Saviour and Lord. The wider sense in which we use it here describes a work of the Holy Spirit by which a commitment which has become merely nominal and formal is rekindled and deepened and by which the fellowship of individual Christians with each other is increased so that not only is the individual Christian revived, but also the whole Christian community. It was this latter type of revival which began in Ruanda in 1933 although its origins have been traced back to the 1890s.[6]

The Ruanda General and Medical Mission was an independent auxiliary of the CMS. Its first station in Ruanda was established at Gahini at the eastern end of Lake Muhazi in July 1925. The site was chosen by Captain Geoffrey Holmes who in 1931 became the brother-in-law of Dr Irvine when he married Mrs Irvine's sister, Ernestine Carr. At Gahini, medical work was begun early and a hospital of seventy-five beds was completed in 1928. In December 1933 the Revival Movement began amongst the staff of this hospital.[7] It soon spread to Kabale in Uganda and throughout the Kigezi province. Over the next few years, teams of the Revival leaders, mainly African but also including some of the Ruanda European missionaries, spoke at conferences and conventions in various parts of East Africa and even overseas. In 1937 the Ruanda Mission seconded Dr Joe Church, who had been associated with the revival from its beginning at Gahini, to work full-time with the Revival Movement. In that same year the first team of Revival leaders visited Kenya and addressed meetings in Nairobi, Kabete, Weithaga and elsewhere. In September 1938 a Revival convention was held at the Alliance High School, Kikuyu for African ministers and evangelists of all the Churches in Kenya. It was addressed by Dr Church and a team of African Revival leaders from Ruanda.

Those outside the Revival Movement originally called its members *abaka*, ('the blazing ones'), but the later and more common name was the Luganda term *balokole*, ('the saved ones'). When the movement reached Kikuyu country, the name used was *ahonoku*, which also means 'the saved ones'. These names witness to the intense impression that its members made on others. In Kikuyu country too, the members of the Revival Movement were often called the *gakundi*, ('the little group or company'), which reflects the ever-present danger of the separation of the members of the Movement from the parent missions or Churches. This was a danger which the Revival leaders were largely able to avoid, to the mutual enrichment of the Movement and the Churches.

The Revival Movement was organised on an informal, unstructured and group-led basis with no officials, bureaucracy or budget. At local village level the Revival Brethren. as they often called themselves, held small group meetings in private homes or Church buildings which they called Fellowship Meetings. Representatives from these groups would meet with other groups on a district, provincial or national level. There were teams of representatives at these different levels which co-ordinated the activities of the Brethren in the various parts of Kenya, but whose main function was to plan and organise meetings at district level or conventions at provincial or national level. At first these were planned and led by European missionaries, but soon the African Revival leadership took over their planning and organisation and the Revival became a truly indigenous movement. All the costs of these meetings and conventions were met from freewill offerings of the Brethren who contributed to what was called in Swahili *Mfuko ya Bwana* ('The Lord's Bag').[8]

The Fellowship Meeting, to which we have just referred, was an important feature of the Revival Movement wherever it came. This Meeting was held every one or two weeks in a convenient place for the members. Although there was no rigid ritual or set form about the activities of the Revival, the Fellowship Meeting often followed a common pattern. As the members assembled they began to sing as they waited for everyone to come. They would sing the Revival chorus *Tukugoca Jesu* ('We are praising Jesus') or some appropriate hymn. Once all were gathered, one or two would lead in prayer. Then followed a period of sharing of experiences since last they had met. This might include the open confession of sin. Such a confession was only accepted if it was accompanied by thanksgiving for forgiveness and victory by the one making the confession. The sharing of experiences was often interspersed with the spontaneous singing of the Revival chorus. Then there followed a Bible reading with comments on its meaning and application and this usually formed the longest part of the meeting. Prayer followed, along the lines suggested by the Bible reading. The meeting closed with a hymn and the Grace said all together, and the members might stay on to share news or chat with any visitors. Finally they went on their way, often singing as they went.[9]

The Revival conventions were much larger gatherings:

> No one who has been to such a convention can forget it - the spontaneous praise, the joy, the orderly way in which physical needs are cared for, and the simplicity which is sufficient. Usually a short verse becomes a motto for the convention, and a message to take back at its end.[10]

Revival Comes to Chogoria

As early as 1924 we find Dr Irvine asking his supporters in Scotland to add 'Revival' to their list of prayer requests for Chogoria saying that they have been praying for several months that a real revival would touch the hearts of the Christians at Chogoria.[11] In 1938 we find Dr Irvine still writing of the need for revival in the life of the Church at Chogoria and in the following years several campaigns and conventions were held at Chogoria or its outstations. Other conventions were held elsewhere in Kenya either on a regional or national basis, and these were usually attended by representatives from Chogoria.

The first local Revival convention was held at Chogoria in May 1940. It was attended by over a thousand people and lasted for eight days. During this convention a memorial to Ernest Carr was dedicated. This took the form of a brick plinth into which was set a large clock and which was flanked by two short walls in which benches were set making a small semicircular enclosure with a brick floor. It was sited on a level place opposite the Church and faced east.

In December 1940 an evangelistic campaign was held at Chogoria with Martin Capon of the CMS as the principal speaker. In May 1942 a joint convention was held at Chogoria for which the CMS staff at Kigari provided a team of four speakers to match a similar team of four from Chogoria. These teams spoke to a specially-invited audience of fifty people from these two mission stations. In addition to those who were specially invited and accommodated, many day visitors came to attend the meetings. These gatherings created a great demand for Bible teaching and so in August 1942 a Bible School was held at Chogoria for communicant members of the Church. It lasted for ten days and over a hundred people attended with the sexes being equally represented. Accommodation was provided for them in the dormitories of the boys' school. It should be mentioned that the subjects covered were not only biblical for Church history and hygiene were included amongst them.[12] This Bible School was such a success that a second one was held in August of the following year and a third one was held in September 1944.

Also in August and September 1944 local conventions were held in four different places in the Chogoria area. These were organised by Silas Muchina and Mary Mowat and met at Chogoria, Ngeru, Chuka and Kanyakine. Then in 1948 a regional convention was held at Embu and was attended by about five thousand people including many from Chogoria. This convention lasted for five days and was organised entirely by African Christians of the Revival Movement. The theme of the convention was "Christ is the head of the Church" (Ephesians 5.23).

Dr Irvine described the year 1948 as the Year of the Revival at Chogoria and called the 1949 edition of the *Chogoria* booklet a Revival number because it contained so many photographs of Revival events. Church buildings were quite inadequate to cope with the crowds who came to the Revival meetings and so they had to be held in the open air, and not in the rainy season! In June 1949 another regional convention was held at Chogoria and was attended by about twelve hundred people. In that same month, Mary Mowat and Dedan Wangai travelled up to Uganda to meet the leaders of the Revival Movement there.

In his report on the year 1948 Dr Irvine includes some general comments on the Revival Movement and its influence in the Chogoria area. The early 'indiscretions' such as the attitude of censoriousness and the tendency to separatism had now been left behind and the movement was now firmly established within the Church. Even amongst the Revival Brethren, racial dislike was still a problem, even between the different peoples who made up the Kikuyu. Dr Irvine had already in 1945 drawn the attention of the local Church members to this problem and in one of his circular letters to them he had written: "Never look at a man's race. Get rid of race-hatred. It is Satan's weapon".[13] Of the three parishes of Chogoria, he notes that Chuka was the one which had most benefited from the Revival, with Mwimbi next and then South Meru. The old African handshake had come into use again amongst the Revival Brethren. This was a threefold grasp consisting of a normal handshake, followed by a grasp of the base of the thumb and then a normal handshake again. This was explained as a greeting in the name of God the Father, the Son and the Holy Spirit.

The Government administrative officers were less happy with the Revival Movement than Dr Irvine was. Their reports for the year 1948 speak of the "fear of an outburst of religious zealotry". The Provincial Commissioner, Central Province, said "there are ominous signs of a spread of sectarianism" affecting Fort Hall, Meru and Machakos. In an obvious reference to the Chogoria area he speaks of "a revivalist movement" in part of Meru District which "is treading dangerous ground".[14]

When Dr Irvine reported on the year 1949 he was able to say that all the Church leaders at Chogoria and many of the teachers were now members of the Revival Movement. The Church had seconded Silas Muchina from his duties in Chuka to work full-time with the Revival Movement in the Chogoria area. In most outstations, weekly or fortnightly Fellowship Meetings were being held and the Revival had given a great stimulus to evangelism throughout the district.[15]

The first national Revival convention in Kenya met at Kabete near Nairobi from August 30th to September 5th 1949. The theme text of the meetings was "Come let us reason together" (Isaiah 1.18). It was the largest Revival convention so far held in Kenya and was attended by about fifteen thousand people from all over the country, including about a hundred from Chogoria district. The Governor of Kenya (Sir Philip Mitchell) flew up specially from Mombasa to address the convention on the Sunday morning. Dr and Mrs Irvine both attended the convention and they bought a caravan in which they lived during the convention. Part of the idea in purchasing the caravan was so that Mrs Irvine could use it to attend local conventions at Chogoria outstations, but it proved to be unmanageable on the narrow, twisting mountain roads and it ended up as additional guest accommodation at Chogoria.

The Revival and the PCEA

The initial reaction of the Missions and Churches to the Revival Movement in most cases had been one of hostility. This was partly due to the early enthusiasm of the Revival Brethren which in some cases had expressed itself in a censorious diagnosis and judgement of other people's spiritual condition, and a tendency to separation from normal Church activities in favour of more specific revival activities. A common practice was for the members of the Revival Movement to gather in a group outside the Church after a normal Church service, and hold a Fellowship Meeting with testimony followed by the singing of the Revival chorus, which only tended to emphasise their difference from ordinary Church members.

Another cause for the opposition of some Church leaders and members was to be found in the personal challenge which they saw in the individual character transformation which was so marked a feature of the influence of the Revival. There was a greater honesty reflected in the restitution of stolen property. There was a greater faithfulness in daily work including a marked responsibility in the use of time. There was a greater readiness to admit to wrongdoing and a new sensitivity to the difference between right and wrong. There was an absence of any racial bitterness and a new feeling of fellowship between the races. Finally, there was a new keenness for Christian things; for Bible teaching, for the conversion of non-Christians, for fellowship with other Christians, and for responsible financial support of the Church and Christian activities.

The reaction of the PCEA was no different from that of other Churches. There was opposition on the one hand and acceptance on the other. Chogoria was the first centre to incorporate the Revival Movement into its own life. Dr Irvine encouraged it from the first and the staff followed suit, especially when they saw and experienced for themselves the liberating and uplifting effect produced by the Revival. By 1948, acceptance at Chogoria was complete. The other PCEA centres at Kikuyu and Kambui were not so sure and at first sat on the fence, but by 1949 they too accepted the teaching of the Revival. Tumutumu remained hostile and in 1949 the Presbytery there refused to continue to sponsor three of their ministers-in-training because they belonged to the Revival Movement. This provoked a crisis and a committee of enquiry was set up to consider the situation. In its report, this committee drew attention to the tendency of the Revival Movement to produce division in Church and family life and to emphasise subjective spiritual experience unduly. On the positive side the committee noted the great zeal for the gospel shown by the Revival Brethren, and their emphasis on the need for repentance and for commitment to upright Christian living. The result was that the committee recommended that the Church should not oppose the teaching of the Revival.[16]

It was at this time that the Revd Solomon Ndambi, whom we have already met as the second African minister at Chogoria and who was now at Tumutumu, admitted that he had been opposed to the Revival. However, he had been so impressed with the effect it had had on his daughter Rachel and her husband Dedan Wangai, the clerk of works at Chogoria, that he had changed his mind.

The Effects of the Revival

Finally, let us summarise the effects of the Revival in the Churches in Kenya almost all of which continue today.[17]

1   It produced hundreds and thousands of conversions, many of them of baptised and nominal Christian men and women.

2   It brought a more radical commitment to Christian discipleship to those already Christians.

3   It deepened the knowledge of the Christian Faith even amongst already committed Christians.

4   It broke down racial and social barriers between black and white.

5   It broke down the tribal and educational barriers between African Christians.

6   It brought members and missionaries of different Churches closer together in a common fellowship.

7   It strengthened and prepared the Church in Kikuyuland for the onslaught of the Mau Mau movement.

CHAPTER TWELVE

POST-WAR DEVELOPMENTS

Shortages still continued for some years after the end of the war. Lack of shipping space continued to limit the import of foodstuffs and other commodities. There were three years of drought from 1944 to 1946 and large-scale food distribution had to be organised by Government to prevent a state of famine, especially in the rural areas. In 1945 Dr Irvine noted that photographic film was still in short supply and even in 1946 sewing materials for the hospital and girls' school were still difficult to get. Rationing of bread, sugar, flour and maize was still in force in 1948. By this time, however, controls on building materials were being relaxed except for corrugated iron sheets and galvanised iron piping. It is good to be able to record that from 1949 there is no mention of any major locust invasions. In 1952 and 1954 small swarms appeared in south Meru but they did not reach Chogoria and were successfully dealt with by the Locust Control Spraying Unit using the chemical contact poison DNOC.

Food, Stone and Administration

By 1946 the price of foodstuffs had more than doubled and food was often hard to get. Chogoria had many mouths to feed. On most days there were about a hundred inpatients to feed in the hospital and ninety pupils in the school. Fortunately none of them objected to dietetic monotony. In one of his reports for 1946 Dr Irvine sets out the daily menu for both hospital and school as follows:

Breakfast: Maize meal porridge with a little sugar.
Midday: Maize, beans, bush peas and plantains
cooked with dripping and salt.
Evening: Meat with potatoes and gravy, followed by
bananas.

Two tons of maize were purchased each month from the Maize Control Board of Kenya and stored in large galvanised iron tanks. Beans and bush peas were bought in large amounts when they were available and stored in a similar way. In both cases, the food was disinfested by using carbon disulphide to destroy weevils and other pests.

During the war and for the years immediately afterwards, no significant building activity had been possible, though the workshop had continued to do essential repairs and maintenance work. In 1946 a source of stone was found about a mile away from Chogoria in an outcrop in the steep hillside overlooking the Kamara River. After prolonged negotiation with the owners of the land, Dr Irvine was able to begin quarrying the stone for use in erecting further school and hospital buildings at Chogoria. Tumutumu supplied a stone-mason and about six men were taken on to quarry the stone. Soon they were producing up to twenty feet of hewn stone daily. The stone, technically known as tuff or tufa, was formed from the compaction over centuries of the volcanic ash which had resulted from the eruptions of Mount Kenya when it was active as a volcano. It was a grey stone, soft and easy to work when first cut, but hardening on exposure to air.

Administration was not Dr Irvine's favourite subject but he realised its importance for the well-being of the Mission. He did all the ordering of things for the Mission, and on one occasion he reminded his supporters in Scotland that this did not just mean Bibles and umbrellas! In fact, the list included food, clothing, drugs, tools, nails, screws, cement and stationery. He also undertook personal orders for individuals for such things as tools, sewing machines, radios, and bicycle spare parts. Both he and other members of staff often returned from Nairobi with the car full of items ordered by local African people. They were sometimes stopped by the police who demanded to see their trader's licence!

All this administration involved the keeping of accounts which Dr Irvine once said he regarded as "a chronic blister". He claimed to be very bad at arithmetic and admitted that he had sat a mathematics examination in the distant past for which he had scored a mark of 1¾%. It also involved the writing of many letters and he records that he and Mrs Irvine between them wrote an average of one hundred and fifty letters each month, mostly after 9pm at night. They had one rule, and that was that they did not write business letters on Sundays.[1] Both Kikuyu and Tumutumu had had full-time lady accountants for some years and Miss Berta Allan of Tumutumu had helped with the Chogoria accounts for several years, but only on an occasional part-time basis. It was a red-letter day for Chogoria and a great relief to Dr Irvine when she arrived on May 24th 1949 on transfer from Tumutumu to become Chogoria's first full-time lady accountant and hospital administrator.

As we mentioned in the previous chapter there had been a recrudescence of female circumcision agitation in 1947. At that time the Meru Local Native Council had passed a resolution that all girls should be circumcised before the age of thirteen years, but parents and the girls must give their consent to this before their local chief.[2] This resolution was re-emphasised by the Council in 1951. However, in 1956 the new African District Council, which had replaced the former Local Native Council, officially banned the practice of female circumcision. This did not however mean that the custom finally died out.

There is also a mention of local political activity in the Chogoria area in Dr Irvine's report for 1947. In September of that year there was a large meeting organised at Mweria market near Chogoria by the Kenya African Union (KAU) at which Jomo Kenyatta spoke. Kenyatta had been elected president of KAU in the previous June.

By the end of 1947, both the chiefs of Mwimbi were members of the PCEA. Chief Jotham Murianki was already chief in Lower Mwimbi and at the end of 1947 Chief Wallace M'Moga was appointed in Upper Mwimbi.

The Semi-Jubilee of Chogoria

In October 1947 the Mission celebrated the semi-jubilee of the Irvines' arrival at Chogoria on Monday October 9th 1922.[3] After twenty-five years there were now forty Christian communities scattered throughout the Chogoria area with over a thousand communicant members of the Church and thirty Sunday Schools catering for almost three thousand children.

The celebrations began on Saturday October 11th at 9.30am with a Fellowship Meeting in the Church organised by the African Church leaders. This meeting for praise and fellowship went on until mid-afternoon with an hour's break at midday for lunch. Dr Irvine had been away for the previous four days on essential business and had only arrived back the previous evening. The result was that he was able to be present at this meeting for only a short time because of his duties in hospital.

Once it was dark enough, the audience returned to the Church and Dr Irvine showed the film which he had made in the 1930s of the people and the work at that time. Many of the audience recognised themselves and their relatives and friends as the film was shown and uttered yells and shrieks of amusement. Pictures of the Mwimbi young men of those early days in pigtails and grease produced particular amusement, for these were long out of fashion, having given way to short-cropped hair and greater cleanliness.

On the Sunday, the celebrations continued with a communion service at 9.30am followed by an extended morning service of praise and thanksgiving. Representatives from the CMS in Embu and the Methodist Mission in Meru attended this service and brought greetings from their people. Dr Irvine preached the sermon at this service and spoke of the changes that the past twenty-five years had brought to Chogoria. In the afternoon there was a service led by the boys and girls of the Chogoria Junior Secondary School which lasted two hours.

What gave Dr Irvine particular satisfaction at this time was that the semi-jubilee celebrations were almost entirely organised by the local African Christians themselves.

Chogoria Becomes a Small Town

The establishment of a mission station inevitably leads to a concentration of population and the introduction of public services to serve that population and the area around. It is not surprising, therefore, to find Dr Irvine commenting early in 1948 that Chogoria was now "a small town".[4]

Chogoria already had a bus service. Nyaga's bus, as it was called after its owner, began to provide a thrice-weekly service in 1945 from Meru to Nairobi. Although Chogoria was about two miles off the main road, the bus came up to the Mission for the convenience of Chogoria people. The main road was still a murram or earth road which led to transport difficulties at the height of the rainy season.

The post office for Chogoria had originally been Embu, but when Chuka-Mwimbi was transferred from Embu District to Meru in 1933 the postal address became P.O.Meru. However in 1949 Chogoria was given its own post office. In February of that year Mr Johannes, the Goan postmaster at Meru, came to Chogoria in order to set up the new post office. Certain regulations concerning security of premises had to be complied with, and these were satisfied by some minor modifications of the Mission office and bookshop which now also became the post office. Simon Peter Waringu who had come to Chogoria from Tumutumu several years before, took charge of the post office and the official address of the Mission now became P.O.Chogoria. Simon had served in the Army and then had been trained as a clerk in which capacity he then came to Chogoria.[5]

The Church Takes Over the Schools

Robert Macpherson and his family left in 1940 and he was replaced by Alex Paterson who in turn was replaced by the Revd John Watt in 1941. Watt went on leave in 1945 and handed over the headmastership of the Primary School to Bernard Mate. Mate was an old boy of Chogoria School and the Alliance High School who had then gone on to Makerere College in Uganda to obtain the Headmaster's Certificate. At this time there were a hundred boys and girls attending Chogoria Primary School.

On the girls' side, Miss Butter-Malcolm was in charge in 1938 and was succeeded in 1940 by Jean Brownlie. By this time half the pupils in Chogoria School were girls. When Jean Brownlie left to go on leave in 1945, her African deputy Tirzah Wallace took charge until she got married. Then her sister Edith succeeded her until her own marriage to Bernard Mate in 1947. Mrs Watt, Mrs Irvine and Mrs Grieve all helped in the girls' school after Edith left until Martha Musa came in 1948. Martha was the daughter of the first Mwimbi Christian at Chogoria to be baptised. In 1951 she became the first woman member of the newly-constituted Meru African District Council.

The village schools had been supervised by Macpherson and then Watt. When Watt left he was succeeded by the Revd George Grieve, the former headmaster of the Alliance High School at Kikuyu. Grieve had retired from the Alliance High School in 1940, but returned to Kenya to serve at Chogoria in 1946. He in turn was succeeded by the Revd Donald Lamont and then by Dr John (Jack) Wilkinson who came in 1949 to combine the post of supervisor of schools with hospital duties. He was assisted by Erasto Mwiricia, formerly headmaster of Kimuchia Primary School.

In 1946 the Church took over responsibility for the Elementary Schools from the Mission. District School Committees were formed made up of representatives of the Church, the Mission and the parents. These Committees now had the responsibility of deciding about the opening of new elementary schools and the posting of teachers. In addition, each school was expected to have its own committee. This move was welcomed by Dr Irvine and his colleagues who up till then had been entirely responsible for the administration and supervision of the schools. It marked the beginning of the transfer to African hands of responsibility for work which had originally been established by the missionaries. As Dr Irvine commented:

> All this is paving the way to our taking the much happier position of co-operators, helpers and senior friends rather than of guides and leaders.[6]

Another welcome change in the work of the schools at this time was that the Government Education Department introduced standard terms and conditions of service with agreed salary scales which were adopted by the Missions. This meant that time was no longer spent in arguments with individual teachers complaining about their salaries when they came in each month to collect their salaries and supplies.

There were nineteen Elementary Schools in 1946 in three separate geographical groups based on Chogoria, Kanyakine to the north of Chogoria, and Kiereni to the south. Eight of these schools were aided by grants from the local education authority, and eleven were unaided and were supported entirely by the fees paid by the pupils. They employed over thirty trained teachers, but also many untrained teachers called 'monitors', and had a total roll of almost three thousand pupils. However, with the opening of the Elementary Teacher Training Centres in Meru and Embu in 1947 more teachers could now be trained and in that year Chogoria produced twenty-two candidates for teacher-training, including fifteen women. As the number of teachers available increased so the standards and numbers in the schools rose. By 1949 there were thirty Elementary Schools employing over eighty teachers for a school population of four thousand pupils. In 1946 the village schools were renamed. They had previously been called Elementary Schools, but were now to be called Primary Schools. This in turn led to a change of name for the school at Chogoria. It had previously been a Primary School, but was now to be called a Junior Secondary School.

At the end of their Primary School course the pupils had to pass the Common Entrance Examination in order to qualify for entrance to the Junior Secondary School. In 1945, seventy-one pupils sat this examination at the Elementary Schools and fifty-six passed, but only twenty-one obtained places in the Junior Secondary School.

In 1947, Edith Ayubu who had been attending Chogoria School, was accepted as a pupil for the new African Girl's High School which was due to open at Kikuyu in January 1948 with Jean Ewan (who later became Mrs Wilkinson) as its first headmistress.[7] Edith was the daughter of the dispenser in charge of the CSM dispensary at Kirindini and was the first Mwimbi girl to qualify for admission to a Senior Secondary School. In 1949, three boys from Chogoria Junior Secondary School were accepted for the Alliance High School so that in 1950 there were eight boys from Chogoria at this Senior Secondary School.

The boarding accommodation at Chogoria Junior Secondary School was greatly improved during this period. In 1946 a new boys' boarding school was built consisting of three dormitories each taking twenty boys. To these were attached a dining hall, a study room and bathrooms. These buildings were built in a semicircle at the opposite end of the football field from the Church. Half the cost of these building was borne by the Government Education Department. A water-tower was added in 1948 in order to improve the water-supply to this new school complex. In 1949 a new dormitory block was built which could accommodate sixty girls for the girls' school and in this case the whole cost was met by the Government. Since, as we have already seen, stone had become available in 1946, all these buildings were now built in stone, and brickmaking ceased to be required.

New regulations from the Government Education Department in 1947 required the Junior Secondary School to have a school farm. This meant that the school needed more land and in March of that year Dr Irvine was able to report that negotiations had been successfully completed for the acquisition of a new plot of land. This plot consisted of that area of land which lay between the two mission plots which had been acquired in 1922. Part of the new plot was used for a school garden and part for growing coffee to provide additional income for the maintenance of the Mission.

In 1941 the Irvines held an At Home in their house for the senior class of the Junior Secondary School and twenty-one pupils came. It was a great success and was repeated on a smaller scale in the following years. The pupils were invited to play games such as darts, draughts, chess and ludo. One game which was particularly popular was pinning the tail on a picture of a donkey put up on the wall. This had to be done blindfold. Then in 1946 the Irvines began to invite two senior schoolboys from the school to tea each Sunday and two senior Africans to supper. This was in order to accustom them to the manners and customs of western society so that they would not feel ill-at-ease when in future they left Chogoria and took their place in a society where these manners and customs were observed, such as in Nairobi.

There is no doubt about Dr Irvine's views on the importance of the kind of education the Chogoria schools were seeking to provide. In the *Chogoria* booklet for 1949 he wrote as follows:

> We believe that education in a Christian school under Christian teachers is essential if Africa is to become a Christian continent.[8]

This explains his great interest in the education and the welfare of young people.

The Hospital Staff Increases

The work of the hospital continued during the years of the war. Sister Clark Wilson left the hospital on May 19th 1942 to join the East African Military Nursing Service, but the troopship on which she was sailing to Colombo in Ceylon was torpedoed in the Indian Ocean and she was drowned.[9] Sister Margaret (Peggie) Fergusson came to replace her and in January 1946 she went on leave to Scotland. Sister Margaret Burt came in May 1947 from the CSM hospital at Kikuyu. At the end of 1948 Dr Irvine was joined by his son Dr Kenneth Irvine who had graduated in medicine in December of that year at Capetown University and had arranged to spend his pre-registration year at Chogoria. In January 1949 they were joined by Dr Wilkinson who because of his youthful appearance was named by the local people, Dr Kamwana ('The boy doctor'), a name that stuck to him throughout the rest of his service in Kenya. His coming meant that there were now three doctors at the hospital and this provoked the senior Dr Irvine's comment, "We shall probably never be so well staffed on the doctor side again!"[10] Little did he know what lay in the future!

Dr Ken went off in August 1949 to relieve the doctor at the CMS hospital at Kaloleni near Mombasa for that month. In December he went to Capetown to be married to Miss Elsabe Murray whom he had met as a student at Capetown University. After the wedding on December 10th, he returned to Kenya with his bride in January and went to the Methodist Mission Hospital at Maua, north of Meru Township, and served there for almost the whole of 1950.

The African members of the hospital staff numbered three medical assistants, ten male dressers and twenty female nurses in 1946. All these had been trained at Chogoria. The senior hospital assistant was Jackson Chabari. Most of the nurses had reached only Standard II or III at school, but they became very competent practically in their work. The theatre nurse may not have been able to write out the list of instruments required for any particular operation, but she always had them ready when they were required for the operation. With the advent of nursing sisters it became possible to hold classes for the nurses in nursing procedures and midwifery. There was, however, a great turn-over in nursing staff because after two or three years in training, the nurses usually got married. This was not regarded as a matter for disappointment, for nursing training was a good preparation for home-making and a real contribution to the life of the community. By 1949, the staff had increased to twenty male dressers and twenty-four female nurses.

Admissions to hospital remained steady at two to three thousand each year with about six hundred patients needing operative surgical treatment. On occasions the hospital wards were so full that tents had to be erected in the grounds in order to accommodate the extra patients. The year 1949, however, saw the admission of 3,690 patients to hospital which was the greatest number of annual admissions so far.

Once the war was over there was an increase in the number of patients. This was due to several factors. Firstly, the introduction of a bus service in 1945 which ran from Meru to Nairobi and back three times a week which we have already mentioned. Secondly, the growing reputation of the hospital which was attracting patients from greater distances. Dr Irvine was particularly glad to see more patients coming from Tharaka and in 1949 he noted that Kamba patients were once again crossing the Tana River to come to the hospital from Kamba country. Thirdly, the standard of care provided in the hospital was improving as more educated youths and girls were coming forward for training and the influence of the Revival on the staff was reflected in a greater concern and care for their patients.

In 1942 a new maternity block was opened with five beds. In that year seventy-five maternity patients were admitted, a figure which had risen to one hundred and sixty-one by 1945. A new children's ward was built in 1949 with twenty cots and a large verandah which could accommodate more cots as required. In that year too, a new operating theatre was erected which was large enough to accommodate two operating tables to allow two operations to be performed simultaneously. Two days a week were now devoted to surgical operations, and operating lists of fifteen to twenty cases were not uncommon.

A new and larger outpatient department had long been required and so the building of a new one was planned and carried out in 1950. Dr Irvine wrote that this "is expected to be the last hospital building needed".[11] However, as we shall see later, this proved not to be the case.

When the CSM hospital at Kikuyu installed a new X-ray machine in 1948, the old one was offered to Chogoria, and a wooden hut was erected behind the original block of wards to house it. Unfortunately when the X-ray machine arrived in February 1949 it was found impossible to restore it to a working condition and so it had to be abandoned. The hut which had been got ready to house it became a second medical consulting-room.

In 1942 the sulphonamide group of drugs became available and on one occasion Dr Irvine recorded that the hospital supply of sulphapyridine (M&B 693) was down to only two tablets. Patients got to know about the effectiveness of this drug and would come to hospital and ask for it by name. By 1946 the new antibiotic penicillin was proving its worth in the treatment of infection. At that time, vials of this substance had to be transported in refrigerated containers and this was not always possible because of the isolated position of Chogoria. Penicillin revolutionised the treatment of tropical ulcer which was so common in the Chogoria area at this time. A short course of injections of penicillin cleaned up the ulcer which could then be skin-grafted in order to complete the healing. The senior African staff became very proficient in skin-grafting these ulcers. Now that this effective short-term treatment was available for tropical ulcers, the workshop erected a number of wooden huts in the hospital grounds to provide hostel accommodation for those patients suffering from tropical ulcer and other short-term ambulant conditions, patients who did not really require hospital accommodation and yet lived too far away to go home during their treatment. These were called "The annexes".

About the same time the new oral treatment for leprosy with the sulphone group of drugs was introduced and replaced the previous method of injection of hydnocarpus (chaulmoogra) oil which had been painful and had little effect on the more severe lepromatous form of the disease. The new drugs could be given by mouth and this made the treatment easier and more acceptable to the leprosy patients. The hospital took part in the therapeutic trials of dapsone in leprosy organised by Dr James Innes who was the Adviser in Leprosy to the East African Governments. The leprosy home at this time had thirty beds.

In 1946 there was an increase in the annual grant to the hospital from the Government Medical Department from £324 to £600 and two years later this grant was increased by £500. At that time fees paid by patients amounted to about £1,000. By 1949 the hospital received only a fifteenth of its annual budget from the FMC in Edinburgh, the rest being found locally from the Government grant and patients' fees.

In accordance with the policy of the Mission Council a Local Hospital Advisory Committee was appointed in 1947 to advise the medical superintendent on matters relating to the Church and the community. This marked a further increase in the involvement of the local African Church and community in the work of the hospital and dispensaries, which Dr Irvine had always welcomed.

Work continued in the dispensaries each of which was staffed by a male dresser trained in the hospital. These men were taken back into hospital for refresher courses from time to time. Also each Wednesday there would be a medical safari to one of eight centres in the Chogoria area. The particular centre to be visited would receive advance warning of the coming of the safari. Then the doctor would leave Chogoria promptly at 8.30am with a team of three dressers or nurses and a carload of drugs and equipment. On arrival the staff would put up trestle tables and set out on them the equipment and drugs they had brought. The doctor worked at one table, another table held the injection equipment and ampoules, and a third held medicines and dressings of different kinds. When penicillin became available it was carried in flasks filled with ice, and since the people had never seen or felt ice, it was the source of a great deal of merriment usually provoked by the doctor! The clinic would begin with a short service and a talk. Music for the hymns was provided by the doctor on his accordion. If only a few patients had turned up for the beginning of the clinic, the service would be held in the middle of the clinic rather than at the beginning in order to have a larger audience. Usually between two and three hundred people were seen at each clinic, of whom about a hundred would be treated for some infection which at this time was often yaws. About fifty per cent of the people needed treatment for tropical ulcers, malaria or intestinal worms. They all paid a small fee, which did not in fact cover the cost of the treatment they were given. The team worked on until dusk and on occasion had to finish their work by the aid of the headlights of the car. Then they packed up and returned to Chogoria often with one or more patients for the hospital, but with a great sense of satisfaction with the work they had done that day.

As more and more of the responsibility for the various departments of the work at Chogoria was handed over to qualified Kenyan staff, Dr Irvine began to consider the need for Kenyan doctors to be trained in order to join the staff of the hospital. With this in mind he began to sponsor the education of a young Chogoria boy named Timothy Riungu. Timothy had been educated at Chogoria and in 1946 had entered the Alliance High School at Kikuyu. In 1949 arrangements were made by Dr Irvine for him to go to Scotland to attend the Royal High School in Edinburgh in order to study and qualify for entrance to a Scottish University. A farewell service was held for him on Christmas Day 1949 and he flew to Edinburgh on New Year's Eve. After his time at the Royal High School he was accepted for the medical course at St Andrews University where in due course he graduated in medicine. He then spent some time in hospital posts in Scotland, after which he returned to Kenya where he joined the Government Medical Service in Nairobi as a pathologist. He died after serving only a few years.

CHAPTER THIRTEEN

THE CHURCH ADVANCES

The decade of the 1950s was a very significant one in the history of Chogoria and in the development of Kenya as a whole. At Chogoria it was a time of advance in all departments of the work there. In the country as a whole, but most particularly in Kikuyuland, it was marked by the emergence of nationalism which finally expressed itself in the militant form known by the name of Mau Mau.

The Revival in the 1950s

The Revival Movement continued in the 1950s and made steady progress in the Church throughout the country, deepening its spiritual life and increasing the commitment of its members. It was also beginning to affect the Kikuyu independent Churches. In the Chogoria area, Revival Fellowship Meetings were held in most outschools one or twice a month, and even weekly in some cases. A second national Revival convention was held in August 1950 at the Church of the Torch on the CSM station at Kikuyu. It took the theme 'Jesus satisfies' based on the saying of Jesus in John 7.37, "If anyone is thirsty, let him come to me and drink". A team of Ugandan Revival Brethren led the large panel of speakers who addressed the meetings. About fifteen hundred people attended including the Irvines. This was the first national Revival convention that Dr Irvine had attended and he commented on how thrilling it was to find "a group of African Christians taking their religion seriously", which is a good definition of revival.[1]

In Chogoria Dr Irvine did all he could to encourage the Revival Brethren. He prepared outline Bible reading notes for use at their Fellowship Meetings, and he wrote circular letters giving advice on pastoral and other problems for their guidance. He attended their meetings whenever he could. He was always impressed by their sense of time. One morning meeting he attended was billed to last from 10.30am to 12.30pm; he records that it ended exactly at 12.31pm!

Later in the 1950s, Chogoria lost two of its most prominent Revival leaders. Dedan Wangai resigned in 1953 to join the Government Public Works Department in his home district of Nyeri. He had come to Chogoria in 1933 as a member of the workshop staff and over the next twenty years had become Dr Irvine's right-hand man in the works department at Chogoria. His administrative duties were taken over by John Braganza, a Goan Government clerk, whom the Government Medical Department had asked Dr Irvine to look after when he developed leprosy. Once he was cured, he had stayed on at Chogoria and assisted Dr Irvine with administration. The other Revival leader who left Chogoria at this time was Silas Muchina. He retired in 1955 and went to live at Karatina near Tumutumu. After his retirement he still took part in Revival conventions, and in August 1956 he returned to Chogoria for a provincial Revival Convention in which the speakers included William Nagenda from Uganda. Silas was also a member of the Revival Movement team which was sent to Malawi by the PCEA in 1962.

The Revival Movement made a vital contribution to the life of the PCEA, as it did to all the Churches which it influenced. As we have already mentioned in Chapter Eleven, it gave the Church roots which were truly indigenous. It brought a new and deeper grasp of Christian truth and revelation to its members and the possibility of direct spiritual encounter with Christ himself in a truly contemporary setting. It brought a new sense of responsibility towards God who demanded holiness of living and uprightness of conduct. It gave an ecumenical dimension to Christian fellowship which ignored family, tribal, national, racial and denominational loyalties. An unforeseen contribution was how the Revival Movement prepared the Church in Kenya to face the onslaught of the Mau Mau Movement in the 1950s, of which we shall speak in the next chapter.

The Presbytery of Chogoria Formed

January 1952 saw the ordination of the first Mwimbi minister. He was the Revd Jediel Micheu whose family lived beside the Mission at Chogoria. He had been trained as a teacher at Kahuhia Teacher Training College, and after service as a teacher had studied divinity at the United Theological College at Limuru. He was ordained by the Presbytery of Tumutumu, the service being conducted by the Moderator of that

Presbytery, the Revd Charles M.Kareri. The Methodist Mission at Kaaga was represented at the service by the Revd Philip M'Inoti, their senior African minister. After his ordination Jediel became the parish minister at Chogoria.

In July of that year the Presbytery of Tumutumu returned to Chogoria to set up a new Parish and Kirk Session at Chuka. Previously all the work in the Chogoria area had been under the supervision of one Kirk Session, that of Chogoria. Now the work at Chuka was to be separated and given its own Kirk Session. Its first minister was the Revd Geoffrey Ngari who was one of the ministers-in-training whose training Tumutumu Presbytery had refused to continue to sponsor in 1949 because of his involvement with the Revival Movement.

In the following year the Synod of the PCEA agreed to the setting up of the Presbytery of Chogoria. As we have already seen, the Synod had been formed in November 1940 as the highest court of the PCEA and had taken over the responsibilities of the former Presbytery of Kenya of the Church of Scotland which had been set up in 1920. The Synod alone had the authority to set up a new presbytery. This was in accordance with the normal polity of a Presbyterian Church, which is organised on a hierarchy of Church courts. The lowest Church court is the Kirk Session which is responsible for the affairs of a parish and congregation; the next is the Presbytery responsible for the supervision of a number of Kirk Sessions; and then above that is the Synod and finally the General Assembly. Up till now there were three Presbyteries in the PCEA - those of Kiambu, Tumutumu and Chania. The first two had been formed as a result of the work of the CSM at its original two stations of Kikuyu and Tumutumu. The last one had been formed in 1946 when the Gospel Missionary Society members joined the PCEA and were organised into a new presbytery. So far, Chogoria had two Kirk Sessions, one at Chogoria itself and the other at Chuka both of which were under the supervision of the Presbytery of Tumutumu. A third Kirk Session was now to be set up and a new presbytery to be formed to supervise the three Kirk Sessions. This meant that Chogoria had now achieved the same status, ecclesiastically speaking, as the other PCEA centres in Kikuyuland.

In September 1953, members of the Presbytery of Tumutumu with their Moderator, the Revd Charles M.Kareri, travelled to Kanyakine about twenty miles to the north of Chogoria on the road to Meru. On

Saturday September 26th they set up the Kirk Session of South Meru and then inducted the Revd Linus Waruiru to the new parish of South Meru. Linus came from the Tumutumu area and was another of the ministers-in-training who had been refused sponsorship by Tumutumu Presbytery in 1949 because he belonged to the Revival Movement. After a successful ministry at Kanyakine, Linus was killed in a road accident in 1969.

On the following day, Sunday September 27th, members of the PCEA Synod (who included those who were also members of the Presbytery of Tumutumu) proceeded to set up the Presbytery of Chogoria and installed Dr Irvine as its first Moderator (Chairman) and the Revd Jediel Micheu as its first Clerk (Secretary).[2]

A further step in the development of the PCEA came in February 1956 when all the work which had been established by the Church of Scotland in Kenya amongst Africans, Indians and Europeans was united into one body.[3] The General Assembly of this newly-united Church was inaugurated at a special service held in St Andrew's Church, Nairobi on February 11th. The General Assembly of the Church of Scotland sent its Moderator (The Right Revd Professor George D.Henderson, DD) to preside over the ceremony of inauguration. The Revd George Calderwood was elected as the first Moderator of the united Church. Professor Henderson taught Church History at the University of Aberdeen. On this occasion he was not simply teaching Church history but making it, so far as the Presbyterian Church in Kenya was concerned.

One of the most important events in the life of the Church in Kikuyuland in the 1950s was the publication of the Old Testament in the Kikuyu language. The New Testament had been published in 1926, and parts of the Old Testament had been made available in Kikuyu since that time. As we have already seen, the translation of the New Testament had been mainly the work of Ruffell Barlow of the CSM and the Revd Harry Leakey of the CMS, and they had continued to translate parts of the Old Testament under the supervision of the United Kikuyu Language Committee. Thus the book of Genesis had been translated by Leakey and published in 1924, and the book of Psalms by Barlow came out in 1936. When the Old Testament was published in February 1951 it was as a separate volume from the New Testament. It was only in 1965 that the two Testaments were published together in one volume in which references and brief notes were also included. Before the two Testaments were brought together into a single volume, the opportunity was taken to revise the New Testament.[4]

School Matters

In August 1950 Bernard Mate, the principal of the Junior Secondary School left for Britain to study at University College, Bangor for a BA degree. His place was taken by Eustace Mutegi. At this time there were sixty boys in the boys' boarding school and over sixty more attending as day boys. In 1951 a private donation was received to enable a swimming pool to be built for the school pupils at Chogoria. This provided an opportunity for the school pupils to learn to swim which otherwise would not have been possible in the Chogoria area where the rivers had few suitable pools in which swimming was possible.

Margaret Bowman came to be principal of the girls' boarding school in 1950 and was assisted by Phyllis Zakayo. In that year there were forty girls in the school and this number increased to sixty in the following year. In order to accommodate these sixty girls, new boarding accommodation was built in 1950. However, in 1952 the girls and boys switched dormitories as the number of girls requiring boarding accommodation was increasing and more boys were now attending as day pupils.

When Dr Wilkinson left on overseas leave in March 1950, Mary Mowat took over his duties as Supervisor of Schools. Erasto Mwiricia continued to serve as Assistant Supervisor until he became Supervisor in April 1951. In 1953 there were forty CSM Primary Schools with about five thousand pupils enrolled, and by 1959 the number of Primary Schools had increased to fifty-five.

This increase in the number of Primary Schools led to a great demand for school furniture which the workshop at Chogoria worked hard to supply. Carpentry was, of course, one of the subjects taught in the Junior Secondary School and so some of the schoolboys were employed in their holidays to make desks, benches, tables and chairs for the schools. In this way they were able to earn money to pay their school fees. Before the different items were sent out to the schools they were inspected by Dedan Wangai, the clerk of works. After he left Chogoria in 1953, the final inspection was carried out by Dr Irvine himself.

African Education in Kenya

The year 1948 saw the publication by the Kenya Government Education Department of the Ten-Year Plan for the Development of African Education. This was the most ambitious plan yet produced. It envisaged the development of the Primary School system over a period of ten years to provide a six-year primary course for half of Kenya's African child population. During these ten years the annual expenditure of local authorities on primary education was estimated to rise from £100,000 to £234,000. Capital expenditure over the same period for the building of new schools and other facilities was expected to be about £800,000. In the same year the Government Salaries Commission recommended salary increases to all Government teachers.

Not surprisingly, the Local Native Councils who since 1945 were the local education authorities for primary education, found it impossible to pay the new salary scales. The Primary School system had already outstripped their financial resources and the long-term planning which they had based on these resources. This situation, combined with the unsatisfactory state of primary education in the country, led to the setting up of a Committee on African Education in Kenya under the chairmanship of Archdeacon Leonard J.Beecher who had originally come to Kenya in October 1926 to join the staff of the Alliance High School, and so had long experience of the educational system of the country.

The report of the Beecher Committee was published with commendable speed in 1949. It found that the Ten-Year Plan had in fact been too conservative and recommended that there should be a rapid expansion of schools for African children up to School Certificate standard together with measures to raise the standard of teacher training. Education should be based on Christian principles and so the Government should continue to work through the Christian Churches and Missions. There should be a great increase in staff for the supervision and inspection of Primary Schools and a greater emphasis on practical aptitudes and skills. Finally, future reorganisation and planning should be based on educational surveys.[5]

The recommendations of the Beecher Report were accepted by the Kenya Government in August 1950 and a new Education Ordinance was passed in December 1952. The result was that as from January 1st 1953, the educational system for African children was divided into three stages covering twelve years of school attendance which began at the age of seven. The first four years were to be spent at a Primary School; the second four years at an Intermediate School; and the final four years at a Secondary School. In 1953 the first eight classes of education were designated Standards I to VIII, and the Secondary School classes were graded into Forms 1 to 4. So far as examinations were concerned, the Kenya Preliminary Examination (KPE) was taken at the end of the eighth year, and School Certificate Examination at the end of the twelfth year.

The result of these changes was the regrading of Chogoria School as an Intermediate Boarding School in 1952, and the upgrading of four of the outschools from Primary Schools to Intermediate Schools, e.g. Ikuu. These schools were then placed under the Meru District Education Board which was answerable to the Government Education Department. At this time, Mr Ariel Njeru took over from Mr Eustace Mutegi the headmastership of the Intermediate School at Chogoria.

Hospital Affairs

When Dr Wilkinson and his family left on leave to Scotland in March 1950, Dr Irvine was once again in sole medical charge of the hospital until his son Dr Geoffrey Irvine arrived in May 1953. Dr Geoff had graduated in medicine at Edinburgh University in July 1951 and then spent his pre-registration year in posts in hospitals in Edinburgh.

Early in 1950 Sister Burt had to return to Britain to care for her elderly parents. She was able to hand over her responsibilities to Sister Louise Morson who arrived three days before she left. Sister Morson came to Chogoria on local appointment after serving at the CMS Hospital at Maseno in the Nyanza Province of Kenya. She had originally intended to stay only a few weeks and ended up by staying for over two years! In July 1950 she was joined by Sister Mary Jane Kamerzel, an American nurse, who had served with the American Red Cross in the Pacific Region. She too was locally-appointed but she travelled to Kenya via Scotland and was able to meet the officers of the Church of Scotland Foreign Mission Committee and the supporters of Chogoria in Edinburgh.

Miss Kamerzel was the first American member of staff of the hospital and her Americanisms sometimes led to amusing situations. For instance, soon after her arrival in July, she went into the main shop in Meru township and asked for 'crackers'. The Indian shopkeeper looked a little surprised, but he was always willing to oblige his customers. He dived into the backshop and emerged with a rather dusty box of Christmas crackers, murmuring, "We thought that people only wanted these at Christmas time!". She had to explain that she was American and 'crackers' was the American word for biscuits. Then she was the first nursing sister to wear a nylon uniform. This so intrigued the schoolgirls that they used to come up and ask if they could feel the nylon material. However, she had a great sense of humour and took all these things in good part.

In 1950 Jackson Chabari retired after twenty-one years' service in the hospital. In recognition of his service it was decided to call the large waiting room in the new outpatient department Jackson Hall. Francis Muruja, who had originally joined the staff in 1941, succeeded him as senior hospital assistant. However, although he had gone into business locally, Jackson soon decided that he would like to come back on to the hospital staff. He was given charge of the hospital pharmacy. The pharmacy was now housed in the building which had been erected in 1929 as the treatment room for the leprosy patients. At that time they used to come there for injections of hydnocarpus (chaulmoogra) oil and for the dressing of their ulcers. With the introduction of sulphone therapy for leprosy, special treatment accommodation was no longer necessary and the building became the hospital pharmacy and store.

The Nurse Training School

From the beginning of the medical work at Chogoria Dr Irvine had trained his own staff, which to begin with was all male. In the early years there was no co-ordination of the training of hospital staff by mission agencies and no commonly accepted syllabus of training.

In 1950, the newly-established Nurses and Midwives Council of Kenya drew up regulations for the training of Kenya Enrolled Assistant Nurses (KEANs). There were to be two grades of this nurse training. Mission hospitals which were able to satisfy the regulations for one of the grades were allowed to apply for recognition as training schools. In February 1951 Dr Irvine asked the permission of the Mission Council to begin to train nurses for the Grade Two Enrolled Assistant Nurse examination and certificate. The Mission Council readily gave their approval recognising that Chogoria had for some years past been training a comparable grade of nurse. Dr Irvine then applied to the Nurses and Midwives Council for recognition as a Grade Two training school and this application was approved. Following this he submitted plans to the Mission Council for the provision of a nurses' home to house the students and these were also approved and quickly erected.

The training course was for two years and the entry qualification was the successful completion of Form 2 of Junior Secondary School. The course began in 1951 with a class of six girls and two boys. In order to distinguish the female nursing students from those who were already trained, the students' white uniform was trimmed with green edging whilst the trained nurses' uniform had red edging. Most of the teaching of the nursing students was undertaken by Sister Morson who proved to be a very enthusiastic and competent teacher. She was assisted in the teaching by the senior African nurses. At the end of the first course three girls and two boys sat the examination and all passed, one after re-examination. In each succeeding year ten students were accepted for the training course, eight girls and two boys on each occasion. Later the two grades were combined into a three-year course and by the time the qualification of the Grade Two Kenya Enrolled Assistant Nurse was phased out in 1961, the Chogoria Nurse Training School had successfully presented one hundred and nine students for the examination, eighty-one of whom were girls and twenty-eight were boys. Some of these nurses were employed by the hospital, but many went into the Government Medical Service.

CHAPTER FOURTEEN

THE PROGRESS OF NATIONALISM

In an earlier chapter we gave an account of the controversy which arose in the late 1920s about the practice of female circumcision and the right of Christian girls and their parents to refuse this practice if they so desired. This controversy was one of the early manifestations of Kikuyu nationalism. Now that we have reached the 1950s in our account of the development of Chogoria, it is appropriate to look at the progress of Kikuyu nationalism as it affected the country in general and the Chogoria area in particular.

Nationalism in Kikuyuland

Nationalism may take various forms. For the purpose of our account of nationalism in Kikuyuland we shall recognise cultural, educational, territorial, political and finally, militant nationalism.

Cultural nationalism is the form of nationalism which we saw at work in the female circumcision controversy. Underlying this form of nationalism was the desire to preserve the traditional rites and customs of the Kikuyu people, which were regarded as threatened by Christian missionary activity and western civilisation. Although the controversy centred on only one item of Kikuyu tradition, namely that of female circumcision, the political leaders of the Kikuyu maintained that the attack on that practice was an attack on the whole Kikuyu way of life. It was on this basis that they appealed to the Kikuyu people to unite in its defence.

The severity of the operation of female circumcision varied from area to area of Kikuyuland. In some areas, the operation was much more extensive and mutilating than was necessary. The result was that from the year 1926 most Local Native Councils were persuaded by Government to pass resolutions restricting the performance of the operation to skilled women recognised by each Council and defining the extent of the tissue which might be removed.[1] Subsequently, the right of girls and their parents to refuse the operation was recognised. Thus, as we have already mentioned, in 1947 Meru LNC passed a resolution allowing female circumcision only if the girl and her parents had agreed to it in front of the local chief. Finally in 1956, both Meru and Embu LNCs passed resolutions forbidding the operation altogether. However, it is doubtful how really effective these resolutions were.

One result of the cultural nationalism we have just described was what we may call educational nationalism. This was based on the recognition by the Kikuyu people of the great advantages of education which gave them the ability to read and write. This ardent desire for education on the part of the Kikuyu people led to the establishment by their political leaders of an educational system independent of the Missions and Government.

Independent schools appeared as early as 1922 in the Fort Hall area and other schools appeared later in the 1920s only to be closed by the Government administration because of their low standards. In 1930 the KCA requested the Government to open schools so that children did not need to attend mission schools. The Government refused. Thus in the 1930s two educational associations came into being in Kikuyuland to provide schools and an education which were not subject to Government or Mission control.[2] The first one was formed in 1931 and was called the Kikuyu Karing'a Educational Association (KKEA).[3] It flourished mainly in Kiambu District where it was closely associated with the KCA. This was a secular body and excluded all religious content from its teaching. It aimed to provide an education which would satisfy Kikuyu nationalist ambitions and was therefore anti-European, anti-Government and anti-Mission.

The second association was the Kikuyu Independent Schools Association (KISA) to which we have already referred in a previous chapter. This Association was set up at Gituamba in the Kandara Division of Fort Hall in 1934.[4] It flourished mainly in Fort Hall District where it had thirty-six schools by 1950. It was not however very popular on the eastern side of Mount Kenya for by the same year there were only six KISA schools in Embu District and three in Meru District.[5] To begin with, KISA sought to retain a recognisably Christian basis. It borrowed heavily from the practice of the Missions and sought affiliation to the African Orthodox Church in South Africa, but eventually broke with this Church and set up the African Independent Pentecostal Church (AIPC) in 1938. This body continued to reject any mission influence and allowed its members to practise female circumcision. It also sought to remain politically loyal to the Kenya Government. However, in the 1940s KISA and the AIPC were gradually infiltrated and eventually taken over by the members of the KCA which had been banned in May 1940 because of alleged subversive activity against the Government. The KISA schools were then used to spread propaganda against the Government and to promote the interests of the Mau Mau Movement. In some cases the children were forced to take the Mau Mau oath and the school buildings and compounds used for oathing ceremonies. The result was that on November 14th 1952 both KKEA and KISA were declared unlawful societies and most of their schools closed in the Central and Rift Valley Provinces. The pupils in these schools were then absorbed into the schools of the Missions or of the local authority.

It was the land question which produced the most intense form of nationalism, which we may call territorial nationalism. From the early years of the British occupation the Kikuyu alleged that land which was rightfully theirs had been stolen from them and given to European settlers. The Colonial Government of Kenya was early made aware of this claim by the leaders of the Kikuyu people and over the years appointed several committees and commissions to investigate it and where found to be justified, to remedy it. The first of these was the Delamere Committee appointed in October 1904 but its conclusions did little to solve the problem. As this problem arose principally from the Kikuyu understanding of land tenure, another committee chaired by G.V.Maxwell was set up in September 1929 to study "the origin and principles of land tenure in the Kikuyu Province". However, the body which conducted the fullest investigation of the land issue was the Kenya Land Commission appointed in April 1932 and chaired by Sir Morris Carter, a former Chief Justice of Uganda and Tanganyika. This Commission examined all the claims made by the Kikuyu leaders and others with meticulous care and produced a voluminous report which was published in 1934. Their report concluded that all the Kikuyu grievances with regard to land could be satisfied by the addition of some twenty-one thousand acres to the existing Kikuyu reserve together with an additional two hundred and forty thousand acres to allow for future expansion of the population. The recommendations of the Carter Commission did not, however, satisfy the political leaders of the Kikuyu people, especially those in Kiambu District where much of the alienation of land to European settlers had taken place.

We come now to consider political nationalism amongst the Kikuyu people. By political nationalism is ultimately meant the desire for independence. To begin with, the Kikuyu people simply wanted a more satisfactory solution to the land question and some say in the government of the country. This was reflected in the formation of the KCA after the First World War, as we have already described. With the outbreak of the Second World War, the Government banned the KCA which they regarded as a subversive organisation. This was done in May 1940 and the leaders of the KCA were arrested and detained at Kapenguria in western Kenya. After the war they were released and resumed political activity as a result of which they formed the Kenya African Union (KAU). This body was formed on October 1st 1944 in order to support Eliud Mathu who had been nominated as the first African member of the Legislative Council.[6] Although membership of this new body was open to all Africans, it continued to be mainly a Kikuyu political organisation led by former KCA members. The leaders of KAU soon began to demand a greater share in government and then eventually self-government.

In order to unite the Kikuyu people in its support, KAU began early in 1949 to enrol members at special secret ceremonies at which people were required to take a special oath and to subscribe money to the organisation. It is about this time that the term Mau Mau began to be used and many people believed that this was just another name for KAU. The meaning of the name Mau Mau is obscure, but a plausible suggestion for its origin is that it is derived from *muuma* which is the Kikuyu word for an oath.[7] However the term *mau-mau* did already exist in Kikuyu as an onomatopoetic description of "the half-snarling, half-gulping noise made by an animal when bolting food" and had been applied to a band of young men who terrorised a locality in the Kiambu district at the end of last century.[8]

By 1951 KAU was divided into moderate and extremist groups. The moderates, most of whom were not Kikuyu, demanded that the organisation denounce Mau Mau, but this did not happen. With the rise of the Mau Mau organisation, Kikuyu political nationalism became militant.

Nationalism Becomes Militant

Kikuyu political nationalism had begun by seeking to use constitutional means to achieve the social, economic and political changes its leaders sought. When they found that this method was not being effective, they turned to the non-constitutional means of militancy and violence. This can be illustrated by the increasing requirements of the Mau Mau oath.

The original oath bound its takers to secrecy. It obliged them to help the organisation with money and practical help and not to sell land to strangers nor to help the Government to apprehend its members. In May 1952 a second oath came to the notice of the Government. This was directed against all enemies and Europeans and required these to be killed if the taker of the oath was ordered to do this. Finally, when the Mau Mau gangs were formed in the forest later in 1952, each member on recruitment was asked to take the *batuni* ('platoon') oath which obliged him to attack European farms, kill European people and Kikuyu enemies even if they were close relatives, and to steal firearms.[9]

There were several groups amongst the Kikuyu people who refused to take the Mau Mau oath and who were therefore regarded by the Mau Mau as its enemies. These included Government administrative staff, those who were loyal to the British administration for one reason or another, those who were committed Christians especially the Revival Brethren, and the old guard traditional Kikuyu who did not recognise the Mau Mau oath as a true Kikuyu oath.

Once the Government realised its true nature, Mau Mau was banned. This occurred in August 1950, but it made little difference to the spread of oath-taking. This continued along with defiance of law and order until late 1952 when the Government on Monday October 20th declared a State of Emergency to exist and called in outside military help from Britain to maintain law and order. Many of the most active leaders of the Mau Mau were arrested and eventually brought to trial.

The declaration of the State of Emergency caught the Mau Mau by surprise, but they soon recovered and appointed new leaders and lieutenants to replace those who had been arrested. The young and active men left their homes and joined Mau Mau gangs which operated especially from the forests on Mount Kenya and on the Aberdare Mountains.

Chogoria and the Mau Mau

Oath-taking was slow to appear in the Chogoria area and it was only in September 1952 that an official report noted that Mau Mau oathing was being recorded in Meru District. By August 1953, oathing ceremonies were being held nearer to Chogoria. Then in the early months of 1954, oathing increased in the Chogoria area as the result of the compulsory repatriation of known Mau Mau supporters from Nairobi back to their own tribal areas.

Once Mau Mau gangs had begun to operate in the forest on Mount Kenya, Chogoria was very vulnerable to their activity since it lay little more than a mile from the forest edge. The question was therefore whether Mau Mau gangs would in fact attack Chogoria. There were several reasons why they might. It was relatively isolated and three miles away from a police station. There were Europeans on the staff there. It was a mission station and well-known as a centre of the Revival Movement. As the Mau Mau were anti-European, anti-Mission and sworn enemies of the Revival Brethren, an attack on Chogoria could be expected.

It was therefore prudent to take security precautions. A security fence was erected around the Mission compound and electric lights were installed at strategic places beside the fence. The fence was patrolled at night, first of all by Dr Irvine, Dr Geoff and the Mission watchmen, and later by a fifteen-strong Home Guard led by former Chief Jotham Murianki, which had been recruited for this purpose. An observation post giving an overall view of the buildings of the compound was built in a tree next to the Church office and manned for most of the night. The security forces stationed a company of British troops on the main road below Chogoria. At one period these were the Royal Inniskilling Fusiliers from Northern Ireland and on several occasions they played football with the Junior Secondary School team at Chogoria, and usually were defeated! After these football matches, their regimental piper would play the bagpipes, much to the fascination of the school boys and girls who had never seen or heard bagpipes before.

The department whose work was most affected by the Mau Mau situation was the hospital. Here the clinical work was almost halved in amount. The numbers of patients coming to the hospital fell because buses ceased running. Also, patients were afraid to venture out on to the roads in case they were attacked by a Mau Mau gang or were taken for questioning by the security forces. There was, however, an increase in the amount of traumatic surgery which the doctors were called upon to perform on patients who had been wounded either by the gangs or the security forces. The greatest increase was in medico-legal work when reports had to be prepared on persons who had been wounded, and postmortem examinations had to be carried out on those who had been killed or found dead. Up to the middle of 1954, thirty-three fatal cases were recorded at Chogoria hospital most of whom died from panga wounds.[10] This medico-legal work usually involved the attendance of the doctors at the court at Meru to give expert witness evidence in cases brought to trial, which often meant being away from hospital for a day or more.

The other department of the work which was affected by Mau Mau activity was that of the Primary Schools, six of which were attacked and burnt down at night. However, they were almost immediately rebuilt by the local community. Other schools were moved temporarily to more secure areas away from the forest or dense bush where Mau Mau gangs could hide. In September 1954 the Intermediate School at Ikuu on the main road to Chuka about ten miles south of Chogoria was attacked and burnt down one night by a gang of thirty Mau Mau. All the nine teachers escaped unharmed except one who was slightly wounded. The seven men teachers hid in the rafters of the school store which was built of stone, and the two women teachers crouched under the floor of their house as the house burnt above them.[11]

Dr Irvine reported in March 1954 that a prisoner had told the police that the Mau Mau intended to attack Chogoria. The result was that two European police officers and a number of African constables were sent to protect the mission station. However, no attack was made, but a gang of twenty Mau Mau was rounded up and captured by soldiers of the Black Watch regiment.

There were numerous cases of individuals being held up in their villages in an effort to force them to take the Mau Mau oath. Some did so when they were threatened with death, but others especially of the Revival Brethren resisted to the end even when a noose was put round their neck to threaten them with death. The first Christian in the Chogoria area to be murdered by the Mau Mau for refusing to take the oath was Mariamu Ndago Samweli who came from Chuka. In 1954 she and another woman were abducted by three terrorists and taken into the bush to be oathed. Her companion agreed, but Mariamu refused and a rope was put round her neck and she was strangled. She was buried beside the Church at Chogoria. She left a husband and a family of six children.

Some of the Revival Brethren in the Chuka area adopted a pacifist position and declared that they would not resist the Mau Mau physically or serve in the Home Guard. Dr Irvine was very concerned about this and was able to persuade some of them to change their minds. There is no doubt that this period was a great testing time for the Church and many nominal Christians succumbed to Mau Mau intimidation.

In general, the Chogoria area escaped the worst aspects of the Mau Mau situation and was not as troubled by gang activity and the measures taken to control it as other areas were. The local people were more loyal and co-operated with the security forces. One result of this was that the policy of villagisation, which was introduced into Kikuyuland in 1954, was not imposed on the Mwimbi people. Under this policy, the population in other areas were obliged to leave their homes and live in large fenced villages under the protection of Home Guards. This was for their own safety but also to prevent their feeding and communicating with the Mau Mau gangs. The policy was partially applied in the Chuka area, but not at all in Mwimbi. Another measure used by the security forces was to declare a mile-wide strip of land bordering the forest, a no-go area which was cleared of vegetation and in which cultivation was then forbidden and any persons found there were liable to be shot on sight. The area above Chogoria was the first one in which this restriction was lifted. This abolition of the mile strip was announced by the Meru District Commissioner in September 1954 when he addressed a large *baraza* (public meeting) of local people at Kiaganguru on the main road, two miles from Chogoria.

The Emergency Ends

KAU was banned in June 1953, but this made little difference to the progress of the campaign against the Mau Mau. However by 1955 the security forces had obtained military control of Kikuyuland and communication between the forest gangs and the so-called passive wing of Mau Mau in the countryside at large had been made hazardous. In October 1956, the police and the administration re-assumed responsibility for law and order as they took back this responsibility from the military.

The Emergency was declared officially at an end on 12th January 1960 when the Governor (who by this time was Sir Patrick Renison) issued a proclamation to that effect.

CHAPTER FIFTEEN

FROM EMERGENCY TO INDEPENDENCE

The terms in the title of this chapter are political and serve to remind us of the context of missionary endeavour and of the work and witness of the Church. We have seen in the last chapter how the Emergency affected the work at Chogoria and we shall see in the next chapter how this work was also affected by the coming of political independence to Kenya in 1963. Meantime this chapter will describe the period between these two events.

Political Developments

The Governor of Kenya who in October 1952 signed the proclamation of the State of Emergency in Kenya was Sir Evelyn Baring. He arrived in Kenya to take up his appointment as Governor in 1952 and left some seven years later. He proved to be a wise choice for "Kenya made great progress during the seven years he was Governor. By the time he came to leave, in the autumn of 1959, the colony's agriculture was transformed, her economy revitalized, and her political institutions properly geared for increasing African participation".[1]

In March 1957 the first elections for African representatives on Kenya's Legislative Council were held. There were eight seats and one of them was allocated to Central Province. The vote amongst the Kikuyu people was restricted to those who held Loyalty Certificates which were granted by the Government administration to those with no known connection with Mau Mau. The people of Meru District held by far the greatest number of these certificates and so it was not surprising that their candidate was elected to represent Central Province. This was Bernard Mate who was elected with a majority of ten thousand votes over his nearest rival, Eliud Mathu, who had previously been a nominated member of the Council. We last met Bernard as the headmaster of Chogoria Junior Secondary School before he left for further education in Britain. Since his return to Kenya in September 1954, he had been on the staff of the Meru Teacher Training College. After his election to the Legislative Council he was appointed Minister of Health.

Discussions on the political future of Kenya continued between Britain and Kenya, and in May 1960 two new African parties were formed. Most of the African members of the Legislative Council, who by now numbered eighteen, formed the Kenya African National Union (KANU) which was dominated by the Kikuyu and Luo peoples. Those who thought KANU too radical and too unrepresentative of the smaller peoples of Kenya formed the Kenya African Democratic Union (KADU) a few weeks after KANU. Elections were held in February 1961 when KANU secured nineteen seats and KADU eleven. KANU refused to form a government whilst Jomo Kenyatta was still in detention, and so KADU formed a minority government. When Kenyatta was released in August 1961, he tried to reconcile the two parties. After he failed to achieve this, he accepted the presidency of KANU on October 28th of that year. In January 1962 he was returned unopposed as the member of the Legislative Council for Fort Hall when the sitting KANU member vacated his seat for him. When fresh elections were held in May 1963, KANU won a large overall majority and Kenyatta was invited to form a government. On June 1st he became the prime minister of Kenya with full powers of self-government over the country. It was at this time that he gave the people his famous rallying cry of *Harambee*, an old Swahili work-chant of the Kenya coast meaning 'pull together'.[2] By this call he hoped to unite the peoples and races of Kenya in order to build a new country and a new society.

At midnight on December 12th 1963, the Union Jack was hauled down in the specially-built Independence stadium in Nairobi and replaced by the new flag of Kenya. Kenya was now an independent state and a year later it became a republic within the British Commonwealth with Jomo Kenyatta as its first president.

Land Consolidation

According to the custom of the Kikuyu peoples, the family land was held by the male head of the family. When he died it was then divided up amongst his sons. The result was that over the years, increasing fragmentation of the family holding occurred in which the size of the plots of land became small and their location often widely dispersed. After the Emergency was ended, the opportunity was taken to abandon this custom and by a process of mutual accommodation under the guidance of land consolidation teams, plots were exchanged to provide a single holding for each landholder in one place. Title-deeds were then issued to each family to make their possession of the holding legally secure. Dr Irvine noted in 1957 that the process of land consolidation was proceeding smoothly in the Chogoria area now that the old Home Guard posts were derelict and the bush was reclaiming their sites.

This reform of land-holding had several results. It produced compact small farms which were easier to work than the former scattered plots. The greater security of tenure of the plot meant that more food and cash crops could be planted and harvested. Also from the point of view of the Church authorities it provided an opportunity to obtain the use of more land for the the Church and its schools and dispensaries, where the local people were willing to help the Church in this way, as many in fact were.

The Growth of the Church

The period of the Emergency had been a difficult one for the Church and its members. Life under curfew conditions had interfered with normal Church activities. Christians as individuals had found themselves assailed from both sides. They were intimidated by Mau Mau gangs and interrogated by the security forces and found it hard at times to maintain their integrity.

With the achievement of its full independence in February 1956 the PCEA entered on a new phase of its existence. All its work was now under the authority of its own General Assembly which met every three years, with its General Administration Committee meeting annually in the years between its meetings.

One of the main problems faced by the Church after the end of the Emergency was the great increase in membership. This increase had significant implications for the Church in terms of the training of ministers and elders, and the pastoral care of its young people.

In order to improve the training of ministers, the Church in January 1955 had combined with the Anglican and Methodist Churches to set up a joint theological college at Limuru under the name of St Paul's United Theological College. It was established on the site of the CMS Divinity School which had been transferred to Limuru in 1930 from its original site at Freretown near Mombasa, where it had been founded in 1903. The new college aimed at providing theological education at a higher level than had been previously available in Kenya. Funds for its development and staff were provided for the most part by overseas Churches and Christian agencies. It was to this college that future ministers of the PCEA would go for training before ordination and posting to parishes of the Church, including those of the Presbytery of Chogoria.[3]

In order to provide more adequate facilities for the training of elders and Church members at large, the PCEA established the Lay Training Centre at Kikuyu in 1962. Elders and others from Chogoria attended courses at this Centre. Also, as well as holding courses at Kikuyu, the staff of the Centre held them at various central locations throughout the Presbyteries, including Chogoria and Kanyakine in the Presbytery of Chogoria.

With regard to the Church's pastoral care of young people, the Presbytery of Chogoria was able to make a significant contribution to its improvement. In 1960 a Mwimbi theological student named Bernard Muindi was engaged in practical work in the Chogoria area as part of his training course at St Paul's United Theological College at Limuru. He and his tutor, the Revd Oswald Welsh, soon realised that young people were not as involved in the work of the Church as they might be. The result was that they and others organised meetings with Church elders in different parts of the Presbytery, and in 1961 the Presbytery formed a Youth Committee. Eventually each parish formed its own Youth Committee in order to promote more adequate pastoral care for the young people in the area for which it was responsible and to involve more young people in the activities of the Church.

In 1951 a small group of PCEA ministers and elders began to revive the quest for Church union which had been abandoned in the 1930s partly due to differing attitudes to the female circumcision issue. They met with the leaders of the Methodist Church in Kenya with the result that the two Churches set up combined offices and a joint community centre in Nairobi. Also, at their initiative a meeting of Presbyterian, Methodist and Anglican representatives was held in Nairobi on October 7th 1961. If the Church union contemplated at this time had gone forward it would have meant that all the three main Protestant Christian agencies at work on the eastern side of Mount Kenya would have been combined into one, but this was not to be.[4]

Changes in the Schools

The further development of African education was one of the casualties of the Emergency. The reorganisation of education on the lines recommended by the Beecher report came into operation at the beginning of 1953 less than three months after the Emergency was declared. However, the additional funds which we have seen were needed for the expansion of primary education were not forthcoming for they were needed to finance the operations against the Mau Mau. The Kikuyu nationalists rejected the Beecher proposals and Mau Mau gangs attacked Primary and Intermediate Schools throughout Kikuyuland. By the end of 1953 no fewer than fifty-five schools had been destroyed and twenty-eight teachers killed.[5] As we saw in our last chapter, six of the schools destroyed were in the Chogoria area.

By the 1950s an increasing number of African students were going overseas for further study and more and more qualified Africans were taking their place in the multiracial society of Kenya. For several years Dr Irvine had spoken in the training colleges and senior schools about the manners and customs of western society. A number of those who heard these talks asked him to write them down. He did so and in April 1958 he published an illustrated booklet with the title *How To Behave*. Many people, both Africans and Europeans, have found this booklet very helpful.[6]

In 1957 the supervision of PCEA schools in the Chogoria area was taken over by one of the educational missionaries of the Methodist Church at Meru. This was an indication of the closer co-operation of the Churches through the Education Committee of the National Christian Council of Kenya. In the following year this Committee became the Christian Churches' Educational Association which co-ordinated the educational work of the Protestant Churches of the country. This Association had for its main objective, "the promotion of Christian religious education in schools and colleges".

Events in the Hospital

During the 1950s there were a few changes in the European staff of the hospital. As we have already mentioned, Dr Irvine's son Geoffrey joined his father in May 1953. In December 1957 Dr Wilkinson returned to the staff and stayed until June 1959 when he left to take charge of the PCEA Hospital at Kikuyu. Sister Burt returned from her extended compassionate leave in April 1954 and took over the duties of Matron again until she went on leave to Scotland in 1958.

In 1957 Raphael M'Thika was appointed to the staff of the hospital as an evangelist. Also a public address system was installed in the hospital so that the Sunday services could be relayed round the wards for the patients who were unable to attend them in the outpatient department.

So far the hospital had had no X-ray machine, although an attempt had been made to install one in 1948 as we have already seen. One problem was that the electric generator which had been installed by Ernest Carr when Chogoria began was a direct current generator and modern X-ray machines required an alternating current supply. So in 1953 Dr Irvine drew up plans to install a diesel engine which would run an alternating current generator and so provide power to allow the installation of an X-ray machine. These plans also included two new buildings; one to house the diesel engine and generator and a second for the X-ray machine and darkroom. Also the diesel would not only supply the new X-ray machine, but would also be used as an alternative source of electricity for the whole station on any occasion when the hydroelectric generator was not working. The diesel engine and a ten-kilowatt electric generator were installed in 1955 on a site near the hospital, and in February 1956 a new Watson Roentgen 50 X-ray machine was installed in a new building on the hospital compound.

The availability of X-ray facilities allowed the diagnosis and treatment of bone injuries and tuberculosis, particularly of the lungs, to be more precise and effective. In 1956 Dr Irvine noted that there were twenty-two patients with tuberculosis in the hospital at that time. In that year the hospital was able to participate in the British Medical Research Council's East African Tuberculosis Treatment Project organised from Nairobi by Dr Pierce Kent, the Government

Adviser on Tuberculosis. This in turn resulted in the establishment of monthly follow-up tuberculosis clinics at Chogoria, Chuka and Kanyekine. The drugs for the treatment of tuberculosis were supplied free by the Government Medical Department.

As we have already mentioned, in February 1956 the PCEA General Assembly took over responsibility for all the work of the Church of Scotland in East Africa, and this, of course, included the three hospitals at Kikuyu, Tumutumu and Chogoria. The result was that an Act was passed by the General Assembly of 1956 setting up a Hospitals' Board to supervise the work of the hospitals on behalf of the Church. This Board had its first meeting in Nairobi on June 19th 1956. Following the setting up of the Hospitals' Board, a Hospital Management Committee was established for the hospital at Chogoria. This Committee was made up of representatives of the Church, the hospital, the local authority and the community.

At this time there was increasing recognition by the Government of the part played by Mission and Church-related Hospitals in the health care of the population. This resulted in the setting up of a special committee by Government in March 1959 to consider the role of the medical services of the Missions in relation to those provided by Central and Local Government. The committee was also asked to advise on criteria to be used to determine the form and degree of assistance that may be needed by Mission Hospitals. The former Director of Medical Services (Dr T.F.Anderson) was the chairman of this committee and Dr Wilkinson was appointed to it as the medical representative of the Christian Council of Kenya. The report of the committee was published in early in 1961 and was accepted by Government as "a valuable contribution towards the future development of Medical Missions". Most of its recommendations were accepted with the proviso that their implementation would depend on additional funds being available for this purpose.[7] One result of the work of the special committee was the setting up by the Government of the Central Advisory Committee on Medical Missions which provided a very valuable means of liaison between the Government and the Medical Missions on subjects of mutual interest and concern.

It was inevitable that the political situation in the years immediately before independence would be reflected in the experience of the hospital at Chogoria. Two examples of this may be given. In 1962 a rumour was circulated that the hospital staff at Chogoria were asking every patient about their political affiliation and refusing treatment to those who said this was KANU. There was of course no truth at all in this rumour. Then in 1963 when KANU had won the election in May, some patients refused to pay their hospital fees on the grounds that KANU had promised the people free medical treatment in their political manifesto and so their treatment should now be free!

Dr Irvine Retires

In December 1961 at the age of sixty-eight years, Dr Irvine retired at the end of almost forty years of devoted service at Chogoria. He and Mrs Irvine left Chogoria to live in Nairobi.

Three years before he retired, Dr Irvine was awarded the highest honour that his University, the University of Aberdeen in Scotland, could bestow in recognition of his work in Chogoria. This was an honorary Doctorate in Divinity (DD). The Dean of the Faculty of Divinity of the University in presenting Dr Irvine for the honorary degree described him as:

> A man of versatile gifts, strong personality and invincible faith, his long and faithful career of medical and missionary service continues a notable tradition of this part of Scotland illustrated by such names as Laws and Hetherwick and claims recognition by his University by the award of its highest appropriate honour.[8]

In the list of honours approved by the Queen and published on New Year's Day of 1962 there occurred the name of Dr Archibald Clive Irvine. He was appointed an Officer of the Order of the British Empire (OBE). On May 8th of that year he went to Buckingham Palace in London to receive the insignia of his appointment from Her Majesty Queen Elizabeth.

After he left Chogoria he arrived in Nairobi on December 15th and opened his copy of *Daily Light*, the devotional book compiled entirely from the words of Scripture. The heading for that day was "Son, go work today in my vineyard" from Matthew 21.28. Dr Irvine took that as a message for himself and for the next twelve years he was actively involved in Christian work in Nairobi and elsewhere helping young people with their personal, spiritual, family and social problems. He gave himself to a ministry of "sustained and methodical prayer", to use his own words.[9] We have already mentioned how he was known as "praying Irvine" at this time by the Christian community in Nairobi. He died in Nairobi on June 6th 1974. His body was brought to Chogoria and buried in the memorial he had erected in 1940 to Ernest Carr, his father-in-law.

After her husband's death, Mrs Irvine continued to live in Nairobi until she went back to England in 1977 to live at Leamington Spa. She died at Warwick on May 20th 1980. Her ashes were placed in the Carr memorial at Chogoria beside the grave of her husband. White marble tablets have been placed on the walls of the memorial to commemorate the service of both Dr and Mrs Irvine.

CHAPTER SIXTEEN

KENYA AFTER INDEPENDENCE

The coming of political independence to Kenya in December 1963 inevitably led to great changes in many areas of public life which had far-reaching implications for the life and work of the Church. These changes included increased foreign capital investment in Kenya and an expansion of Kenyan involvement in commerce and industry. This meant increased opportunities for material and social betterment for many African people. Therefore there arose a great demand for education and the various forms of training which would allow the people to take advantage of these opportunities.

Education after Independence

In Chapter Thirteen we saw how the Kenya school system was reorganised by the Education Ordinance of 1952 on the basis of the recommendations of the Beecher Report of 1949. According to these recommendations, education was to be provided on morally sound Christian principles in schools which were to be graded as Primary, Intermediate and Secondary Schools.

By 1956 the education system as a whole was arranged on an 8-4-4 formula with eight years of primary education which would consist of four years in a Primary School of Standards I-IV and four years in an Intermediate School of Standards V-VIII. Then would follow four years in a Secondary School with Forms 1-4. The last four years would then be spent at University or in some other form of higher education such as teacher training. However, later in 1956 Standard VIII was withdrawn from most schools and the primary and intermediate grades were combined into one primary grade. From 1961 Forms 5 and 6 were added to certain Secondary Schools and the period of higher education was reduced by one year. The complete educational formula thus became 7-4-2-3. This meant seven years in primary education; then six years in secondary education which was made up of two parts (four years in

Forms 1-4 and two years in Forms 5-6), and finally three years in higher education.[1]

After Independence, the new Government decided to set up the Kenya Education Commission to review the whole field of education in the country. It was chaired by Professor Simeon H.Ominde of the Department of Education at Nairobi University. The Commission published its report in 1964 and recommended a secular basis to education in Kenya and a departure from the practice of using Missions and Churches to manage Primary Schools. These schools were to be transferred to the control of the District Education Boards. Three new ideas were emphasised in the Report. First, that the call for *Harambee* should have a place in the provision of educational facilities. Second, that education should be the seed of the economic development of the country. And third, that education should be regarded more as a benefit to the State than to the individual.[2] The recommendations of the Ominde Report were embodied in the Education Act (No. 5 of 1968). This Act put all Primary Schools under the local County Councils and defined the relationship of the former Church or Mission managers of these schools as that of 'sponsorship'. It laid down the rights of sponsors as three in number: the right to be consulted by the Government Teachers' Service Commission on the assignment of teachers to a school; the right to use the school premises when not in use for other purposes; and the right to provide religious instruction at the school.

By 1969 the County Councils had found themselves in difficulty over the management of Primary Schools, and in the following year their management was taken over by central Government. School fees were now to be collected by the Provincial administration. In 1971 the Government agreed that an annual fee of KSh 72 would be charged for attendance at a Primary School. However, in 1974 the Government announced that no fee would be charged for the first four years of primary education, but the parents would be expected to pay for school buildings, uniforms and books.

Secondary Schools were to continue to be managed by Boards of Governors as they had been before Independence. These Boards would be directly responsible to the Ministry of Education and their membership would represent the various interests of the local community. The appointment of each member had to be approved by the Ministry of Education.

The Schools at Chogoria

These changes in policy had, of course, a marked effect on the Chogoria school system. This was most marked in the case of the Primary Schools. In 1968 the management of these schools was transferred from the Church to Meru County Council and then later to the Ministry of Education when this Council found it could not cope with its new responsibility.

The Presbytery now assumed the new role of sponsor and appointed one of its ministers as Education Secretary. The first of these was the Revd Jediel Micheu. He was followed by the Revd Leonard Mburugu, and then by the Revd Elias Kabii.

The preparations for the establishment of the Chogoria Boys' Secondary School under its own Board of Governors were made in 1961 and the new school opened on January 29th 1962. It consisted of a Form 1 of thirty boys who were accommodated at the school. At first only twenty-one beds were available, and nine had to be borrowed temporarily from the equipment of the former Girls' School. This first Form 1 proved to be a very enthusiastic class. They called themselves the Pioneers and chose as the school motto the words *Thiaga mbere na kio* ('Press on with zeal'). Each year an additional class was added until by 1965 the school consisted of four Forms. The first headmaster of this school was Ephantus Mpungu who shortly after his appointment became an Assistant Education Officer with the Ministry of Education. His successor was Percy Bell who guided the school through its early years and laid a solid foundation for its development. Dr Wilkinson was the first chairman of its Board of Governors and when he left Chogoria in December 1965, he was succeeded by Ashford M'Rucha who over the years has made a great contribution to the education of both boys and girls in the Chogoria area.

After the establishment of the Chogoria Boys' Secondary School in 1962, the Girls' Intermediate Boarding School continued for another two years. Then at the end of 1963 it was closed on the grounds that there were now enough day school places available in the area for pre-secondary education. The Ministry of Education then gave permission for a Girls' Secondary Boarding School to be opened at Chogoria in 1965.

The first Form 1 consisted of thirty-six girls, who were welcomed to the new school in March of that year under the charge of Margaret Bowman. An additional Form was added each year until the school consisted of four Forms as in the case of the Boys' School. The girls at first used the old buildings of the former Girls' Intermediate School. By 1970 the school compound had been extended by the addition of more land beside the main road to allow the building of more teaching accommodation and recreational facilities together with a school farm and fish ponds.

The Ominde Report had recommended that President Kenyatta's call for *Harambee* should find a place in the development of education, and this was increasingly coming to pass throughout the country. By 1965 a third of secondary schools in the country were *Harambee* in origin, but those which were visited by the Ominde Committee were not satisfactory. They were understaffed and their classes were too large. This situation was not allowed to continue and gradually a policy of 'cost-sharing' was adopted by which the Government appointed and paid the teachers, and the community provided the school facilities and equipment in the spirit of *Harambee*. The result was a great expansion of both primary and secondary education throughout the Chogoria area.

Health Care in Kenya

In the years preceding Independence, Government expenditure on education had far outstripped that on health care. The Anderson Committee in its report of 1960 indicated that whilst ten years previously the annual recurrent budgets of the Education and Medical Departments had been similar, by 1960 the education vote was almost three times the medical vote.[3] This meant that the new Government faced problems in the financing and staffing of the health care services of the country. These problems were compounded by the election promise of free medical treatment made by the party which had won the election and now formed the Government. This promise was partly honoured in 1965 when President Kenyatta announced on June 1st that all outpatient treatment and children's inpatient treatment would be provided free at all Government medical units.

At Independence, the Churches and Missions in Kenya provided almost a third of the total number of hospital beds available to the population, as well as a large proportion of the primary health care services in the rural areas.[4] The Ministry of Health acknowledged the contribution which these hospitals and services made to the health care of the people, and although it gave grants to Church and Mission Hospitals to help with their recurrent costs, these rarely covered more than a quarter of these costs.

In view of this situation, the Ministry of Health's Central Advisory Committee on Medical Missions in 1966 set up a sub-committee under the chairmanship of the Deputy Director of Medical Services of the Ministry of Health (Dr P.J.Munano) to consider "The Closer Integration of the Health Services of Kenya". The report of this sub-committee was published in April 1968 and recommended closer integration of Government and Church health care services as well as increased Government grants to the Church health care services.[5] Although the Government was sympathetic to the recommendations of this report, their implementation foundered on the same rock as those of the Anderson Report of 1960, namely, the non-availability of the necessary finance.

Meantime the Churches and Missions had not been idle in their consideration of the problems which their own health care services were facing. In 1961 the Protestant Churches' Medical Association had been formed to co-ordinate the health care work of the Protestant Churches and to form a forum in which its problems might be discussed. The PCEA was a leading member of this organisation and provided Dr Wilkinson to be its chairman.

The PCEA was responsible for three of the largest Church hospitals in Kenya and was finding their support and management increasingly difficult. At the meeting of the PCEA General Administration Committee held in June 1965 a special commission was set up with the Revd Johanna Mbogoli of the Methodist Church as its chairman. The main question which this commission was asked to consider was whether the PCEA could continue to run its three hospitals at Kikuyu, Tumutumu and Chogoria in view of their staffing and financial problems.[6] The commission recommended that all three hospitals should be retained and developed. About ten years later another commission was appointed to consider the future of the three hospitals. It reported to the Church in April 1975 when its principal recommendation was that the hospitals should become more involved in community health care. We shall see in the next chapter how seriously Chogoria Hospital took that recommendation. Meantime, the hospital itself needed some attention.

Chogoria Hospital Redevelopment

In common with the other two PCEA hospitals, Chogoria Hospital had played an important part in providing health care for the area in which it was located, but it was now over forty years old. By 1965 it was evident that the work had completely outgrown the site and the buildings of the hospital.

Over the years since its establishment, the inpatient accommodation of the hospital had grown piecemeal as money had become available and as the health care needs of the population appeared to demand it. The needs of the population placed an increasing burden on the facilities of the hospital as any provision of new facilities only led to a greater uptake by the population of the services provided. By 1966 the percentage daily occupancy of beds in the wards of the hospital was 104% and by 1970 this had risen to 160%. There were other problems too. The water supply and the sewage disposal systems were becoming inadequate and demands were being made on the electric power and lighting supply with which it could barely cope.

In March 1965 the water supply to the hospital and the staff houses was improved by the installation of a water treatment plant consisting of a sedimentation tank together with an alum-precipitation and chlorination purification system. The installation was carried out by Davis and Shirtliff, a civil engineering firm in Nairobi.

In the course of 1966, information reached the Protestant Churches' Medical Association about new capital grants which were being made available from western Germany for the building of Church institutions in Africa. These grants were financed from the Church tax which the German Government levied on its people for the support of the State Church and its activities in that country. The German Government had now agreed that these grants could be used for the development of Church institutions overseas. A special agency had been set up in Germany to administer these grants which was called the *Evangelische Zentralstelle für Entwicklunghilfe* (The Protestant Central Agency for Development Aid).

Spurred on by this information, the General Assembly of the PCEA in March 1967 commissioned the staff of Chogoria Hospital to prepare plans for the phased redevelopment of the hospital. The PCEA Head Office also arranged that a representative of the Central Agency should visit Chogoria to confirm that this redevelopment would be eligible for a grant from his organisation. He agreed that it would be. The problem now arose of which of the three PCEA hospitals should be the first to be redeveloped since all were in a similar physical condition.

In February 1968 this problem came before the PCEA Hospitals' Board for consideration. A motion was proposed by Dr Wilkinson (who was at that time the medical superintendent of Kikuyu Hospital) that Chogoria Hospital should be the first of the three PCEA hospitals to be redeveloped. He gave three reasons for his motion. Chogoria was the busiest of the hospitals; it was the most isolated and distant from other health care facilities; and it enjoyed very good community support. The Board agreed to this motion and the General Administration Committee of the Church accepted their recommendation in the following month.

Once the choice of Chogoria as the hospital to be redeveloped was finally approved by the PCEA, a formal application was made to the Central Agency in Germany for a grant to provide the following:

1   The rebuilding of the hospital with two hundred beds, i.e., one bed per thousand of the population.

2   The establishment of a department of health education and preventive medicine.

3   The expansion of the community nurse training school to cater for seventy-five trainees instead of the current fifty.

The Central Agency accepted this application and called for the submission of detailed plans. These were prepared by Watson and Crowder, a Nairobi firm of architects, who were briefed by the hospital staff who visited several other hospitals in Kenya and Tanzania to obtain fresh ideas in hospital construction. To help with all the extra work and to prepare for the commissioning of the new hospital, several extra members of staff were recruited on a temporary basis from Britain, Germany and Australia to assist the permanent staff.

One of the conditions of a grant from the Central Agency was that twenty-five per cent of the cost of any scheme to which they gave aid should be financed from local sources. This meant that in addition to the preparation of building plans, arrangements had to be made to raise money locally to form the twenty-five per cent local contribution. A widespread appeal for contributions was mounted under the patronage of the Provincial Commissioner of the Eastern Province, Eliud Mahihu.[7] He was tireless in his solicitation of contributions which came from numerous sources including President Kenyatta, the Ministry of Health, the representatives of commerce and industry, the hospital's own funds, the local coffee co-operative societies and from members of the local community. Contributions also came from overseas donors in Scotland, England, Canada, Holland and Germany. Eventually more than the required twenty-five per cent contribution was raised.

The plan was that the old hospital buildings would become the nurse training school, and the new hospital would be built on the land lying between the old hospital and the main road. The Church had agreed to allocate this area of land to be the site of the new hospital together with additional land for staff housing. The building contractors were Messrs Channa Singh and they arrived on the site on Christmas Day 1969 ready to begin the building of the new hospital. The foundation stone of the new outpatient department was laid by President Kenyatta on February 27th 1970. He returned over a year later to open the first phase of the redevelopment of the hospital on March 5th 1971, and on Sunday July 11th the new buildings were dedicated by the Revd Elias Kabii, the Moderator of the Presbytery of Chogoria. These new buildings included an outpatient department, wards for men and women, an operating theatre and an administration block together with the essential infrastructure of services to provide them with water, electricity, sewage disposal and adequate communications. It was at this time too that a mains electricity supply from the national grid reached Chogoria allowing the old hydroelectric plant to be disposed of locally. This plant had given faithful service to Chogoria for over forty-six years.

Another important event of 1971 was the appointment of the first Kenyan matron in January of that year in the person of Mrs Helen Karimi Raini. After nursing training in England, Mrs Raini had joined the staff of the hospital in March 1970. She was the daughter of

Christopher Mwongera who was a senior member of the workshop staff at Chogoria.

With the completion of the first phase of the redevelopment plan, the number of beds provided in the hospital increased from 119 to 174. Nevertheless, the bed occupancy hardly fell below one hundred per cent. This illustrated the need to press on with the completion of the second phase of the plan which included a children's ward and other essential services such as the kitchen and the laundry. By 1975 the total capacity of the hospital was 246, but the bed occupancy was still not far short of one hundred per cent and temporary hostel type of accommodation had to be brought into use for inpatients. The annual report of the hospital for 1977 records that the three phases of its redevelopment were now "virtually complete". The same report records that bed occupancy for that year was 110% with the admission during the year of 6,079 inpatients!

However, as we have traced the history of the hospital it has become obvious that its development has never been complete, but always continuous. This will continue to be seen as still more new buildings and new services are added to the hospital in the next two decades as we shall describe in our final chapter.

The Challenges to the Church

As we have seen, the PCEA had become an independent body in 1943, and in February 1956 had assumed full responsibility for all the work which had been established by the Church of Scotland in Kenya. In the 1960s, however, the PCEA became conscious of certain challenges which it faced in the new politically-independent Kenya. Not all of these challenges arose out of the new political situation.

The first challenge came from the greatly-increased membership of the Church which we mentioned in the previous chapter. This increase reflected the high rate of population increase in the country as a whole, but also the effectiveness of the faithful witness of the Church. The continuing influence of the Revival Movement also played a large part in attracting people to membership of the Church. The result was that the territorial organisation of the Church had to be revised in order to produce smaller parishes and smaller presbyteries. The first sign of this at Chogoria came in 1966 when the Presbytery was given permission to subdivide Mwimbi Parish into two to form the Parishes of Chogoria and Lower Mwimbi. The subdivision of other parishes followed, until in 1977 the Presbytery of Chogoria had nine parishes and was itself divided in March 1978 and a new Presbytery of Imenti was formed on March 13th of that year with its headquarters at Kanyakine. It was agreed that the boundary between the two presbyteries should be the line of the Mutonga River.

The second challenge came from the need to provide additional pastoral care and Christian education for the new members of the Church. This meant that the Church had to secure an educated ministry capable of communicating the Christian Faith to all levels of society and of applying Christian principles to the new ethical situations facing its members in the economic and social life of the new Kenya. In the first instance, therefore, the need was for more ordained and well-trained ministers. The response to this challenge is reflected in the larger number of candidates from Chogoria Presbytery who now began to come forward for training at St Paul's United Theological College at Limuru.

However, it was clear that the PCEA would have to consider methods of improving the pastoral care of its members. The result was that in 1965 the Church began to plan for the introduction of a 'tent-making ministry' in which candidates would be trained and ordained whilst still continuing in secular or non-parochial Church employment.[8] Not until 1980 was the final scheme introduced, when four candidates came forward from Chogoria Presbytery. One of these was the Revd Geoffrey Bundi who was ordained at Chogoria on November 27th 1984 and continued in his employment with the Community Health Department of the hospital.

Meanwhile another step had been taken in order to provide more pastoral care. The Eighth General Assembly in 1976 agreed that there was "no Biblical or theological reason" against the ordination of women to the ministry of the Church, and recommended that this should become the practice of the PCEA.

The third challenge came from the new relationship to its Primary Schools which the Church had been given by the Education Act of 1968. As we mentioned above, prior to this Act becoming law, the Church had been responsible for the management of the Primary Schools which it had established, but under this new Act they were to be regarded as 'sponsors' with certain limited responsibilities which we have already defined. The Church was unprepared for this change and for a time appeared to lose interest in the schools. However, in 1974 the PCEA appointed full-time religious education advisers for each Presbytery but in 1979 found it could not afford to pay them. Meantime the Christian Churches' Educational Association prepared teaching material for the religious education lessons in the schools and ran in-service courses for teachers of these lessons.

Sunday Schools had existed from the beginning of the work at Chogoria and had played an important part in the Christian education of the young. However, it was not until the 1960s that they found a secure place in the organisation of the Church. At first they were the responsibility of the Presbytery Youth Committee set up in 1961 as we saw in the previous chapter. The result was that in 1964 the first Church School Committee was formed in Chogoria Presbytery and effective arrangements began to be made for the support and supervision of the Sunday Schools, which were now referred to as Church Schools. A full-time Church School organiser was appointed by the Presbytery and the Church School Committee provided him with a motor cycle to enable him to visit the Church schools. With the removal of the management of the Primary Schools out of the hands of the Church by the Education Act of 1968, the importance of these Church Schools for the religious education of the young people of the Church came to be recognised.

CHAPTER SEVENTEEN

COMMUNITY HEALTH CARE AT CHOGORIA

There were three parts to the plan drawn up in the late 1960s for the redevelopment of the health care work at Chogoria. First was the complete rebuilding of the hospital. Second was the establishment of an improved community health care service for the population of the Chogoria area. Third was the expansion of the nurse training school of the hospital. In the last chapter we described how the hospital was rebuilt. Now we look at the second and third components of the plan and in order to provide continuity in our narrative we shall follow their development through into the 1990s.

The Chogoria Dispensary System

From the beginning of his work at Chogoria, Dr Irvine saw the need to get out amongst the people if the Mission's task of evangelism, education and health care was to be effectively carried out. Within only six months of his arrival he reported that a number of educational centres had been established around Chogoria and that medically-trained 'dressers' had been posted to two of them. In addition, when he went on evangelistic safaris he took medical supplies, and often a dresser to treat any sick people he met.

Eventually the common pattern of early mission medical services emerged in which the central hospital at Chogoria was surrounded by a number of static satellite dispensaries at varying distances from the hospital. These dispensaries were built of the local materials of mud and wattle and were usually staffed by a dresser who had been given some training in the hospital and then sent out with some simple medical supplies with which to treat the sick. The first two dispensaries of this kind appear in photographs taken about 1925.

Over the years, the number of dispensaries increased until by 1970 there were eight, each one staffed by at least one qualified enrolled nurse trained in the hospital's nurse training school. These dispensaries provided daily clinics for the treatment of sickness and injury. In addition to these permanent static centres, 'mango tree clinics' were also held in the open-air in markets or other suitable locations by mobile teams which went out from the hospital on weekly safaris as we have mentioned in an earlier chapter.

The result of the establishment of static dispensaries and the mango tree clinics was to provide a network of recognised health care centres throughout the district. In due course, this network formed the basis on which the outreach work of the new Community Health Department of the hospital could build and expand.

The Community Health Department

Community health is a term which may be used to describe the type of curative and preventive outreach health care which was provided by the dispensaries such as we have just described. However, in recent years it has come to mean a much more comprehensive and organised service than they were able to provide, and a service in which the local community was encouraged to participate in terms of training, fundraising and health promotion.

The beginnings of the practice of community health in this more comprehensive sense at Chogoria dates from June 1970 when Sister A.J.Faro, who was a trained health visitor, joined the staff of the hospital as a full-time nurse educator. In September of that year, she and Mrs Jane Miriti formed a team to provide Health Education in all its aspects in the hospital and in several of the dispensaries on a regular basis.

By 1972 a whole series of outpatient clinics were being held at the hospital in addition to the daily curative outpatient clinics. Some were the continuation of pre-existing clinics, but others were new. The annual report for this year lists the following: antenatal, child welfare, family planning, tuberculosis, leprosy, epilepsy and physically handicapped.

The foundation of a separate Community Health Department (CHD) within the work of the hospital came in 1974 as part of the physical redevelopment of the hospital buildings and compound, when the Department was provided with its own headquarters building. The later years of the 1970s were spent by the Department in recruiting and training suitable staff and in organising an expanded outreach programme which initially was based mainly on the use of mobile clinics. However, in the rainy seasons it was often difficult to maintain the mobile clinic service since most of the centres visited were on dirt roads which the rains sometimes made impassable. In 1976 regular safaris for the control and treatment of leprosy were begun using dapsone as the sole drug.[1] In the following year this became part of the Meru District Leprosy/Tuberculosis Control Project which covered the whole District.

By 1978 the original eight static clinic centres of 1970 had been increased to twenty-four and at each of these centres regular Family Health Clinics were held at which curative medical services were provided along with child welfare, antenatal and family planning. These services were available on an integrated basis as the staff were now being trained to provide all of them at each Family Health Clinic. This integration of clinic services is a unique feature of the Chogoria health care organisation and is a great convenience for patients as they do not need to attend on separate days for different services. They know that on whichever weekday they attend, all four of these services will be available, and they will not be asked to come back another day if they want a specific service such as immunisation or antenatal care.

Meantime, progress was being made in the involvement of the local communities in their own health care. Initially, clinic-building committees were established in order to involve the local people in the erection of a suitable building in which a Family Health Clinic could be held where this did not already exist, or had become inadequate, and in the provision of suitable accommodation for the resident Clinic nurse. By 1980 these committees were being encouraged to become Area Health Committees and to take over the management of their own clinic and responsibility for the health care of their area. They also chose Volunteer Health Workers for training by the Community Health Department so that they could then serve the people of their own area.

Chogoria Attracts International Attention

In order to obtain support for the community health care programme at Chogoria, applications for funds were made to international aid agencies during the 1970s. The information provided attracted the interest of these agencies who then provided financial support for different aspects of the programme. The initial funding which led to an enormous expansion of community health care work came from donors interested in the encouragement of family planning. For instance, in 1975 the Family Planning International Assistance (FPIA) of the USA allocated funds to develop the family planning clinic service, in particular to employ salaried field educators to promote family planning in the community.

In 1983 the FPIA funding came to an end and the United States Agency for International Development (USAID) requested that an evaluation of the results of the programme should be made because the records showed a remarkably high uptake of preventive health care services, especially family planning. The eventual outcome of this request was the conduct of a Chogoria Community Health Survey in 1985. This survey was conducted by a team made up of representatives of the Chogoria CHD and two members of the staff of the Division of Reproductive Health of the Centers for Disease Control of Atlanta in Georgia. It was jointly funded by FPIA and SIDA (The Swedish International Development Agency).

The survey covered a sample of 1,880 women aged 15-45 of whom 96% of those selected were interviewed. The result showed that the level of use by the women of the maternal and child health services including family planning was 'extremely high' with 34% of couples using modern methods of family planning.[2] This in turn showed that smaller families were not unacceptable to East African culture as some authorities had argued. The publication of the results of this survey enhanced the reputation of the Chogoria Hospital Community Health Department amongst international aid agencies and led to further successful applications for support for the Department and its programmes.

During the 1980s the expatriate staff of CHD became very successful at raising money from overseas aid agencies and initially it was the policies of these agencies which determined the nature of the projects which were undertaken. With increasing experience, the CHD staff become more selective about the money they accepted and the nature of the projects they supported, so that later projects were more directed to fulfilling the real needs of the community served by Chogoria rather than simply following the policies and priorities of the donor agencies.

The main sources of funding for the Department since its foundation have been aid agencies in USA and Sweden. Other countries which have supported specific projects or provided specialist equipment or transport include Canada, Germany, Holland, Japan, Norway and the United Kingdom. So far as staff are concerned, the Church of Scotland provided the senior professional staff of the Department until October 1991 when Joyce Riungu succeeded Dr Colin Fischbacher as

Director of the Department. Mrs Riungu had obtained a Master's degree in Public Health at Liverpool University in 1990.

The Community Health Care Programmes

During the 1980s the services provided by the CHD were organised into four main programmes, or units as they are called in the annual reports of the hospital. In 1990 the aim of all these programmes as of the CHD itself was defined in the following terms:

> We would like to see a responsible community that is able to involve its members in the process of improving living standards for all by identifying their needs, prioritizing, planning, organising for implementation and evaluating their own work, using the resources available to them to achieve self-reliance.[3]

The first of these programmes is the **Rural Health Unit** which continued and developed the original service provided by the dispensaries of which we have spoken above. This unit was eventually responsible for primary health care activities and integrated clinic services at forty different sites in the catchment area of the hospital whose population will soon number 500,000 people. It also undertook the training and support of volunteer health teams which included community health workers, traditional birth attendants (TBAs), and members of the Area Health Committees. The TBAs attended over half the domiciliary births in the Chogoria area. By 1989 the unit had established fifty-four Area Health Committees, and had trained 538 community health workers and 614 TBAs. The salaried field educators who had originally been employed to promote the family planning service had gradually become involved in other aspects of health care in the community including the supervision of the volunteer health teams. By 1991 this function was taken over by the Area Health Committees and the employment of salaried field educators was finally phased out in June 1992. The cost of these field educators had been borne by the Swedish aid agency SIDA since 1983.

Some measure of the activity of the Rural Health Unit can be obtained from the number of the patient attendances recorded at the various rural health clinics for which it was responsible and which were all within a thirty-mile radius of Chogoria. In 1993 almost 256,000 patient attendances were recorded at these clinics, made up of over 184,000 attendances for curative services and over 71,000 for preventive services (child health, family planning and antenatal). It is of interest to note that by 1992 only three of these rural health clinics were mobile.

The **Health Education Unit** was established in 1982 as a programme to introduce family-life education into schools and Churches. It has trained marriage counsellors and teachers to help young people to meet the problems of sexual behaviour, family life and parenthood. In 1985 it produced a special issue of *VIVA*, a Kenya magazine for girls and young women, which dealt with the problems of adolescence, marriage and pregnancy as well as giving advice on how to maintain health.[4] It was widely circulated round girls' secondary schools and proved very acceptable. Latterly, the unit has turned its attention to the prevention of HIV infection and promoted an AIDS-awareness programme in the community. In August 1988, folk-media programmes were introduced as a method of health education and a number of troupes were trained to use traditional song, dance, drama and story-telling to educate the local people in methods and issues of health care. A manual on family-life education for teachers was published in 1989.

The 1985 Community Health Survey had drawn attention to the much poorer health found among the people who lived in Tharaka, the semi-arid lower eastern part of the Chogoria catchment area. So in 1986 a special **Tharaka Unit** was set up within the CHD in order to improve the health and social service provision there. Area Health Committees were set up and in 1989 a training centre was opened at Marimanti to accommodate up to thirty people attending training courses in health care and community development. An innovation in Tharaka has been work with traditional healers and circumcisers following a recognition of their important influence on the beliefs and behaviour of the people there.[5]

The **Enterprise Development Unit** is the fourth unit of the Department and was founded in 1987 to assist Area Health Committees to generate income in order to cover clinic and community-based health care costs. It was funded by the Kenya Rural Enterprise Programme which aimed at improving the local economy of an area by providing loans to small projects or businesses which had no other access to credit facilities or technical advice or assistance. This scheme was financially supported by the US-based World Education Programme. By the end of 1993, the unit had forty-four Market Business Groups and had given loans to 905 people. The kind of projects which have been supported by the unit include those of tailoring, carpentry, maize-milling and poultry-keeping. By the end of 1993, the unit was able to record a loan repayment rate of over 96%.

In view of all these varied activities it is not surprising to find that by 1986, the Community Health Department was the largest department of the hospital in terms of both paid and voluntary staff.[6] In 1992 it was described as providing one of the largest operational community health programmes in the country of Kenya.[7] It certainly was one of the Kenya programmes best known to international aid agencies worldwide, as we have already seen.

One significant result of the increasing experience of the department was the spate of articles and reports published by its staff on all aspects of community health care in the Chogoria area. Thus the annual report of the hospital for 1986 lists no fewer than thirteen articles written and published by the staff in that year.[8]

The Community Nurse Training School

In Chapter Thirteen we described how in 1951 Chogoria Hospital began to train Kenya Enrolled Assistant Nurses (Grade Two). In 1961 this qualification was phased out and replaced by the Kenya Enrolled Nurse (KEN) certificate which was awarded on successful completion of a three-year course - a year longer than the previous course. This new course was successfully introduced into the training programme at Chogoria and Sister Morson returned to take charge of the training in May 1961, staying until October 1963. In 1967, the Nursing Council gave conditional recognition of the training school for the training of enrolled midwives, but the school apparently found it could not fulfil the required conditions.[9]

The number of enrolled nurses in training at Chogoria in 1968 was fifty and in the plans for the redevelopment of the hospital it was agreed to increase this number to seventy-five. No new accommodation was to be built, but the buildings of the old hospital were to be refurbished and adapted for use as dormitories and classrooms. This duly took place and was paid for by a grant from the West German aid agency, *Brot für die Welt* (Bread for the World).

However, about this time the realisation arose in nursing circles throughout the world that the kind of enrolled nurse training which was being required by national professional bodies in Africa and elsewhere, was not appropriate to the work they were expected to do in rural health care services. The curriculum for this training was usually based on that of the United Kingdom and was confined to the subject of general nursing. In Africa particularly, enrolled nurses needed also some training in midwifery and health visiting. So discussion arose about 'the multipurpose nurse' and the concept of the community nurse was introduced.

The result was that training for the KEN qualification was phased out and replaced by a new course for the certificate of the Kenya Enrolled Community Nurse (KECN). This course was to be of three and a half years' duration and would include general nursing, midwifery and health visiting (community nursing). The duration of the course was reduced to three years in 1987.

At Chogoria this change of course took place in 1975. The timing of the change could hardly have been more appropriate for it occurred when the new Community Health Department had just been set up in the hospital and was beginning to plan its community strategy. Part of that strategy was the establishment of Family Health Clinics through the district which provided excellent practical training facilities for the community nurse trainees.

The Nursing Council of Kenya continued to monitor the suitability of its requirements for the training of the Enrolled Community Nurse, and in July 1990 introduced a new curriculum. This was called the Kenya Enrolled Community Health Nurse (KECHN) National Curriculum and was designed to cover a period of two and a half years' training. It was described as "a competency-based curriculum" and was expected to produce a nurse with a better standard of competency in general nursing, community nursing and midwifery than the previous curriculum had done. This new curriculum was introduced by the nurse training school at Chogoria in 1991 and the previous three-year KECN course was phased out and ceased at the end of 1992 so that full implementation of the new curriculum was able to begin in 1993. There were forty-six students on the last KECN course at Chogoria and all passed the Nursing Council examination, eleven with credit.

However, by 1991 the wisdom of continuing to train basic grade KECHNs at Chogoria was beginning to be questioned by the staff of the hospital and the nurse training school. Kenya was now producing an adequate number of KECHNs for its needs. Each year about thirty of these nurses would qualify at Chogoria and only three or four could be employed by the hospital. Many of the others found difficulty in obtaining employment elsewhere. By contrast, registered nurses were in very short supply, especially those with public health training. It seemed only prudent, therefore, to plan for the introduction of registered nurse training at some future date providing the financial and staffing requirements of such a change could be met. The hospital annual report for 1993 recorded that plans for such a change had now been made, and all that was required was funding for this to occur.

As part of their contribution to nursing education, the staff of the hospital and training school published in 1989 a *Procedure Manual* for Nurses and Midwives.[10] This was a substantial volume of over four hundred pages which was intended to provide a practical manual for nurses and midwives who worked in tropical hospitals and community health units similar to those at Chogoria.

In view of Dr Irvine's interest and involvement in the training of nurses, both men and women, from his earliest years in Chogoria, it was entirely appropriate when in 1983, the Nurse Training School at Chogoria was renamed *The Clive Irvine School of Enrolled Community Nursing*. In 1989 the word Enrolled was dropped and the name became *The Clive Irvine School of Community Nursing*.

In keeping with the hospital's general policy of encouraging and developing Kenyan leadership, when the post of Principal Tutor of the School became vacant in March 1993, a Kenyan Principal was appointed, Jane Karonjo. Mrs Karonjo had been to Atlanta in the USA to study community health there in 1991.

CHAPTER EIGHTEEN

CHOGORIA AFTER 1980

The main event of the 1970s at Chogoria was the rebuilding of the hospital and there is little to report from the other departments there for that period. By contrast, the 1980s showed increasing activity in several aspects of the work there.

Community Development

Access to Chogoria from the outside world has always been by the south-north road which runs along the eastern side of Mount Kenya and is now called the B6. This road forms part of the road system which runs right round the mountain. On its eastern side, the road twists its way in and out of the valleys which have been carved out by the numerous rivers and streams which flow down the mountainside. Sections of this road had been re-aligned and tarred in recent years until the only section which remained untarred was that which ran northwards from the Thuchi River to Nkubu township. This was the section on which Chogoria was situated. The tarring of this section was finally completed with British financial aid and technical assistance in 1985 and included the tarring of the first mile of the side-road up to Chogoria.

The completion of the tarmac road and its extension to the gate of the hospital has had a number of results quite apart from the dramatic changes its realignment brought to the road network of the area around Chogoria.[1] Chogoria is now much less isolated than it has been in the past and Nairobi is now only three hours away by road. Motor traffic has increased on the road and this has led to an increase in traffic accidents with which the hospital has had to deal.

Another result has been that the area where the tarmac road ended at Chogoria has developed into a market area with shops and stalls. These are all situated up and down the road on the opposite side to the hospital. Previously the local market had been at Kabeche, about half a mile to the north of Chogoria, but now the shopkeepers have mostly moved down to Chogoria. Small hotels have been built beside the shops to provide overnight accommodation and guide services for the increasing number of climbers who come to ascend Mount Kenya using the Chogoria route. The end of the tarmac also became the main local bus-stop for buses and taxis (*matatus*) which ran from Chogoria to Meru in the north, and to Embu and Nairobi to the south. Because of its use as a bus stop, the area has become known locally as 'The Stage'.

A further indication of the increasing development of Chogoria was the expansion of the post office there in the mid-1980s and the installation of post-boxes whose numbers ran from 0 to 599. To accommodate its expanded services, the post office moved into the building which had been originally built as a nurses' home.

One of the beneficial effects of the upgrading of the main road for the hospital was the acquisition of a guest house for the use of its many visitors. The contractors who worked on the road had been a British firm called the Keir Construction Company and in the course of their work on the road they had asked permission to build a house on the hospital land at Chogoria to accommodate some of their engineers. When they had completed the work on the road, they handed over this house to the hospital and this became the hospital guest house. Because of its origin it was named Keir House.

The 'Urbanisation' of Chogoria

In 1948 Dr Irvine had commented that Chogoria had become a small town. It was, however, some forty years later that this was officially recognised when in 1991 Chogoria was officially designated as an Urban Area with its own Urban Council and Office. The Urban Area was to run from the forest edge down to beyond the new tarmac main road. This designation was the result of the Government desire to promote local urban development and to stem the drift of the population from the rural areas towards the cities.[2]

In the following year Chogoria found itself in a new Administrative District. The new District of Tharaka-Nithi was separated from the southern part of Meru District and given its own District Commissioner with his headquarters at Chuka, less than ten miles to the south of Chogoria. This meant that Chogoria staff now had a much shorter distance to travel to consult their District Commissioner. Also it meant that the Government administration was able to support and supervise the people of Tharaka more effectively than before.

The Hospital Services Expand

The hospital began the decade of the eighties with 236 beds and ended it with 306 beds. The increase in the number of beds was due to increased patient demand. The inpatient admissions were just over six thousand at the beginning of the decade and rose to well over eleven thousand during the decade, and have shown a corresponding increase in the 1990s. In 1993 the total number of patients admitted to hospital was 12,669 whose average duration of stay in hospital was 10.7 days giving a total bed occupancy of 118% for that year. The increased demand for the outpatient services at the hospital is also shown by the rise in numbers. The total number of outpatient attendances at the hospital in 1980 was about thirty-five thousand and by 1985 it had reached well over fifty thousand, a level which it maintained into the 1990s. In 1993 the number was 62,913 including eye and dental unit attendances.

The numbers of staff employed also increased until in 1993 the total number of people employed in the health care service and training there reached 493. This total was made up of 346 employed in the hospital, 128 in the community health department and 19 in the nurse training school. Over 98% of the staff were Kenyan. The hospital is now one of the largest private sector employers in the Tharaka-Nithi District.

During the decade of the eighties a number of specialist services were added to those services already provided by the hospital. In March 1982 two new specialist clinics were begun. The first was a dental clinic which became so popular that a purpose-built dental unit was added to the outpatient department. This was taken into use in November 1986 and contained two dental surgeries and a denture laboratory. The unit is usually staffed by one dental officer and three dental assistants. In 1993 well over six thousand patients were seen at the unit, and about two hundred and fifty dentures were supplied by the dental laboratory. Soon after it was set up in 1982, the unit began to hold dental sessions at schools and Family Health Clinics. These sessions became increasingly popular, and in 1993 almost two thousand patients attended them.

The second new specialist service was an eye clinic staffed by a clinical officer who had been trained in eye work at the Government Medical Training College in Nairobi. The accommodation for this clinic was also extended in 1986 to provide four rooms for clinical use and for the fitting of spectacles. In the same year the clinical officer went to the PCEA Hospital at Kikuyu for training in cataract extraction. This allowed the holding of two well-attended week-end 'eye camps' for cataract extractions which were held at the hospital in 1989 and 1990. From 1987 the unit has been supported by the German *Christoffel-Blindenmission*. This organisation provided funds for the further training of the staff and supplied new items of equipment including a slit lamp. In 1993 a total of 3,930 outpatients were seen, over twelve hundred of them at the mobile clinics. The spectacle workshop dispensed 1,087 pairs of spectacles in that year.

For some years a clinic had been held at the hospital by the Kenya Association for the Physically Disabled every second month. This clinic supervised mainly the rehabilitation of patients who had been left with disability following an attack of acute poliomyelitis. The hospital was able to obtain elementary training in physiotherapy for some of its staff on an occasional basis. However, in August 1987 a physiotherapy department was set up by a volunteer physiotherapist from overseas and a room was equipped with the appropriate apparatus to assist in the rehabilitation of both inpatients and outpatients.[3] In 1988 a full-time physiotherapist was seconded to the unit by the Government Ministry of Health.[4]

The hospital annual report for 1988 mentions the psychiatric service offered by the hospital. At this time there were four psychiatric nurses on the staff and the Government psychiatrist based at Meru Government Hospital was paying monthly visits to advise on patients. Chogoria Hospital had also seconded a Kenyan doctor for training in psychiatry in Nairobi.

The main clinical service not so far offered by the hospital was that for disorders of the ear, nose and throat. However in 1989 a clinical officer returned to Chogoria after specialist training in ENT in Nairobi for which he had been sponsored by the hospital. In 1992, negotiations were under way with the Kenya Ear Foundation to set up a permanent community-based ear service at Chogoria, but so far this has not proved to be possible.

In 1986 a second operating theatre was built to accommodate the increasing surgical demands on the hospital. This theatre was used mainly for eye operations, but was also used for caesarean sections, and the tubal ligations which formed part of the family planning programme.

A number of items of specialised medical equipment were acquired by the hospital in this period. These included a cardiac monitor from Holland which was given in 1984, and a gastroscope which came as a gift from friends in Scotland in March 1986. The gastroscope allowed the investigation of chronic abdominal pain of gastric origin and gave rise to a research project on chronic gastritis which was funded by the Imperial Cancer Research Fund of the United Kingdom. A new X-ray tube and cables were donated by aid agencies in Holland in 1988. However, during the year 1991 the static X-ray machine was frequently out of order and in 1992 a new machine was donated by these agencies. A second-hand ultrasound machine was bought from the United States in 1991 for diagnostic use in surgery and obstetrics.

Computerisation of the Community Health Department records became possible in 1985 when four IBM-compatible microcomputers were donated to the hospital by USAID and installed in the CHD. This allowed clinic attendances to be monitored so that defaulters could be identified and visited in their homes. In 1990 a computer was obtained for the administrative office of the hospital.

In 1983 the long and close connection of the Irvine family with Chogoria came to an end when Dr Geoffrey Irvine left the staff of the hospital to become the Medical Co-ordinator of the Protestant Churches' Medical Association which in 1987 changed its name to the Christian Health Association of Kenya (CHAK). He retired from this post in 1989 but continued as chairman of the Mission for Essential Drugs and Supplies (MEDS) which had been established in September 1986 as a joint venture of CHAK and the Medical Department of the Kenya Catholic Secretariat. This organisation was set up on a non-profit-making basis to undertake the bulk-buying of medicines and medical supplies and soon became the main source of medical supplies to the Christian medical institutions and services which joined its membership.

The financial position of the hospital had rarely been secure since its foundation but in this period it became much worse. The hospital ended the year 1985 with the largest deficit it had ever had, totalling well over one million Kenya shillings. Various measures were introduced to try to reduce the continuing annual deficit, and in 1989 these had managed to reduce the deficit by twenty-five per cent. There were a number of causes of this recurrent deficit: a Government Ministry of Health grant which was reduced each year and in 1993 was to disappear altogether; increasing inability of ordinary patients to pay the hospital fees which had provided the major part of the hospital income (formerly over sixty per cent, but in 1993 only thirty-six per cent); and the increasing cost of staff salaries and medical supplies. This financial situation was not unique to Chogoria Hospital but was similar to those faced by other health care services in Kenya both public and private and reflected the economic difficulties of the country as a whole.[5] These difficulties can be illustrated by the rising rate of inflation, which in 1993 reached over one hundred per cent. This led to the phased introduction of an increase of fifty per cent in hospital fees in that year. Nevertheless no patient in real need was ever refused treatment or admission to hospital if they were genuinely unable to pay the hospital fee.

In 1990 the hospital management adopted the slogan: "The most important person in the hospital is the patient". On this basis the staff were encouraged to seek to improve the hospital services, already, it should be said, of a high quality. The need for compassion was emphasised and also the need to treat the patient as whole and not just the diseased part.

As an expression of this continuing concern for the welfare of its patients, the hospital established a Patient Welfare Fund in August 1993. The aim of this fund was to give the community served by the hospital the opportunity of contributing directly to the welfare and comfort of patients. It was intended to replenish the fund from time to time by holding fund-raising events at the hospital. The first major event of this kind was held in February 1994 which concluded with a service of thanksgiving in the hospital chapel for its success.

Two income-generating projects were introduced in 1991. The former children's isolation ward (Imenti Ward) was turned into an amenity ward for patients able to pay higher fees for better accommodation or whose fees were paid by the Kenya National Hospital Insurance Fund. The other children's ward (Shinda Ward) was extended to take more patients to compensate for the loss of beds due to the change of use of Imenti Ward. The second project was the building and opening of the Lenana Restaurant just inside the main gate of the hospital to provide snacks and meals for staff and visitors.

Other projects have been introduced in order to increase the self-sufficiency of the hospital. Land has been purchased in the Kamara valley below the hospital in order to grow vegetables for the hospital kitchen. The hospital report for 1992 said that the vegetable production for that year had been excellent. Also, in 1991 the hospital bought several milch-cows and built a milking shed in order to provide its own supply of milk, a commodity of which about two hundred litres are required each day. To these were added pigs and then a small herd of sheep. The sheep were bought when the last hospital lawnmower broke down beyond repair in 1993, in order to keep the grass under control and also to form an occasional contribution to the hospital dietary menu.

Yet further projects have been aimed at enabling patients to pay the hospital fees when these are required. In 1991 the hospital introduced its own health insurance scheme in conjunction with a Nairobi insurance firm. This scheme enabled hospital staff and local people to obtain insurance cover for outpatient and inpatient treatment for the payment of a relatively low annual premium. After a slow start, the number of policies issued under this scheme by the end of 1993 reached one thousand four hundred, providing health insurance cover for about eight thousand people. A Vegetable Wholesale Supermarket Project has also been started to provide an avenue for local vegetable growers to sell their produce in Nairobi. This increases their income and also allows them to pay hospital and school fees where these are required.

As a result of all these efforts to reduce costs and generate income, the hospital annual report for 1993 was able to record at the end of that year that "the hospital income and expenditure began to look more balanced".

The Hospital Chaplaincy Team

In 1989 the Presbytery of Chogoria appointed the first full-time hospital chaplain to the staff of the hospital. The pastoral care of the patients in hospital had originally been the responsibility of Dr Irvine and his assistants. This work was shared by the local evangelists and when a parish minister was appointed to Chogoria in 1926 he was encouraged to include the pastoral care of the hospital patients and staff amongst his duties.

As we mentioned previously, the hospital first employed a full-time evangelist in 1952 when Raphael M'Thika joined its staff. He was succeeded by Ezekieli Kanampiu who retired in 1990 and was succeeded by Phinehas Kiruja. It was about this time that the Presbytery decided that its pastoral link with the hospital should become more official and made the full-time appointment of the Revd Francis Kiania as hospital chaplain. He was succeeded in October 1990 by the Revd Elias Kabii. Miss Milka N.Waruhiu was commissioned as a Church sister in 1992 and appointed as the third member of the chaplaincy team whose work is now supervised by a chaplaincy committee set up by the hospital.

Sunday services were held in the outpatient department or in the open-air and were relayed to the wards by the public address system which had been installed in 1957. There was no separate hospital chapel until 1983 when one was built in the centre of the new hospital compound and dedicated in August of that year.

Three Grades of School

By the early 1980s three grades of school were recognised in Kenya and all of these were represented at Chogoria itself. The younger children of the staff of the institutions at Chogoria were able to attend the nursery school which had been established on an informal basis in the early 1970s and had proved very popular.

Primary education was represented by the Chogoria Girls' Boarding Primary School which was opened on February 9th 1981. Sixty-five Standard V girls turned up on that day and spent their first night on mattresses on the floor of the former Church Office building at Chogoria.[6] Soon, however, five wooden classrooms and a dormitory were built on the two acres of land which had been allocated to the school by the Church. Eventually a three-storey classroom block was built in stone to accommodate twelve classes, and by 1991 over four hundred girls were enrolled by the school in Standards V to VIII. The school attracted pupils from all over the country and has established a fine reputation for itself. The staff are paid by the Government Teachers' Service Commission but all other fees and costs must be paid by the parents and by special fund-raising efforts. This arrangement is in accordance with the 'cost-sharing' policy adopted by the Government Ministry of Education.

With the success of the Girls' Primary Boarding School at Chogoria there arose a demand for a similar school for boys. However, sufficient land was not available at Chogoria itself for one to be built there and so plans were made to build the Mwimbi Boys' Primary Boarding School at Kianjagi near Chogoria which was opened in January 1994.

We have already spoken of the origins of the Boys' and Girls' Secondary Schools at Chogoria. There is little more to say of them in the 1980s except to record their increase in size with the erection of more buildings and the increase in the numbers of their pupils and staff members. In both cases their name was changed to that of a High School. In 1993 the enrolment of both schools was over five hundred pupils in three streams from Form 1 to Form 4, all of whom are boarders. The costs of both these schools are met on the basis of the 'cost-sharing' policy of the Government as in the case of the Primary School.

To celebrate the jubilee of the Boys' High School in 1987, its former pupils and the local community subscribed towards the building of an impressive new two-storey Jubilee Block containing classrooms and offices, and a jubilee monument. The monument commemorated two jubilees: the semi-jubilee of the Secondary school itself which was founded in 1962 and the golden jubilee of the beginning of the Chogoria Primary School in 1937. The original brick building of 1937 had largely fallen into disuse because its classrooms were now too small to accommodate the larger classes of pupils which had become normal, as compared with the size of class for which the classrooms had been built originally.

As we have seen, the schools in the district were no longer the responsibility of the PCEA except as the Church served as sponsors for them in the sense already described. In 1985 the Presbytery of Chogoria reported that they were sponsors for fifty-five Nursery Schools, eighty-two Primary Schools and twenty Secondary Schools. With the formation of the Presbytery of Chuka in 1988, sponsorship of a number of these schools became the responsibility of that Presbytery. Even so, the Presbytery of Chogoria could record in 1993 that they were the sponsors of fifty-six Primary Schools, thirteen Secondary Schools and four Polytechnics.[7]

In 1983 the PCEA proposed that it should enter the field of higher education and establish a Teacher Training College under its auspices. Permission to proceed with this project was given by the Government

Ministry of Education. The site chosen for this College was Rubate in the Chuka area where the existing Secondary School was extended to accommodate over a hundred students for a Primary Teacher's training course lasting two years. No Government aid was promised for this venture, but so great is the shortage of trained teachers in the country that the Church expected those trained at the Rubate College would find no difficulty in obtaining employment in the Government education service. After ten years of negotiation and preparation, the College opened on October 12th 1993 with a roll of one hundred and thirty students, sixty-six of whom were women, and a full-time teaching staff of twelve.

The Church and Its Mission Areas

At Chogoria itself, the Church building continues to be the living centre of the Christian community. Although it was built in 1930 its fabric is still in good condition. There have been changes, of course, for the open-meshed windows have all been glazed and the benches have been replaced by proper pews. Also, a public address system has been installed. In October 1968 a stone pulpit was built on the north side of the outside of the Church for use when the congregation is larger than can be accommodated in the Church itself and the service has to be held in the open air.

The Church is in frequent use especially on Sundays. A notice on the main road invites the passer-by to share in the Sunday worship of the Chogoria congregation and announces the services as follows:

DURING SCHOOL TERMS

8.30-9.15am	Girls' Boarding Primary School
9.15-10.15am	Boys' High School
10.15-11.15am	Girls' High School
11.15am	Regular Vernacular Service

We have already mentioned how in 1977 the parishes in the Presbytery of Chogoria began to be subdivided, and that a new Presbytery of Imenti containing six parishes was formed in 1978. This process of reorganisation continued in the 1980s and in November 1988 the Presbytery of Chuka was set up by removing three parishes from jurisdiction of the Presbytery of Chogoria, which was then left with six parishes. The line of the Tungu River became the boundary between the two presbyteries. This reorganisation, of course, posed problems of manpower and staffing for the Church especially as it was generally recognised that a minister should be expected to care for not more than ten congregations and for not less than five.[8]

Each of the three presbyteries included what were called *Nendeni* or mission areas.[9] These were areas outside the normal bounds of the presbytery for which the Church felt called to have a special concern. Thus the Presbytery of Imenti had Meru Township and Isiolo Township as its Nendeni areas because there existed in these two places what could be regarded as a PCEA congregation amongst their inhabitants.

Tharaka had for long been an area of special concern to the staff at Chogoria and we have seen how Dr Irvine used to go there frequently on his evangelistic and medical safaris. The Presbytery now decided to put the work there on a more permanent footing and in May 1980 declared Tharaka to be its Nendeni area. In 1981 it set up the Kajiampau Rural Development Project and obtained a grant of land to be used for building a centre and to provide agricultural demonstration plots. In 1985 the Presbytery posted a minister to Tharaka on a permanent basis.

As we mentioned in the previous chapter, the hospital also shared in the development of the work in Tharaka alongside the Church by setting up the Tharaka Project of the Community Health Department in July 1986, and by the building and staffing of the Marimanti Community Health Training Centre which was opened in September 1989.

The Woman's Guild

In 1987 the PCEA Woman's Guild celebrated its sixty-fifth anniversary and Chogoria shared in those celebrations. The Guild was not, however, formed in Chogoria until 1930 when the foundation members were Mrs Irvine, Mrs Macpherson and Mrs Marion Musa. Others joined the Guild and in 1935 a Chogoria committee was formed with Mrs Lydia Zephania as chairman, Mrs Julia Ephanto as secretary and Mrs Marion Musa as treasurer. In 1953 the first Chogoria Presbyterial Council was formed and this was followed in 1979 by the formation of the Imenti Presbyterial Council, and then in 1987 a Presbyterial Council was set up for the new Chuka Presbytery. Over the years the Guild has financed numerous projects for the Church and the hospital, and helped to supply many of the needs of the work at Chogoria. For instance, it built an antenatal ward at Chogoria hospital, a manse at Kajiampau and houses for Church workers in various places, to name but a few of the projects it has financed and supported.

The Woman's Guild derived its name from the corresponding women's organisation in the Church of Scotland. This body was set up in 1887 with the aim of uniting together "all women who are engaged in the service of Christ in connection with the Church, or desire to give help to any practical Christian work in the parish".[10] In Scotland the Guild became a national movement united in its service and support of the Church. In the same way, the PCEA Woman's Guild has become an important part of the work and witness of the Church in Kenya nationally, and locally in Chogoria and elsewhere.

EPILOGUE

The three activities of evangelism, education and health care appear like three intertwined strands running through the story of the origins and development of Chogoria. In practice they involved the preaching of the gospel, the establishment of schools and the provision of health care services.

By the gospel is meant, of course, the good news that in the life, death and resurrection of Jesus Christ, God offers to men and women forgiveness of sin and the opportunity to live in fellowship with him in their daily lives. It was the desire to share this good news which sent the first Kikuyu evangelists to the Chogoria area in 1916, to be followed six years later by Dr and Mrs Irvine. This desire was the basis of all the work at Chogoria and the inspiration of all those, both European and Kenyan, who have been responsible for its development over the years. As a result of preaching the gospel there came into being a Christian community which was organised along Presbyterian lines in keeping with the tradition to which the early missionaries, both Kenyan and European, belonged.

The other two activities were the implication of the preaching of the gospel which is also concerned to develop the mind and to preserve the health of the body which God had created. The first evangelists were also teachers who taught the people to read and to write and to understand the world around them, as well the truths of the Christian Faith. They began by gathering together small groups of interested people in the villages, and then built mud-and-wattle school buildings in which they could hold classes for teaching. From these small beginnings arose the extensive system of schools of different grades which exists in the Chogoria area today.

In the beginning, elementary health care was provided by dressers who had been trained by Dr Philp at Tumutumu Hospital.

They were called 'dressers' because much of their work was the dressing of wounds and ulcers in the early days of health care. With the arrival of Dr Irvine, this side of the work at Chogoria was further developed. Soon after he arrived, he built four small mud-and-wattle huts to form a hospital and began to train his own dressers to work in this hospital and in the dispensaries he eventually established around Chogoria. From these small beginnings came the large modern hospital which exists at Chogoria today, and the comprehensive community health care service which is based on it. The health care service provided by the hospital and its community health department now enjoys an international reputation for its excellence and effectiveness.

As we have already seen, the story of Chogoria is part of the biography of Dr Clive Irvine. He was a man of many talents and boundless energy who for forty years provided the continuity of policy and direction which allowed the work at Chogoria to develop on an orderly plan. Many of the improvements in the life of the community at and around Chogoria can be traced to his interest and initiative. First and foremost he was an evangelist, but he was also an educator concerned with both literary and practical education and with the building and staffing of local schools. He was keenly interested in the welfare of the local community and sought to improve the local economy. One of his most successful efforts to achieve this was the introduction of the growing of coffee to the Chogoria area which for many years has been the basis of its economic prosperity.

This book has concentrated on the history of Chogoria but this should not be allowed to obscure the fact that the work at Chogoria forms part of the organisation and work of the Presbyterian Church of East Africa. This Church traces its historical origins to the year 1891 when Scottish missionaries established their first station in Kenya at Kibwezi. In the year 1991, therefore, the Church was able to celebrate the centenary of its foundation.

That year was also the year in which the Thirteenth General Assembly of the Church was held in Nairobi. This Assembly elected as its Moderator one whom we have already met in this book, the Revd Bernard Muindi. He was born and educated at Chogoria and was the first Mwimbi minister to have been elected Moderator of the PCEA General Assembly. As a result of his election in 1991, he presided over the centenary celebrations of the Church. His election at this time was an appropriate recognition of the place of Chogoria and its people in the history of the Presbyterian Church of East Africa.

APPENDIX ONE

SIGNIFICANT DATES IN THE HISTORY OF CHOGORIA

1913 CMS approached by Dr Arthur of Kikuyu to allow CSM to take over missionary responsibility for the Chuka-Mwimbi area (September).

1915 Mweria chosen as site of Mission by Dr Stanley Jones (October).

1916 African evangelists arrive at Mweria: Daudi Makumi from Kikuyu and Samsoni Maingi from Tumutumu (March).

1922 Dr Arthur and Ernest Carr decide to move Mission to Chogoria in Chief Mbogoli's location (February). Prefabricated bungalow taken to Chogoria from Nairobi (March). Dr & Mrs Irvine arrive at Chogoria (October 9th).

1923 Mud-and-wattle Church building erected and dedicated (June). Educational and medical work begun.

1924 Baptism at Chogoria of first eighteen Mwimbi Christians by Dr Arthur (September 28th).

1926 The Revd Jeremiah Waita arrives at Chogoria as first African minister (March). First permanent (brick) hospital building opened with two wards and ancillary rooms (March). Small leprosarium built at Gatheru. New Testament published in Kikuyu language.

1927 Coffee first planted at Chogoria by Dr Irvine. First Christian marriage celebrated (December).

1928 The Revd Solomon Ndambi succeeds the Revd Jeremiah Waita at Chogoria (June). Deacons' court set up for oversight of Church affairs. Foundation stone of new Church laid by Mrs Ernest Carr (August 4th).

1929 Female circumcision controversy reaches Chogoria with signing of the Chogoria promise (September 28th).

1930 Completion and dedication of new brick Church building at Chogoria (January 17th). Robert Macpherson arrives (August). The Chogoria Woman's Guild formed. First number of the annual *Chogoria* booklet produced by Dr Irvine.

1932 Kirk Session set up for the Chogoria congregation by Church of Scotland Presbytery of Kenya (February 14th).

1933 Dr Irvine ordained to the ministry of Church of Scotland by the Presbytery of Aberdeen (January 1st).

1935 Erasto Mwiricia becomes first Chogoria boy to go to the Alliance High School at Kikuyu (January).

1936 Chogoria Primary School officially approved by Government Education Department and new school building built at Iteri.

1939 New block of hospital buildings erected including two wards and an operating theatre. Sister Jean Clark Wilson arrived as the first nursing sister at Chogoria Hospital (April).

1940 First Revival Convention held at Chogoria (May).

1942 Sister Clark Wilson leaves to join East African Military Nursing Service and is replaced by Sister Peggie Fergusson (May).

1943 Ordination of the Revd Joseph Gathoga at Chogoria and his induction as parish minister at Chogoria (January 3rd).

1945 Bernard Mate becomes headmaster of Chogoria Primary School. Synod of the PCEA (formed in 1943) meets at Chogoria.

1947 Sister Margaret Burt joins staff of hospital (October). Semi-jubilee celebrations at Chogoria (October 12th).

1948 Edith Ayubu becomes first Chogoria girl to go to the Alliance Girls' High School at Kikuyu (January). Dr Irvine describes 1948 as "The Year of the Revival" at Chogoria.

1949 Chogoria given its own Post Office (February). New outpatient department built at hospital.

1950 Francis Muruja becomes senior hospital assistant as Jackson Chabari retires from this post.

1951 Official recognition of enrolled nurse training obtained for Chogoria Hospital (February). Old Testament published in Kikuyu language (February). Erasto Mwiricia becomes Supervisor of Schools at Chogoria (April).

1952 Ordination of the Revd Jediel Micheu as first Mwimbi minister

(January). Formation of Parish and Kirk Session of Chuka (July).

1953 Formation of Parish and Kirk Session of South Meru (September 26th). Presbytery of Chogoria established (September 27th). Dr Geoffrey Irvine joins staff of the hospital.

1956 First X-ray machine installed in the hospital (February).

1961 Dr & Mrs Irvine retire and go to live in Nairobi (December).

1962 The Chogoria Boys' High School opens with Form 1 (January).

1965 The Chogoria Girls' High School begins with Form 1.

1968 The PCEA decides to develop Chogoria Hospital. Management of Primary Schools transferred to local authority.

1970 President Kenyatta lays foundation stone of the new hospital (February 27th).

1971 Helen K.Raini appointed matron of the hospital (January). President Kenyatta opens the first phase of the hospital development (March 5th). Revd Elias Kabii dedicates the new hospital buildings as Moderator of Presbytery of Chogoria (July 11th).

1974 The Community Health Department established by the hospital. Death of Dr Clive Irvine in Nairobi (June 6th) followed by burial at Chogoria.

1975 Nurse Training School begins to train new grade of Kenya Enrolled Community Nurses.

1978 Presbytery of Imenti formed with centre at Kanyakine (March 3rd).

1979 The Revd Bernard Muindi becomes Secretary-General of the PCEA (April).

1980 Mrs Irvine dies in England (May 20th) and her ashes are buried at Chogoria beside her husband. Francis Muruja retires from post of senior hospital assistant.

1981 Chogoria Girls' Boarding Primary School opens (February 9th). New Church office built at Chogoria.

1983 Dr Geoffrey Irvine leaves hospital to become Medical Co-ordinator of the medical supply agency MEDS in Nairobi.

1985 Completion of realignment and resurfacing of road from Embu to Meru with side-road extension to Chogoria.

1987 Jubilee of Chogoria Boys' High School celebrated.

1988 Presbytery of Chuka formed with centre in Chuka township (November 11th).

1991 The Revd Bernard Muindi elected as Moderator of the Thirteenth PCEA General Assembly (April 15th). Nurse Training School changes to training Kenya Enrolled Community Health Nurses. Joyce Riungu succeeds Dr Colin Fischbacher as Director of the Community Health Department (October).

1992 Chogoria placed in the new administrative district of Tharaka-Nithi with headquarters at Chuka. Chogoria officially designated an Urban Area (December 22nd).

1993 Jane Karonjo takes over as Principal Tutor of the Community Nurse Training School (March). Rubate Teacher Training College opened (October).

APPENDIX TWO

SENIOR STAFF AT CHOGORIA HOSPITAL

MEDICAL SUPERINTENDENTS

Dr Clive Irvine	October 1922 to December 1961
Dr John Wilkinson	December 1961 to November 1965
Dr Andrew Young	December 1965 to November 1967
Dr Geoffrey Irvine	December 1967 to April 1983
Dr Scott Murray	April 1983 to December 1988
Dr Alastair Sammon	December 1988

MATRONS

Miss Rita Butter-Malcolm	1929 to 1939
Sister Jean Clark Wilson	April 1939 to May 1942
Sister Peggie Fergusson	May 1942 to September 1947
Sister Margaret Burt	October 1947 to April 1970
Sister Helen Karimi Raini	January 1971 to December 1976
Sister Jane Paxton	January 1977 to January 1979
Sister Helen Karimi Raini	February 1979

HOSPITAL ADMINISTRATORS

Miss Berta Allan	May 1949 to 1962
Miss Elizabeth Alexander	1962 to 1968
Mr Henry McCombe	December 1969 to Dec. 1972
Mr Gerrard Murunge	January 1973 to September 1974
Mr Leslie Glidden	October 1974 to Sept. 1976
Mr Gerrard Murunge	September 1976 to March 1984
Mr Ephantus Mpungu	March 1984 to December 1986
Mr Festus Nkonge	January 1987

SENIOR HOSPITAL ASSISTANTS

Mr Johnstone Kiambati	1929 to 1941
Mr Jason Baranya	1941 to 1950
Mr Jackson Chabari	1950 to 1980
Mr Francis Muruja	

The post of Senior Hospital Assistant was discontinued in 1980.

NOTES & REFERENCES

Key to Abbreviations:

CB	The *Chogoria* booklet published annually by Dr Irvine
CHAR	The Chogoria Hospital Annual Report
FMK	Jomo Kenyatta, *Facing Mount Kenya: The Tribal Life of the Gikuyu* (London: Secker & Warburg, 1938)
GAR	Reports to the General Assembly of the Church of Scotland
JMBK	Jeremy Murray-Brown, *Kenyatta* (London: Fontana/Collins, 1974)
KN	*Kikuyu News*. Quarterly journal of the Kenya Mission of the Church of Scotland (1908-1958)
PCEA	The Presbyterian Church of East Africa
PCEA GACM	PCEA General Administration Committee Minutes
RM	Robert Macpherson, *The Presbyterian Church in Kenya* (Nairobi: PCEA, 1970)

Chapter References

Chapter One: From Krapf to Kikuyu

1 W.S.Price, *My Third Campaign in East Africa: A Story of Missionary life in Troublous Times* (London: William Hunt, 1890), page v.

2 Eugene Stock, *The History of the Church Missionary Society: Its Environment, Its Men and Its Work* (London: CMS, 1899), vol.1, p.71.

3 J.L.Krapf, *Travels, Researches and Missionary Labours in Eastern Africa* (London: Trübner, 1860), p.127.

4 *Ibidem*, p. 544. Krapf's report of seeing the peaks of Mount Kenya in 1849 was confirmed only in 1883 when the Scottish explorer Joseph Thomson became the second European to see these peaks as he crossed the northern end of the Aberdare Mountains on his journey from Mombasa to Lake Victoria Nyanza. See J.Temple & A.Walker, *Kirinyaga: A Mount Kenya Anthology* (Nairobi: Mountain Club of Kenya, 1974), p.3.

5 Roland Oliver, *The Missionary Factor in East Africa* (London: Longmans Green, 1952), p.7.

6 W.G.Blaikie, *The Personal Life of David Livingstone* (London: John Murray, 1917), p.190.
7 W.S.Price, *op.cit.*, p.258.
8 East African Scottish Mission (EASM): *Instructions to Mission Party*, May 1891, p.1.
9 James Stewart, *EASM Report no.1, p.7*.
10 *Ibidem*, p.8.
11 RM, p.31, n.22.
12 JMBK, p.341, n.1. *Thogoto* is possibly "a corruption of the word Scotch". But there is a Kikuyu word similar to it which can mean "to make faltering attempts to speak a foreign language" and so 'Thogoto' may be a pun linking Scotch men speaking broken Kikuyu. The Mission was also sometimes called *Kwa Thigochi* (The place of the Scotch).
13 His full name was David Clement Ruffell Scott. At Kikuyu he was nicknamed *Watenga* because of his frequent use of the word *tenga*, clear away. This word came from Mang'anja (as Chinyanja or Chichewa was then called), the language used in Blantyre where Scott had served before he came to Kikuyu. The word also occurs in Swahili with the same meaning.
14 Henry Scott's nickname in Kikuyu was *Chichia* which means 'the one who watches', because he wore spectacles.
15 Dr Philp published the first medical handbook in the Kikuyu language with the title *Ibuku ria Maundu ma Thipitari* (A Book of Hospital Matters). It contained sixty-eight pages and went into a second edition in 1920. See KN 73 (July 1920), pp.17-18.

Chapter Two: Into Chuka-Mwimbi Country

1 Roland Oliver & Gervase Mathew (eds), *History of East Africa* (Oxford: Oxford University Press, 1963), vol.1, p.80.
2 A.M.M'Imanyara, *The Restatement of Bantu Origin and Meru History* (Nairobi: Longmans Kenya, 1992).
3 Godfrey Muriuki, *A History of the Kikuyu 1500-1900* (Nairobi: Oxford University Press, 1974), chap.2 (esp. pp.55-61).
4 H.E.Lambert, *The Systems of Land Tenure in the Kikuyu Land Unit* (Capetown: School of African Studies, University of Capetown, 1950), Communications no.22, p.32.
5 L.S.B.Leakey, *Mau Mau and the Kikuyu* (London: Methuen, 1952) p.2.
6 FMK, p.24.
7 Godfrey Muriuki, *op.cit.*, p.47, note 32.
8 *Native Land Tenure in Kikuyu Province*. The Maxwell Report (Nairobi: Government Printer, 1929), endmap.
9 A.R.Barlow, *The Mountain of Light*, KN 19 (May 1910), pp.5-7. Other names for the mountain are *Kirimara* (The spotted mountain) and *Kiriira* (The white or chalk mountain).
10 JMBK, p.339.
11 J.W.Arthur, *A Journey Made in View of Extension*, KN 53 (January/February 1915), pp.1-15.
12 J.W.Arthur, *The Kikuyu Missions Volunteer Carrier Corps*, KN 63 (May-July 1917), pp.1-8.
13 Geoffrey Hodges, *The Carrier Corps: Military Labour in the East African Campaign, 1914-1918* (New York: Greenwood Press, 1986), p.179.
14 *Ibidem*, p.111.

15 Gordon Hewitt, *The Problems of Success: A History of the Church Missionary Society 1910-1942* (London: SCM Press, 1971), vol.1, p.183.

Chapter Three: The Prospect of Help

1 This diary is amongst the Arthur papers in the Edinburgh University Library Special Collections Department, Gen.762/64. The actual diary entry reads as follows: "Got to Matikiro at 8.30.... On arrival rotten time hunting for water. At 12 young doctor Irvine, son of UF manse in Aberdeen and would-be missionary came down and introduced himself" (KMV Diary, p.73).
2 Lyn Irvine, *So Much Love, So Little Money* (London: Faber & Faber, 1957).
3 Elizabeth Irvine, Obituary of Archibald C. Irvine in *Aberdeen University Review*, vol.46 (1975-76), p.235.
4 Information supplied by Aberdeen University archivist from University records.
5 Elizabeth Irvine, *loc.cit.*
6 Church of Scotland Foreign Mission Committee, Minutes of Meeting of 18/11/1919, p.28.
7 J.W.Arthur, Obituary of Ernest Carr in KN 150 (December 1939), p.293
8 Mrs Henry E.Scott, *A Saint in Kenya: A Life of Marion Scott Stevenson* (London: Hodder & Stoughton, 1932), pp.208-209.
9 The East African Standard reported the wedding in its issue of Saturday May 7th 1921.
10 Church of Scotland Foreign Mission Committee, Minutes of Meeting of 28/2/1922, p.22.

Chapter Four: In Chuka-Mwimbi

1 Church of Scotland Foreign Mission Committee Minutes of Meeting of 18/4/1922, pp.18-19.
2 KN 53 (January/February 1915), p.13.
3 It has been suggested recently that the original name of the Chogoria site was *Ndemere*, and that the name Chogoria was a mis-spelling (by Ernest Carr) of the word *Cirigwa*. This word was the name of the age-grade of Mwimbi boys initiated at the time when Chogoria was founded. See J.T.Stephens, *In the Shadow of Mount Kenya* (Oberlin, Ohio: privately printed 1993) p.27.
4 KN 82 (December 1922), p.13.
5 KN 85 (March 1923), pp.13-16 and GAR 1923, p.204-205.
6 GAR 1924, p.226.
7 Zabulon J.Nthamburi, *A History of the Methodist Church in Kenya* (Nairobi: Uzima Press, 1982), p.62.
8 Chogoria Jubilee booklet, p.1.
9 KN 119 (March 1922), p.21.
10 Chogoria Jubilee booklet, p.2.
11 *A Standard Swahili-English Dictionary* (Oxford: Oxford University Press, 1939), p.546, s.v. *Zungua*.
12 A.R.Barlow, Cyclostyled *Memorandum on Kikuyu and Christian Beliefs*. See also RM pp.7-12.

13 The word *Ngai* comes from the Masai *En-kai* and means primarily a supernatural being or power or the source of anything wonderful or inexplicable (RM p.10).
14 FMK p.238.
15 RM p.11 and FMK pp.243-252.
16 KN 109 (September 1929), p.20.

Chapter Five: Early Days at Chogoria

1 KN 128 (June 1934), pp.29-31.
2 Zabulon J.Nthamburi, *A History of the Methodist Church in Kenya* (Nairobi: Uzima Press, 1982), pp.57-62.
3 KN 83 (March 1923), p.15.
4 KN 89 (September 1924), p.18.
5 KN 177 (September 1946), p.768.
6 Elizabeth F.Irvine, Obituary of Archibald Clive Irvine in *Aberdeen University Review*, vol. 46 (1975-76), p.235.
7 Clive Irvine, *Telephone to Heaven* (Achimota, Ghana: African Christian Press, 1967).

Chapter Six: The First Seven Years (1922-1928)

1 CB 1959, p.2.
2 GAR 1929, p.320.
3 GAR 1925, p.232.
4 GAR 1930, p.580.
5 GAR 1924, p.226.
6 GAR 1928, p.397.
7 In his article written on the occasion of the diamond jubilee of the arrival of the Scottish missionaries at Kibwezi in 1891, Dr Arthur records how John Paterson and Dr David Charters share the credit of initiating the coffee industry of Kenya when they began to plant coffee at Kibwezi. See KN 197 (September 1951), pp.1182-1184. Some of the coffee seedlings were later transplanted to Kikuyu and became the first coffee plants to be grown in the Kenya Highlands (See cyclostyled memorandum by Dr J.W.Arthur dated June 2nd 1930 and entitled, 'The origins and development of the education of the Kikuyu in Kenya'). Paterson left the Mission in 1903 and became a farmer and coffee planter in Kiambu District,
8 KN 145 (September 1938), p.167.
9 KN 106 (December 1928), pp.21-23.
10 KN 177 (September 1946), p.786.

Chapter Seven: The First Seven Years (cont.)

1 KN 120 (June 1952), p.6.
2 KN 83 (May 1923), p.15.
3 GAR 1924, p.226.
4 GAR 1926, p.312.
5 KN 120 (June 1952), p.6.
6 A.C.Irvine, 'The Running of a Small Leprosarium in Kenya', *East African Medical Journal* 1951; vol. 28; pp.280-282.
7 KN 91 (March 1925), p.16.

8 GAR 1925, p.232.
9 GAR 1926, p.310.
10 Church of Scotland Foreign Mission Committee Minute of Meeting of 2/3/1926, p.77.
11 H.R.A.Philp, *God and the African in Kenya* (London: Marshall, Morgan & Scott, 1936), Chapter X, 'The Rev. Solomon Ndambi', pp.83-92.
12 GAR 1929, p.318 & CB 1930.
13 GAR 1929, p.320.
14 KN 84 (June 1923), p.28.
15 GAR 1930, p.581
16 Mrs Henry E.Scott, *A Saint in Kenya: A Life of Marion Scott Stevenson* (London: Hodder & Stoughton, 1932), p.252.
17 *Ibidem*, p.125. This nickname *Nyamacheki* arose out of an incident at Kikuyu when Miss Stevenson's cheque book was stolen from her house by some youths who had seen her signing cheques to pay accounts and thought they could use them in the same way to obtain money. An alternative meaning of 'the thin lady' has been suggested, but this is hardly supported by the existing photographs of Miss Stevenson at this time.
18 *Ibidem*, p.255.
19 Zabulon J.Nthamburi, *A History of the Methodist Church in Kenya* (Nairobi: Uzima Press, 1982), p.59.
20 GAR 1929, p.319.

Chapter Eight: Opposition Arises (1929)

1 FMK, p.25.
2 L.S.B.Leakey, *Mau Mau and the Kikuyu* (London: Methuen, 1952), p.9
3 RM, p.28.
4 F.D.Corfield, *The Origins and Growth of Mau Mau: An Historical Survey* (Nairobi: Government Printer, 1960), p.13.
5 *Ibidem*, p.14.
6 GAR 1930, p.579.
7 RM, p.105.
8 H.R.A.Philp, 'Native Gynaecology', *Journal of the Kenya Medical Service* 1924; vol.1; pp.3-4 (January), and 'Artificial Atresia in Kikuyu Women', *Kenya Medical Journal* 1925; vol. 2, pp.86-87 (June). See also J.A.Verzin, 'Sequelae of Female Circumcision', *Tropical Doctor* 1975 vol 5 pp 163-169 (October).
9 Today the official medical term used by the World Health Organisation is 'female genital mutilation'. See WHO, *Female genital mutilation* (Geneva: WHO 1993), Press release WHA/10. See also Editorial. 'Female genital mutilation', *British Medical Journal* 1993, vol.307, no.5902, p.460 (August 21st).
10 As was maintained by F.D.Corfield, *op.cit.* p.41. See also Julian Huxley, *Africa View* (London: Chatto & Windus, 1932), pp.194-198. In a letter to the Kenya Director of Education in January 1939, Dr Arthur wrote as follows: "I would like to say that this circumcision has been a dead letter in our mission for years; it has now become a live issue because the Kikuyu C.A. have made it a political issue". This letter is now in the Kenya National Archives in Nairobi.
11 F.B.Welbourn, *East African Rebels* (London: SCM Press, 1961), p.142.

12 JMBK, pp.134-135.
13 KN 110 (December 1929), p.14.
14 CB 1930, p.1.
15 GAR 1930, p.579.
16 RM, p.114.
17 RM, p.113.
18 RM, p.119, n.26.
19 RM, p.113.

Chapter Nine: Recovery and Progress (1930-1939)
1 GAR 1932, p.668.
2 KN 123 (March 1933), p.14.
3 KN 115 (March 1931), p.12.
4 GAR 1930, p.581.
5 KN 113 (September 1930), pp.23-26.
6 J.N.Ogilvie, *Afric's Sunny Fountains* (Edinburgh: Blackwood, 1921), pp.67-68.
7 KN 118 (December 1931), p.14 and CB 1936, p.2.
8 Church of Scotland Foreign Mission Committee Meeting of 19/4/1932, Minute no. 1444 (4).
9 Church of Scotland Presbytery of Aberdeen, Minutes of Meeting of 6/12/1932, p.185 (Service of Licensing) and Meeting of 1/1/1933, p.189 (Service of Ordination). These Minutes are in Aberdeen City Archives, reference no. CH 2/1/30.
10 GAR 1934, p.670 & KN 128 (June 1934), p.11.
11 CB 1936, p.2.
12 GAR 1937, p.738.
13 KN 108 (June 1929), p.29.
14 KN 111 (March 1930), pp.18-21.

Chapter Ten: Recovery and Progress (cont.)
1 RM, Chapter 7, 'The Gospel Missionary Society', pp.84-92.
2 CB 1934, p.5.
3 GAR 1936, p.602.
4 J.S.Smith, *The History of the Alliance High School* (Nairobi: Heinemann, 1973), p.15.
5 KN 116 (June 1931), pp.31-35.
6 KN 141 (September 1937), p.68.
7 GAR 1930, p.580.
8 This building does not occur in any photographs before 1930 and it is first mentioned in CB 1931, p.6.
9 CB 1930, p.8.
10 KN 133 (September 1935), p.10.

Chapter Eleven: War and Revival (1939-1949)
1 RM, pp.124-125.
2 KN 168 (June 1944), p.595.
3 KN 179 (March 1947), p.789.
4 KN 181 (September 1947), p.833.

5 Zabulon J.Nthamburi, *A History of the Methodist Church in Kenya* (Nairobi: Uzima Press, 1982), pp.78-81.
6 Kevin Ward, 'The Balokole Revival in Uganda' in Zabulon J.Nthamburi (ed), *From Mission to Church: A Handbook of Christianity in East Africa* (Nairobi: Uzima Press, 1991), pp.113-114.
7 A.C.Stanley Smith, *Road to Revival: The Story of the Ruanda Mission* (London: CMS, 1946), p.57.
8 George Mambo, *Kenya Churches Handbook: The Development of Kenyan Christianity, 1498-1973* (Kisumu: Evangel Publishing House, 1973), pp.113-144.
9 Max Warren, *Revival: An Enquiry* (London: SCM Press, 1954), Appendix II, pp.118-121.
10 Jocelyn Murray, *Proclaim the Good News: A Short History of the CMS* (London: Hodder & Stoughton, 1985), p.194.
11 KN 90 (December 1924), p.18.
12 KN 162 (December 1942), p.492.
13 CB 1945, p.1.
14 *Report of African Affairs Department for 1948* (Nairobi: Government Printer, 1949), p.43.
15 KN 192 (June 1950), p.1098.
16 RM pp.126-127.
17 See two articles on the East African Revival by Robert Macpherson in KN 190 (December 1949), pp.1044-1046 and KN 193 (September 1950), pp.1107-1113.

Chapter Twelve: Post-War Developments (1944-1952)

1 KN 177 (September 1946), p.768.
2 KN 185 (September 1948), p.930.
3 The main semi-jubilee celebrations in 1947 were held on Sunday October 12th and this date was frequently quoted by Dr Irvine later as that on which he and his family first arrived at Chogoria in 1922. In fact, as we have already seen, they arrived at Chogoria on Monday, October 9th as Dr Irvine records in a contemporary letter in *Kikuyu News*. See KN 82 (December 1922), p.13.
4 KN 183 (March 1948), p.864.
5 KN 190 (December 1949), p.1049.
6 KN 177 (September 1946), p.768.
7 In 1964 this School was renamed The Alliance Girls' High School.
8 CB 1949, p.11.
9 KN 168 (June 1944), pp.575-576. Sister Clark Wilson was drowned on February 12th 1944 when the troopship *Khedive Ismail*, in convoy en route from Mombasa to Colombo, was torpedoed by a Japanese submarine in the Indian Ocean. The ship sank in less than two minutes with the loss of 1,297 lives. The sinking has been described as one of the worst maritime disasters of the Second World War. See the report in *The Times* of February 12th 1994, p.11.
10 KN 192 (June 1950), p.1099.
11 CB 1950, p.11.

Chapter Thirteen: The Church Advances (1952-1960)

1 KN 202 (February 1953), p.1288.
2 KN 205 (February 1954), p.1360.
3 RM, p.133.
4 A.R.Barlow, 'The Story of the Kikuyu Bible', KN 196 (June 1951), pp.1160-1163. The revised version of the Kikuyu New Testament bound up with the Old Testament in 1965 has remained the standard version. However, in 1991 another version in simpler Kikuyu (*Gikuyu kihuthu*) was published by the Living Bible International and is now available.
5 *African Education in Kenya*. The Beecher Report (Nairobi: Government Printer, 1949).

Chapter Fourteen: The Progress of Nationalism (1929-1960)

1 JMBK, p.136.
2 JMBK, p.147.
3 The Kikuyu word *karing'a* means 'pure' and was applied to those who were regarded as pure-blooded Kikuyu. See L.G. and G.S.B. Beecher, *A Kikuyu-English Dictionary* (Nairobi: CMS Bookshop, 1938), p.82, s.v. *karing'a*.
4 J.B.Ndungu, 'Gituamba and Kikuyu Independency in Church and School' in B.G.McIntosh (ed), *Ngano* (Nairobi: East African Publishing House, 1969), pp.135.
5 *Ibidem*, p.147.
6 JMBK, p.226.
7 C.G.Rosberg Jr & John Nottingham, *The Myth of Mau Mau. Nationalism in Kenya* (New York: Praeger, 1966), p.331.
8 Robert Macpherson, *Mau Mau and the Church* (Edinburgh: Church of Scotland Foreign Mission Committee, 1953), p.5.
9 CR, pp.165-167.
10 John Wilkinson, 'The Mau Mau Movement: Some General and Medical Aspects', *East African Medical Journal* 1954, vol.31, pp.295-314.
11 KN 207 (October 1954), p.1401.

Chapter Fifteen: From Emergency to Independence (1956-1963)

1 JMBK, p.298.
2 JMBK, p.309.
3 RM, p.140.
4 RM, pp.132 & 142,
5 *Kenya Education Department Annual Report for 1953* (Nairobi: Government Printer, 1954), p.27.
6 Clive Irvine, *How to Behave* (Nairobi: ESA Bookshop, 1958). By 1970 this booklet had reached its ninth edition which is an indication of its popularity and usefulness.
7 *Report of the Committee Appointed to Consider the Role of the Medical Services rendered by the Missions in Relation to those Provided by Central and Local Government: The Anderson Report* (Nairobi: Gov't Printer, 1960), p.6.
8 *Aberdeen University Review*, vol. 37 (1957-1958), p.39
9 Clive Irvine, 'Retire to a New Job' in *Outlook*, the house journal of the Nairobi Baptist Church (1970).

Chapter Sixteen: Kenya after Independence (1964-1970)

1 J.S.Smith, *The History of the Alliance High School* (Nairobi: Heinemann 1973), p.274. The 7-4-2-3 system of education came to be regarded as too academic and in 1981 a Government-appointed education task force recommended a return to the previous 8-4-4 system which occurred in 1985 when the Standard VIII was re-introduced into Primary Schools.

2 *Kenya Education Commission Report:* The Ominde Report (Nairobi: Government Printer), Part One (December 1964); Part Two (July 1965).

3 *The Anderson Report*, p.11.

4 *The Closer Integration of the Health Services of Kenya:* The 'Pink' Report (Nairobi: Ministry of Health, 1968), Appendix III. This report gave the bed provision in Church-related hospitals as 29.1% of the total number of beds available to the population of Kenya in 1964. However, when the primary care services of the Churches were taken into account, it was reckoned that the Churches provided at least fifty per cent of the total health care available to the population of Kenya.

5 *Ibidem*, pp.43-45

6 PCEA GACM, April 1965, Minute 1190.

7 Chogoria was now in the new Eastern Province of Kenya which was formed in April 1963 with its headquarters at Embu.

8 PCEA GACM, April 1965, Min.1160. The 'tent-making ministry' was one in which the minister continued in his former occupation after ordination. It is so named from the apostle Paul's still working as a tent-maker on his missionary journeys as recorded in Acts 18.3.

Chapter Seventeen: Community Health Care at Chogoria (1970-1993)

1 In January 1987, multiple drug therapy for leprosy was introduced in Meru District using the three drugs rifampicin, clofazimine and dapsone over a period of six months to three years. This new method of treatment has been remarkably successful and has reduced the incidence of leprosy in Meru District.

2 *1985 Chogoria Community Health Survey: Report of Principal Findings* (October 1987), p.104, table 8.6. If all methods are included, the figure rises to 43%.

3 CHAR 1991, p.24.

4 *VIVA Chogoria Special Issue* by Chogoria Hospital Youth Programme (Nairobi: Trend Publishers Ltd., 1985).

5 CHAR 1988, p.22.

6 CHAR 1986, p.15.

7 CHAR 1992, p.21.

8 CHAR 1986, p.45.

9 CHAR 1967, p.4.

10 Olwen C.A.McNeil (ed), *Procedure Manual for Nurses and Midwives* (Nairobi: African Medical & Research Foundation/Macmillan, 1989).

Chapter Eighteen: Chogoria after 1980

1 Tony Airey, 'The Impact of Road Construction on Hospital Inpatient Catchments in the Meru District of Kenya', *Social Science & Medicine* 1989, vol. 29, pp.95-106.

2 CHAR 1991, p.6. See Meru District Development Plan 1989-1993.

3 CHAR 1987, p.15.
4 CHAR 1988, p.19.
5 CHAR 1991, p.12.
6 The use of the former Church Office was possible because the Church had built a new office block for the Presbytery and Parish near the Church at Chogoria, which was opened in 1981.
7 The figures for 1985 are taken from the report of the Presbytery of Chogoria to the Eleventh General Assembly of the PCEA held in April 1985. Those for 1993 are from the Minutes of the Presbytery of Chogoria (Minute 11/93 of the meeting of January 3rd 1993).
8 PCEA GACM, April 1987. Report of Chogoria Presbytery, p.2.
9 The Swahili word *nendeni* is the second person imperative plural form of the verb *enda* meaning 'go!' and was adopted by the PCEA as a missionary slogan in 1963 when the sixty-fifth anniversary of the beginning of the CSM at Kibwezi was celebrated. The origin of the slogan is the Swahili version of Jesus' command to his disciples in Mark 16.15: "Go *(Nendeni)* into all the world and preach the good news to all creation".
10 Mamie Magnusson, *Out of Silence: The Woman's Guild 1887-1987* (Edinburgh: St Andrew Press, 1987), p.55.

INDEX

Aberdeen University   23, 53, 122, 143, 186-8
Africa Inland Mission   18, 60, 98
Allan, Berta   109, 183
Alliance Girls' High School   113
Alliance High School   89-90, 100, 111, 113, 118, 124
Anderson Report   142-3, 148, 189-90
Area Health Committee   158, 160-2
Arthur, Dr John W.   16-17, 22, 28, 40, 55, 70, 72, 81, 179, 186
Ayubu, Edith   113, 180

Bantu peoples   11-13
Barlow, A.Ruffell   10, 18, 28-29, 56, 90, 122
Beecher Report   124-5, 140, 145
Bell, Percy   147
Bible translation   2, 36, 56, 122-3, 191
Bowman, Margaret   123, 148
Brickmaking   44-45, 52
Brownlie, Jean   111
Bruce, Alexander L.   4, 7
Bundi, Geoffrey   154-5
Burt, Sister Margaret   115, 125, 141, 180
Butter-Malcolm, Rita   60, 91-93, 111, 183

Calderwood, George   40, 55, 86, 122
Carr Cottage   79
Carr, Ernest   23-29, 31, 45, 47, 60, 78-79, 86, 90, 102, 141, 144, 179, 186
Carrier Corps   17-18, 22-23, 54, 64, 79
Central Agency (EZE)   151-2
Chabari, Jackson   92, 115, 126
Charteris, Dr David   6, 47, 187
Chogoria   28-29, 43, 186
Chogoria booklet   43, 75, 92, 102, 114, 180
Christian Churches' Educational Association (CCEA)   141, 155
Christian Health Association of Kenya (CHAK)   169-71
Chuka   13, 16, 19, 25, 40, 51, 59, 77, 97, 102-3, 121, 134, 167
Church building   54, 57, 79, 83-86

194

Church Missionary Society   1, 3-4, 15-16, 18, 24, 56, 62, 67, 70, 99, 102, 110, 139
Church of Scotland   7, 16, 19-20, 23, 27, 37, 43-45, 47, 55, 61, 67, 76, 81, 91, 97, 117, 121-2, 126, 142, 153, 160
Circumcision, female   66-68, 88, 109, 127-9, 139, 179, 188
Cobb, G.C.   45
Coffee-growing   47, 50, 114, 178-9, 187
Community Health   157

Dagoretti   5-6
Deacons' Court   57, 71, 81
Dispensaries   49, 113, 117, 156-7
Donkeys   49-50
Dressers   79, 115, 117, 156, 177

East African Revival   99-101
East Africa Scottish Mission   4, 8, 97
Evangelistic safaris   56, 61, 79-80, 83, 88, 98, 156, 175

Family planning   159, 169
Faro, Sister A.J.   157
Fergusson, Sister Peggie   149
Fischbacher, Dr Colin   160

Gaitungu   45
Gathoga, Joseph   82, 97, 180
Gospel Missionary Society   87, 121
Grieve, George   112

Harambee   137, 146, 148
Harvey, Gwen Martin   82
Health education   157, 161
Hospital chaplaincy   172
Hospitals' Board   142
Hospital Management Committee   142
How to Behave   140

Imperial British East Africa Company   4, 26, 64
Irvine, Anthony (Tony)   xi, 25, 29, 42, 95
Irvine, Dr Clive   x, 22, 178
---appointment   22
---army service   21

195

---arrival at Chogoria 29, 190
---death 144, 181
---education 22
---graduation 23
---honours (DD, OBE) 141
---marriage 25
---meeting with Dr Arthur 22, 186
---offer for missionary service 23
---ordination 81
---retirement 143-4, 181, 191
---service at Tumutumu 23, 25
Irvine, Dr Geoffrey xi, 42, 45, 95, 125, 132, 141, 169, 182
Irvine, Joy 25, 29, 31, 38-40, 46, 53, 55, 60, 85, 99, 104, 144, 176, 181
Irvine, Dr Kenneth 42, 95-6, 115

Jiggers 82-83
Jones, Dr Stanley 16-17, 25, 28, 179

Kabii, Elias xi, 147, 152, 172, 181
Kamara River 31, 52, 83, 108
Kamerzel, Sister Mary Jane 126
Kanampiu, Ezekieli 172
Kanini, Willie 58, 81, 97
Kareri, Charles M. 121-2
Karonjo, Jane 164, 182
Kenya African National Union (KANU) 137, 143
Kenya African Union (KAU) 109, 130
Kenya, Mount 3, 11-15, 33, 40-41, 54, 70, 78, 95, 108, 132, 140, 165-6, 184-5
Kenyatta, Jomo 64, 68, 109, 137, 148, 152, 181
Kibwezi 5-6, 47, 178, 187
Kikuyu Central Association (KCA) 64, 67-75, 90, 128-30
Kikuyu hymnbook 57, 82
Kikuyu Independent Schools Association (KISA) 129-30
Kikuyu Mission 7-9, 17, 23, 46, 58, 60, 72, 81, 109, 117, 119, 139
Kikuyu Missions Volunteers 17-19, 22
Kikuyu people 11-13
Kilimanjaro, Mount 2, 15
Kirinyaga 14
Kirk Session 81, 121
Kirore 73-74
Krapf, Johann L. 1-2, 9, 61, 184

196

Lamont, Donald   112
Land consolidation   137-8
Leakey, Harry   56, 122
Leprosy   52-53, 80, 86, 92, 117, 120, 126, 158, 179, 192
Livingstone, David   3-4, 8
Locusts   37-38, 63, 75, 107

Mackinnon, Sir William   4, 7, 26
Macpherson, Robert   87, 111, 180
Mahihu, Eliud   152
Maina   30, 45, 57
Maingi, Samson   17, 27, 30, 179
Makumi, Daudi   16, 27, 70, 179
Malaria   53, 79-80, 118
Mate, Bernard   111, 123, 136, 180
Mathu, Eliud   130, 136
Mau Mau Movement   106, 119-20, 130-5, 140
Mbogoli, Chief   16-17, 28, 179
Mburugu, Leonard   147
Medicine man (*mundu mugo*)   32-35, 39, 93
Methodist Mission/Church   32, 40, 61, 86, 98, 110, 115, 121, 139-40, 149
Micheu, Jediel   xi, 120-2, 147, 181
Mission to Lepers (The Leprosy Mission)   52, 86, 92
M'Moga, Wallace   109
Morson, Sister Louise   125, 127, 162
Mowat, Mary   102-3, 123
Mpungu, Ephantus   147
M'Raria, Daudi   82
M'Muga, Musa   81
M'Rucha, Ashford   147
M'Thika, Raphael   141, 172
Muchina, Silas   97, 102-3, 120
Muindi, Bernard   xii, 139, 178, 181-2
Mukangu, Gerishom   57, 81
Murianki, Jotham   97, 109, 132
Muriithi, Jonathan   71, 81
Muruja, Francis   xi, 126, 180-1
Musa, Marion   55, 176
Musa, Martha   111
Mutonga, Phares   82, 98
Mwiricia, Erasto   89, 112, 123, 180
Mweria   x, 16-17, 28, 109, 179

Nagenda, William   120
Ndago, Mariamu   134
Ndambi, Solomon   57, 70, 79-80, 105, 179
Nendeni area   117, 193
Ngai   33-35, 186
Ngari, Geoffrey   121
Nguiai, Ayubu   30, 44
Njeru, Ariel   125
Njuri ncheke   98
Nurse training   126-7, 156, 162-4
Nyamacheki   60, 188

Ominde Report   146, 148
Ordination of women   155

Parents' Union   90
Paterson, Alex   111
Paterson, John   47, 187
Penicillin   117
Philp, Dr Horace R.A.   10, 17, 23, 25, 40, 55, 177, 185
Post Office   38, 111, 166, 180
Prayer   41-42, 54, 101, 144
Presbyterian Church of East Africa (PCEA)   87, 97, 105, 121, 124, 138, 142, 153-5, 174, 178
Presbytery of Chogoria   62, 121-2, 139, 147, 152, 172, 174-5
Presbytery of Chuka   174-5
Presbytery of Imenti   154, 175
Presbytery of Kenya   55, 72, 81, 121
Presbytery of Tumutumu   97, 105, 121-2
Protestant Churches' Medical Association (PCMA)   149-50, 169

Raini, Helen K.   153, 181
Revival at Chogoria   79, 101-4, 116, 119-20, 133-4, 154
Revival in Ruanda   98-100
Revival at Tumutumu   24, 99
Riungu, Joyce   157, 181
Riungu, Timothy   118
Rubate Teacher Training College   174, 182

St Paul's United Theological College, Limuru   121, 139, 154
Scott, Dr Clement   8-10, 17, 26, 82, 185

Scott, Dr Henry   9, 16, 185
So Much Love: So Little Money   22
Sponsorship of schools   146-7, 155, 174
Stevenson, Marion   60-61, 67, 188
Stewart, Dr James   4-5
Stone, discovery of   41-42, 108, 114
Sunday Schools   81, 109, 155

Tent-making ministry   154, 192
Telephone to Heaven   42
Tharaka   11-12, 46, 62, 80, 116, 161, 166-7, 175-6
Thogoto   7, 185
Traditional birth attendants (TBAs)   160
Tuberculosis   53, 92, 142
Tumutumu Mission   9-10, 23-25, 30, 40, 42, 46, 51-52, 60, 65, 67, 73, 99, 108-9, 177

Waita, Jeremiah   55, 57, 179
Wallace, Tirzah   111
Wangai, Dedan   79, 103, 105, 120, 124
Waringu, Simon Peter   111
Waruiru, Linus   122
Watson, Thomas   6-7, 63
Watt, John   111-2
Waweru, Wilson   17, 27, 30, 59
Welch, Dr Janet   53, 61
Wilkinson, Jean   113
Wilkinson, Dr John   112, 115, 123, 125, 141-2, 147, 149, 151
Wilson, Sister Jean Clark   93, 115, 180, 190
Woman's Guild   176, 180
World War, First   17, 24, 64, 130
World War, Second   44, 95-96, 107, 115, 131

X-rays   93, 117, 141-2, 169, 181

Yaws   53, 79, 91, 118

Zakayo, Phyllis   123

NOTE: In order to accommodate a postscript by the author's daughter, some pages have been re-set. The index has been adjusted, but there will be a few cases where the reference may be one page out, especially round about pages 117-127.

By the same author:

Health and Healing:
Studies in New Testament Principle and Practice
(Handsel Press - out of print)

Healing and the Church
(Handsel Press - out of print)

Christian Ethics in Health Care:
A Source Book for Christian Doctors, Nurses and other
Health Care Professionals *(Handsel Press - out of print)*

Making Men Whole:
The Theology of Medical Missions
(CMF, 157 Waterloo Rd, London SE1 8XN)

The Coogate Doctors:
The History of the Edinburgh Medical Missionary Society *(EMMS, 7 Washington Lane, Edinburgh EH11 2HH)*

The Bible and Healing:
A Medical and Theological Commentary
(Handsel Press and Eerdmans)

The Medical History of the Reformers
Calvin, Luther and Knox
(Handsel Press)

More information from
handsel@dial.pipex.com

POSTSCRIPT

Since this book was written, there have been many more developments at Chogoria.

The town of Chogoria has continued to expand, becoming ever busier with more shops and kiosks, vehicles and *matatus* (bus/taxis), more concrete buildings, more open-air evangelism involving many different Christian denominations based in the area and beyond.

The Presbyterian Church in Chogoria has also continued to grow. By 1999 there were 11 congregations in Chogoria Parish alone. No one building was big enough to gather all congregations together, so later it was decided to build a new and larger church at Chogoria, in an L-shape around the old church building. At the time of writing this building is not yet complete.

In the hospital, more specialist services have been developed and expanded, in response to needs within the community. In the surgical unit, the scope of investigation and treatment expanded with donated endoscopic equipment, a new ultrasound machine, a rehabilitation service provided by a visiting orthopaedic surgeon. A gynaecologist arrived to develop the maternity and gynaecology services. Short- and longer-term medical staff and specialists from several countries provided services and training in each clinical department over the years. A psychiatric clinic was started and run by a trained pyschiatric nurse. The ENT clinic was started and run by a trained Clinical Officer, but faltered when he left after some years.

1995 was an eventful year. As well as setting up the intravenous infusion production unit to provide the hospital with safe and inexpensive IV fluids, there were two major changes in training programmes. After years of preparation, the *Clive Irvine School of Nursing* started to offer the Kenya Registered Community Health Nurse (KRCHN) curriculum, and the first intake of students began the course in the now renamed *Clive Irvine College of Nursing*. The college continued to run bridging courses, and later, distance learning courses, to enable experienced nurses to upgrade their qualification.

In the same year, the Kenya Government's Ministry of Health approved training for pre-registration doctors at Chogoria, Tenwick and Kijabe Hospitals, working together with members of CMF Kenya (Christian Medical Fellowship) and MAP (Medical Assistance Programme). Medical Graduates from Nairobi University, many of whom were committed Christians, were able to undertake their pre-registration year for the first time in a church hospital. A significant number stayed on as medical officers for varying lengths of time. Others went on to work in different parts of Kenya, in government or church hospitals, using their medical skills in those communities. This training programme continues to be a rewarding responsibility for the hospital.

The same three hospitals, Chogoria, Tenwick and Kijabe, together with CMF Kenya, put much time and energy, over several years, into developing a postgraduate training programme for a M.Med. (Master of Medicine) in Family Medicine, to teach broad-based medical and surgical skills, with the aim of better equipping Kenyan-trained doctors to work in rural areas. However, when this programme finally got off the ground in 2005, in collaboration with Moi University in Eldoret (in western Kenya), Chogoria did not have the required number of medical staff with the stipulated postgraduate qualifications in Family Medicine / General Practice, and had to withdraw, until the right doctors could be recruited.

Throughout the 1990s there was a steady decline in patient numbers, and it became clear that in much of the catchment area, new medical clinics, both government and private, were springing up near the Chogoria clinics. This "competition" necessitated a review of services provided, and much thought on preventing costly duplication while still making services accessible, and appropriate to community needs.

Local fundraising for hospital needs, such as bedlinen, continued to be organised by the Patient Welfare Committee. Several sponsored walks, and a sponsored climb of Mt Kenya by hospital staff, raised a significant amount in 1998, and involved many in the community.

A bigger event involving the whole community in 1999 was the fund-raising Harambee attended by the then President of Kenya, His Excellency Daniel arap Moi. This raised KSh 13.5 million for the renovation of the hospital buildings, work which went on for much of the next year. The President also publicly confirmed the support of the Government for the work in Chogoria, support which provided the services of a surgeon, two medical officers, two nurses, a physiotherapist and a radiographer.

It was recognised that to attract good staff, there needed to be good schools for their children and so the Chogoria Complex Primary School was established in 1998 on the Chogoria mission "complex", offering a high standard of education to senior staff children without the need for them to board. With now around 300 pupils, the school continues to provide sound teaching, and a strong link with a primary school in Scotland has provided an added dimension.

The increasing impact of HIV / AIDS in Kenya through the 1990's was felt in the Chogoria community as much as elsewhere. The Community Health Department was very involved in health education, teaching facts and ways to reduce the transmission of this deadly disease. But it was not until around the year 2000 that medicines became available at an affordable price, and the hospital HIV/AIDS programme began in a small way. At the same time, in the maternity department, began the programme to reduce mother-to-child transmission of the virus. At last a ray of hope could be offered. Gradually the HIV/AIDS Programme has expanded, largely with funding from the USA, enabling drugs to be given to both adults and children who fulful the criteria, and care to be provided at home when needed. And the stigma and despair diminishes.

A Palliative Care Programme has been developed in parallel with this. Run by specialist nurses, with funding from the UK, it cares for the terminally ill, many of whom have cancer, with families who do not know what best to do, and who cannot afford to do much. Providing adequate pain relief, a waterproof mattress, and a caring presence may be what is most needed.

The Chaplaincy Team continue to be much involved in the care of patients and staff. The Rev. Elias Kabii retired in 2004, and the Rev. Elyseus Iguna took his place. One valuable opportunity for the chaplaincy team is the time spent with the significant numbers of boys who come for circumcision, between leaving primary and starting secondary school. It is a time traditionally used for education for manhood, and the days that the boys are in hospital have been an important time for learning life skills, health education, and bible-based teaching.

As more types of treatments are provided on an outpatient basis, more specialist clinics are developed, and numbers of outpatients rise, so pressure on accommodation increases. To help meet the demands, a two-storey annexe to the Outpatient Department was built with donated funds. It was named "The Dr Wilkinson (Kamwana) Wing" to honour the service given by the author of this book, and was dedicated in November 2005 in the presence of his daughter, the writer of these pages.

Over the years the leadership of the hospital has changed. Medical-Officers-in-Charge Dr Alastair Sammon (1998 – 1995), Dr Gordon McFarlane (1995 – 1999), Dr John Potts (2001 – 2005) handed on, after a change in the constitution, to a Hospital Director who is not necessarily medically qualified. Mr Samuel Mwaria (2005 – 2007) was the first to act in this role, followed by the appointment of Mr Jediel Sendeyo in 2007. He is supported by a new Hospital Board, most of whom are now required to be professionally qualified. So the leadership is now entirely in Kenyan hands. As it should be.

But the original vision has not changed.

Dr Alison J Wilkinson MB ChB, FRCOG

Gynaecologist in Chogoria Hospital 1992 - 2006
as mission partner of the Church of Scotland

Stirling, Scotland
October 2008

1   Dr Clive Irvine (1962)

2   Mrs Joy Irvine

3   Dr Geoffrey
    Irvine

4 The Bungalow (1922)

5 The first Church (built 1923)

6   The Church at Chogoria (built 1930)

7   The Chancel

8 The Deacon's Court (1928)

Filipo
Musa
Maina
Revd S.Ndambi
Dr Irvine
Gerishom
Willie
Jonathan
Ayubu

9 Group after the signing of the Chogoria promise (Sept 29th 1929)

Dr Arthur is in the centre of the back row

10 The Chogoria Kirk Session (1935)

11 The Chogoria Revival Team (1949)

Mary Mowat
Silas Mûchina
Dedan Wangai
Rachel Wangai

12 The Woman's Guild (1936)

13 The Boys' Primary School (built 1936)

14 Mr Grieve teaching Class of Standard VI Boys

15 Chogoria Boys' High School (Jubilee Block 1987)

16 Chogoria Girls' Boarding Primary School
Headmistress, Mrs Irene Ndiga

17 Girls' Boarding School at Chogoria (built 1937)

18 Chogoria Girls' High School (Admin. Block 1970)

19 The First Permanent Hospital Building (1926)

20 The Five Hospital Orderlies (1927)
Ezra, Samson, Suleiman, Paulo, Mtuwangari

21 The First Leprosarium at Gatheru (1926)

22 The Leprosy Dispensary (1929)

23 The Quadrangle of the Old Hospital (about 1950) now the Nurse Training School

24 The Injection and Dressing Shelter (built 1930)

25   Sister Clark Wilson, Dr Irvine & Staff (1939)

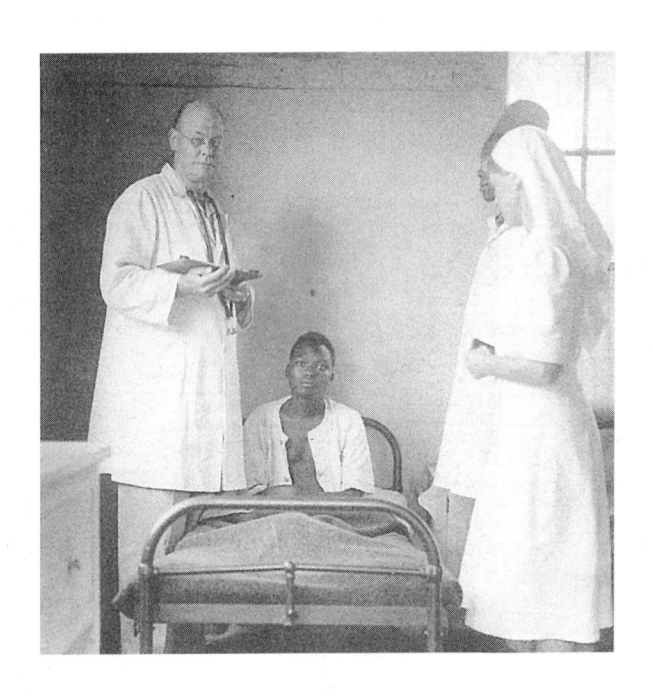

26   Dr Irvine, Sister Fergusson & Adiel with male patient

27 Sister Margaret Burt

28 Jackson Chabari

29 Francis Mûruja

30   Dr Irvine Taking a Service at a Dispensary

31   Dr & Mrs Wilkinson at Mûkûûni Dispensary
(1949)

32 The Women's Ward (1941)

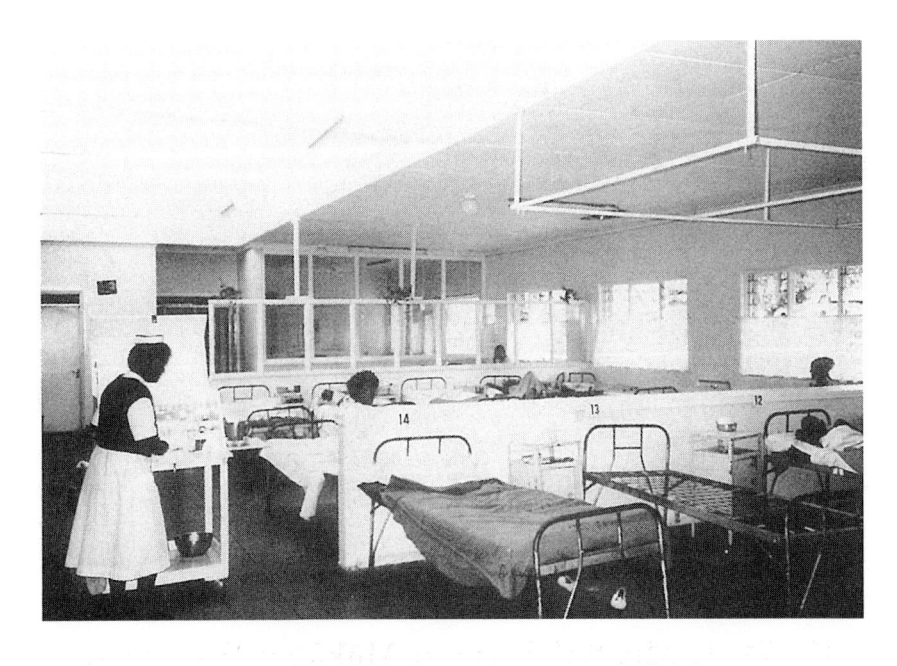

33 The Women's Medical Ward (1971)

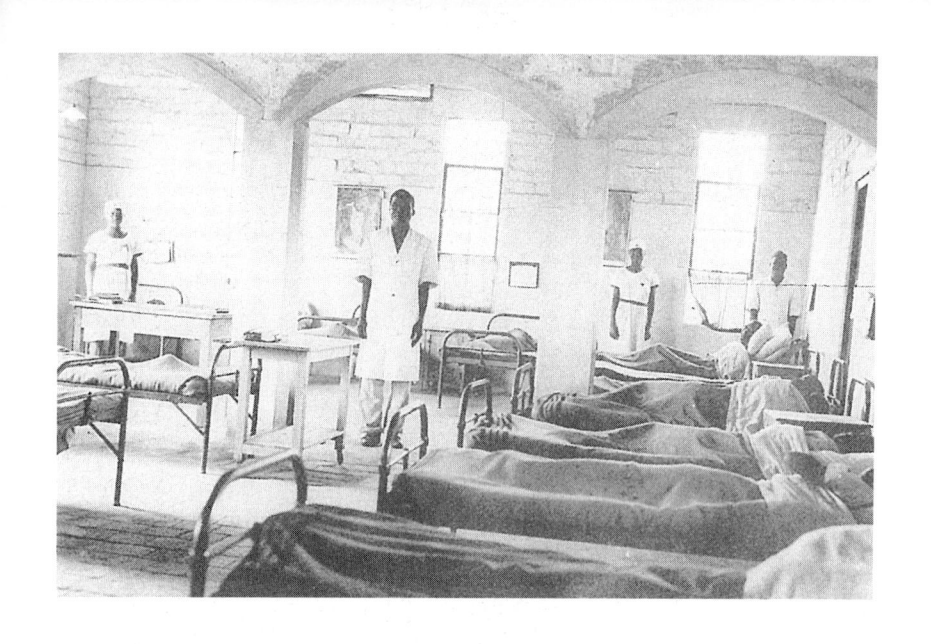

34   The Men's Ward   (built 1939)

35   The Surgical Wing   (built 1971)

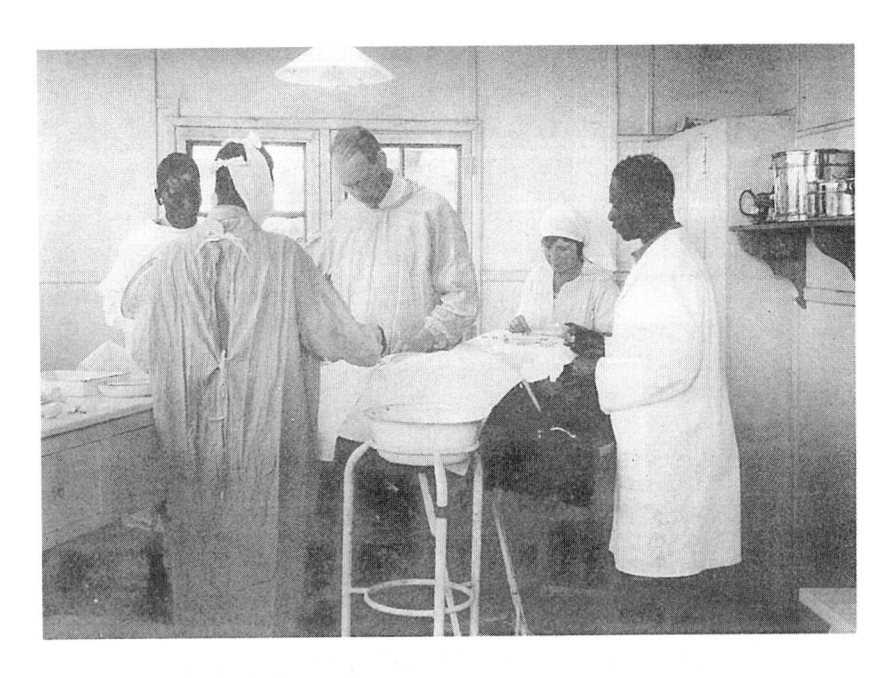

36 The Old Operating Theatre (built 1926)

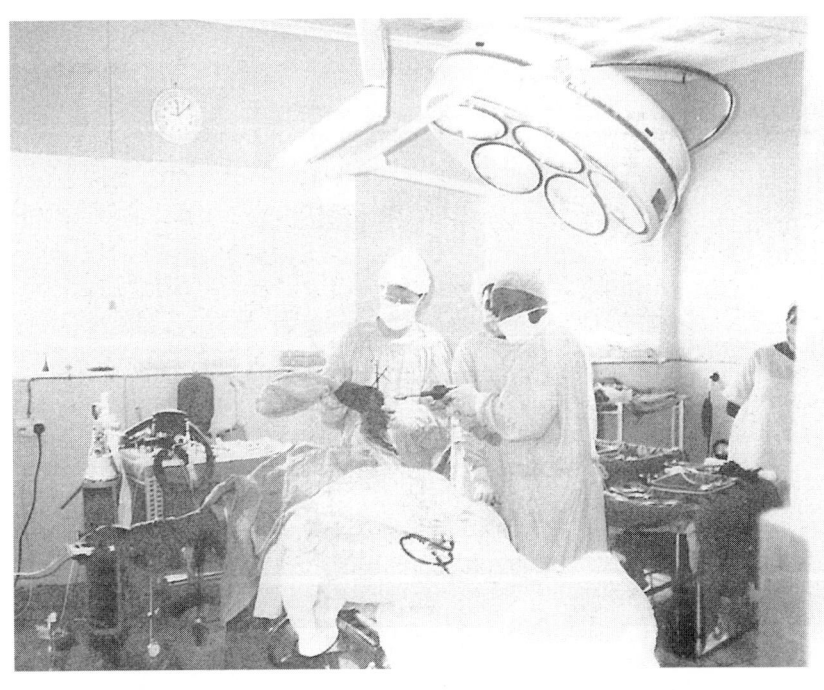

37 The Modern Operating Theatre (built 1971)

38   The Medical Wing   (built 1971)

39   The Hospital Chapel   (built 1983)

40 Mrs Helen Raini (Matron)

41 The Outpatient Clinic

42 Dr Alastair Sammon

Medical Officer-in-charge from 1988

43 Mr Festus Nkonge

Hospital Administrator